# Images
## of American Society
## in Popular Music

B. Lee Cooper

# Images
# of American Society
# in Popular Music:

## A Guide to
## Reflective Teaching

Nelson-Hall nh Chicago

Library of Congress Cataloging in Publication Data

Cooper, B. Lee.
  Images of American society in popular music.

  Bibliography: p.
  Includes index.
  1. School music – Instruction and study – United
States.  2. Music, Popular (Songs, etc.) – Instruction
and study.  3. Music and society.  I. Title.
MT3.U5C747      784.5'00973      81–18790
ISBN 0–88229–514–4 cloth        AACR2
ISBN 0–88229–798–8 paper

Manufactured in the United States of America

10  9  8  7  6  5  4  3  2  1

The paper in this book is pH neutral (acid-free).

To Jill, Laura, Julie, and Michael

# Contents

# Acknowledgments

I wish to express my appreciation to the following editors and journals for granting me permission to reprint portions or revised versions of my articles listed below:

"Examining Social Change through Contemporary History: An Audio Media Proposal" *History Teacher* 7 (August 1973), 523–34; "Review of *American Graffiti*" *History Teacher* 7 (February 1974), 283–84; "Review of *Chuck Berry's Golden Decade*" *History Teacher* 8 (February 1975), 300–301. Reprinted with permission of Keith Ian Polakoff, editor; the original copyright is reserved by *History Teacher*.

"Exploring the Future through Contemporary Music" *Media and Methods* 12 (April 1976), 2–35ff. Reprinted with permission of Kay Blumenthal, assistant editor; the original copyright is reserved by the North American Publishing Company, 401 Broad St., Philadelphia, PA 19108.

"Futurescope" *Audiovisual Instruction* 21 (January 1976), 42–48; "Popular Music: A Creative Teaching Resource" *Audiovisual Instruction* 24 (March 1979), 37–43; "The Traditional and Beyond: Resources for Teaching Women's Studies" *Audiovisual Instruction* 22 (December 1977), 14–18ff; and "Using Popular Music in Social Studies Instruction" *Audiovisual Instruction* 17 (November 1972), 86–88. Reprinted with permission of Carol Bruce, managing editor; the original copyright is reserved by the Association for Educational Communications and Technology.

"The Image of American Society in Popular Music: A Search for Identity and Values" *Social Studies* 64 (December 1973), 319–32; and "Oral History, Popular Music, and Les McCann" *Social Studies* 67 (May/June 1976), 115–18. Reprinted with permission of Barbara Ferkiss, managing editor.

"The Image of the Black Man: Contemporary Lyrics as Oral History" *Journal of the Interdenominational Theological Center* 5 (Spring 1978), 105–22. Reprinted with permission of John C. Diamond, Jr., editor; the original copyright is retained by the *Journal of the Interdenominational Theological Center.*

"The Image of the Outsider in Contemporary Lyrics" *Journal of Popular Culture* 12 (Summer 1978), 168–78. Reprinted by permission of Ray B. Browne, editor.

"Social Change, Popular Music and the Teacher" *Social Education* 37 (December 1973), 776–81, 793; and "Images of the Future in Popular Music: Lyrical Comments on Tomorrow" *Social Education* 39 (May 1975), 276–85. Reprinted with permission of Daniel Roselle, editor.

"An Opening Day Collection of Popular Music Resources: Searching for Discographic Standards" and "William L. Schurk—Audio Center Director: A Close Encounter with a Librarian of a Different Kind" are reprinted with permission from Fred E. H. Schroeder, editor, and Ray B. Browne, publisher.

"Popular Culture: Teaching Problems and Challenges" In *Popular Culture and the Library,* edited by Wayne A. Wiegand (Lexington: University of Kentucky, 1978), p. 10–26. Reprinted with permission of the editor.

"Rock Music and Religious Education: A Proposed Synthesis" *Religious*

*Education* 70 (May-June 1975), 289–99. Reprinted with permission of the Religious Education Association, 409 Prospect St., New Haven, CT 06510.

"Teaching American History through Popular Music" *AHA Newsletter* 14 (October 1976), 3–5. Reprinted with permission of the American Historical Association and Kathleen D. Swiger, editor.

"Teaching Contemporary History from an Audio Perspective—'The Image of American Society in Popular Music'" *Library-College Experimenter* 2 (November 1976), 22–34; "Popular Music Resources— Audio Collection Guidelines" *Library-College Experimenter* 4 (May 1978), 11–22; and "Contemporary Singers as Subjects for Biographical Study" *Library-College Experimenter* 5 (May 1979), 13–28. Reprinted with permission of Library-College Associates, Inc., and Sandy Sheppard, editor.

I also wish to thank the following colleagues, critics, friends, and loved ones for encouraging me to write this book: Larry Bagford, Liz Bellavance, Vivian Blevins, Donna Brummett, Roger Buese, Charles and Kathleen Cooper, Gary Crist, Bob and Patty Douglas, Larry Haverkos, Esther Hayhurst, Gordon Henry, Jim Hinchey, Robert Jewett, Bob Oliver, Lynn Ryan, Margie Schumaker, Bill Schurk, Virginia Senn, John E. Sukovich, Verdan D. Traylor, and especially Wayne A. Wiegand.

# Introduction

Why should high school and college teachers be interested in a series of essays that explore various approaches to stimulate reflective thinking through the study of popular music? Why should students be encouraged to examine the images of American society contained in contemporary song lyrics? Why should librarians be responsible for acquiring and cataloging recorded commentaries by Stevie Wonder, Joni Mitchell, Phil Ochs, Janis Ian, Neil Diamond, Paul McCartney, Bob Dylan, Chuck Berry, Paul Simon, and other popular songwriters?

Music is the universal language of mankind. . . .
  —Henry Wadsworth Longfellow

The function of popular music has not received much notice from sociologists, who perversely have spent more time assessing the impact of television despite the fact that many people from the ages of ten to twenty-five are more heavily exposed to radio and records. For many people in this age group, popular music provides a sense of change, as records and styles replace each other in the instant history of the hit parades. At any time in this history, each listener has a few records that enrich his feelings, extend his sense of love or despair, and feed his fantasies or fire some real relationship. . . . Absorbing this music without necessarily thinking much about it, the generations of popular music audiences since 1956 have formed quite different sensibilities from the preceding generations which are raised on sentiment and melodrama.

  —Charlie Gillett

Most historians feel reasonably comfortable in drawing on literature, visual arts, and architecture to supplement their work, but usually shy away from using music. Thus an important dimension of human expression and creativity is ignored.

—John W. Barker

. . . Music is central to our time and the great musicians are, in this culture more than in any other in recent times, the true shamans, the religious and secular spokesmen, the educators, and the poets.

—Ralph J. Gleason

The songwriter has a special place in this scheme, for at his best he verbalizes the state of society, either directly by openly questioning or protesting things, or indirectly by depicting the private life and interior feelings of someone who moves within that society.

—Jack McDonough

In the twenty years or so "it's" been with us, rock has metamorphosed from the teenager's jalopy to something very much like the family car. It is now the mainstream of American popular music, with everything else reduced to a tributary status.

—Peter Reilly

Music is a world within itself, with a language we all understand. . . .

—Stevie Wonder

The ideas developed in popular songs should be examined in contemporary classrooms because the attitudes, values, and beliefs expressed in modern tunes depict the major concerns of our time—personal identity, ecology, freedom, militarism, political protest, women's liberation, and so on. In short, the lyrics of popular songs are valuable tools for accomplishing the twin educational goals of self-evaluation and social analysis. This text is specifically designed to assist students and teachers to achieve these two objectives.

I am a teacher, not a musician. I teach with recorded music, primarily through lyric review. I do not pretend to conduct formal analysis with my students because I think that this research approach is too systematic and too restrictive to introduce in a survey-level classroom environment. What I attempt to generate is a reflective environment that opens student minds to philosophic inquiry. I am more interested in what the music means to each learner than in what lyric configurations say statistically or in even what the recording artist may have originally intended to say through his or her song. The "receiver" is the person I am concerned about, and, as one of several receivers in the classroom, I feel free to introduce my position just as I expect my students to reflect their positions to me. In essence, the thesis that I have tested while teaching with popular music is that the pluralistic belief patterns of American society are accurately reflected by the music.

Specifically, what are the problems confronting an instructor who initiates teaching approaches with popular music? There are five typical belittling faculty responses. I am not presenting them in any particular order, and I don't want to imply that one is more of a problem than another. I do want to depict these responses in a kind of psychological or medical framework, though, because I feel that they represent fairly distinctive syndromes of behavior.

The first one I call the "Pandering to Student Whims" syndrome. Proponents of this position argue that popular music can't possibly be a valuable teaching resource precisely because students like it. This argument is grounded in an ancient learning theory proposition – that all *real* education is misery. The best thing that can be said about a particular course is that it makes students "miserable"; the next best thing that you can say about a faculty member – apparently – is that he or she is miserable and boring.

The second belittling faculty response is the "You Must Be Ignoring the Really Significant Material" syndrome. I hear this frequently from my fellow historians. My colleagues contend, "We can barely cover all the necessary material in our classes now, so how can you expect us to introduce that junk music and still get through the Louisiana Purchase and the Tea Pot Dome Scandal?"

The third response is the "Let him alone. He'll get over it" syndrome. The idea expressed in this response is that creative people will sometimes go off the deep end with a particular educational experiment, but they'll eventually drift back to academic reality.

The fourth falls into the "I'd love to try it, but I've got a tin ear" syndrome. Here the unspoken assumption is that one must be musically talented to employ music in the classroom: "I don't play the piano, so I can't use music." It takes quite a bit of explanation on my part to convince a skeptical colleague that I don't sing or play either.

The fifth challenge is the one I consider to be the most serious. This syndrome should be labeled, "It's a fine course enrichment idea for a confirmed pop music freak, but I don't know a damned thing about rock and roll." This position asserts that a teacher must have an avocational interest in popular music in order to convert it into an academic resource. "It's easy for you to go to your personal album collection, pick out six records, take them into your class, and demonstrate to your students the differing attitudes toward religion in contemporary society. But what about folks like us who don't have backgrounds in popular music?" Of course, the depressing thing about this contention is that these teachers are actually saying, "We can't possibly learn enough about contemporary music to use it!"

Since I am also committed to employing popular culture beyond the realm of contemporary music as teaching resources, I decided to test myself. My goal was to approach a popular culture area that I didn't know anything about, that I never liked as a youngster, and that I could therefore experiment with in terms of attempting to master it sufficiently to utilize it in my classes. Well, I like television, love motion pictures, and collected baseball cards and comic books as a child; but I had never read more than a couple of science fiction stories in my life. The sf genre had simply never appealed to me. So, I spent six weeks of one summer vacation period doing nothing but reading science fiction books.[1] What an experience! I consider myself to be living proof that a person can learn new fields of interest. I also feel quite strongly that it is imperative for teachers to avoid the "I Don't Know That; Therefore, I Can't Do It" position. If teachers can't learn new tricks, then it gives a lie to the entire educational process they are directing.

Teachers and librarians face similar problems in searching for popular culture instructional resources. These difficulties are magnified when the materials being sought are related to contemporary music. Hit songs of today may be purchased from record shops, discount and department stores, and national record clubs (Columbia Record Club or RCA Record Club). After carefully assessing the newest copyright law interpretations, an academic librarian may develop an audio tape collection of popular music by recording from radio or television programs or by requesting teachers and students to permit him or her to construct tapes of records from their personal collections. The desire to broaden a collection's profile from current hits to "oldies" can be accomplished through the purchase of television-advertised "greatest hits" collections. In addition, there are several record outlets throughout the United States that specialize in buying and selling records from the 1950s and 1960s.

But why purchase records when they can be acquired at no cost? Donated collections, though undeniably nonselective in composition, can be a library budget's godsend. The primary sources of donated recordings are private collectors, radio stations, and professional musicians. It's a common situation when a record collector dies that his or her family doesn't know what to do with all the 33⅓, 45, or 78 r.p.m. "junk" that had been the collector's "treasure." Librarians and teachers should be standing at graveside with open arms to receive these vinyl pieces of oral history. Deejays and radio station managers will often send promotional copies of recordings to libraries; and, if long-term relations can be established with them, they might even send non-promo albums to local schools and colleges rather than dumping them into their record storage vaults. Occasionally, a teacher might even be fortunate enough to establish a record-giving relationship with a pop performer. I wrote an article about jazz pianist Les McCann in 1976 and his wife kindly sent me complimentary copies of all his recent albums. My point is that there are numerous ways for educators to acquire popular records.

The next question that usually arises is, "Where can a librarian or teacher go to find sample teaching units using popular music?" I can't supply an easy answer to this request. I can suggest some journal resources — *Social Studies*, the *Popular Culture Association Newsletter*, *Audiovisual Instruction*, *Social Education*, *Media and Methods*, *Popular Music in Society*, the *Journal of Popular Culture*, and the *English Journal*. Each of these magazines has, in the past decade, presented one or two fine articles dealing with the construction of popular music teaching resource units. There simply is not much instructional guidance material currently available. Most scholars tend to write about the educational benefits of popular music in a strictly theoretical vein, ignoring the resource/methodology issues so crucial to classroom teachers. As far as drawing ideas from functioning instructional models, most people who actually teach with recordings are too busy organizing for their classes to publish anything about what they are doing. That's a shame because the successes they are achieving ought to be communicated to larger teaching publics.

In contrast to the scarcity of teaching units, lyric resources are plentiful. The Charlton Publishing Company of Derby, Connecticut, has been producing *Hit Parader, Song Hits, Rock and Soul Hits,* and numerous other monthly lyric journals for more than three decades. The lyrics that appear in these Charlton magazines may not always be exactly the same as those actually sung on the popular record, but it's much easier to transcribe lyrics from recordings if you have a publication available that contains at least three-fourths of the correct words. Album covers and protective slip sheets bearing lyrics are usually the most accurate lyric sources for students and teachers. Recently *Billboard* magazine reported a burgeoning publishing market for the lyrics of pop tunes in music stores.[2] Although the focus of song book production is primarily on instrumentation, lyrics are generally provided for each of the anthologized tunes.

Disciplinary investigations of popular music—usually unrelated to teaching—are more common today than ever before. This scholarly activity is indicative of the general growth in popular culture study. The areas of sociology, economics, music, English, and history have already produced some fine works,[3] and much more will be written in the next decade. A much wider perspective on the popular music scene—well beyond the singers and songwriters who are influential in the contemporary music industry—is certain to stimulate some very interesting research and publication on the "nonstar" aspects of popular music.[4]

This book is designed to serve several purposes. It should be entertaining to teachers, scholars, librarians, and popular music fans. It should also provide resources—both literary and audio—to both students and teachers as they pursue the nature and meaning of contemporary American society. Finally, it provides this author with an opportunity to share fifteen years of teaching, writing, and research experience with popular music resources with a large reading audience.

# PART ONE

# Popular Music
# in the
# Classroom

# ONE

# Popular Music as an Instructional Resource

Many question the value of listening to, let alone studying, popular songs. Their doubts are usually based on surface observations about modern music. The volume is deafening; the lyrics seem repetitive and unimaginative; and disc jockeys who scream jingles, blow horns, and heap senseless praise on tunes that are here today and gone tomorrow are annoying if not intolerable. Yet during the past decade a variety of scholars — music theorists, psychologists, cultural historians, teachers of poetry and literature, sociologists, and linguists — have begun to examine carefully the meaning and social impact of popular music. This serious study is no mere quirk. It marks an attempt to understand the reason for the immense popularity and influence of contemporary singers, songwriters, and their songs.

Although experts on popular music disagree on many issues, there is consensus among them that the music of today is notably different from music produced during any other period of history. There are at least three reasons for this. First, the well-organized commercial distribution and radio broadcasting of popular recordings has created a vast listening public that is constantly exposed to tunes in cars, homes, elevators, department stores, and recreational areas.[1] The popular song is a universally available phenomenon. Second, technological advancements in musical instruments and other sound-producing equipment (tape recorders, multi-track tapes, speakers, and amplifiers) have enabled singers to produce such high-quality recorded material that, as a recent audiocassette advertisement declares, "You can't tell whether it's

Ella Fitzgerald live or on Memorex."[2] Finally, the quality of song lyrics has increased so dramatically that many English teachers refer to popular songwriters such as Bob Dylan, Paul Simon, Carole King, Don McLean, and Paul McCartney as poets.[3] But while the lyrics of some contemporary songs have earned rich praise as poetry, the words of other popular tunes have been condemned by politicians, theologians, and journalists as sinister propaganda tools.[4] The fact that so many modern singers, unlike their pre-1960 "forefathers," tend to deal lyrically with controversial social and personal issues has created concern about the influence of popular music. Antiwar chants, religious tunes, women's liberation melodies, and social protest songs have dramatically depicted the image of the United States through lyrical means. It is this descriptive aspect of contemporary music that is particularly valuable to social studies teachers.

## WHAT IS POPULAR MUSIC?

The general field of modern music is usually segregated into several categories of songs or singing styles. Commentators frequently use terms such as *blues, rock, jazz, country, folk, rhythm and blues, pop, bluegrass,* and *soul* to delineate different popular music sounds. Each of these terms has an element of descriptive validity; yet each category can be potentially misleading. The task of defining the performing styles of singers such as Johnny Cash, B. B. King, Phil Ochs, Pete Seeger, or the Archies is fairly easy. The real problem arises when a student of popular music attempts to narrowly classify the styles of such versatile singers as Elvis Presley, Ray Charles, or Barbra Streisand. The fact that these three artists have performed songs in a variety of vocal styles inevitably creates confusion. To avoid such classification difficulty, though, the general term *popular music* employed here ignores stylistic variation and includes those songs that have attained public acceptance since 1950 as noted in the Top 100 rating charts of *Billboard* magazine. Put simply, the idea that a song is popular means that it is played frequently in private homes as well as in public places – at dances and restaurants, on radios and jukeboxes, or anywhere else people gather.

When social studies students examine a popular song, that song's melody, rhythm, harmony, acoustics and form are of secondary importance to its lyrics. This does not mean that instrumental performances are of no significance as popular music. The learning potential of a modern song, however, is often found in the quality of the message delivered through the lyrics. Content creates images. The image of society depicted in a song frequently exerts a stronger hold on a listener than the social reality that surrounds him. That is, songs of love, peace, and joy can create a sense of well-being in an individual's mind even though he or she may be suffering from personal or social problems. Likewise, songs may challenge the status quo in order to stimulate the notion that things aren't going well.

## Why Use Popular Music in the Classroom?

Social studies instruction should develop the ability of a student to anticipate, understand, direct, evaluate, and live with constant social change. Most historians agree that the only thing that is less stable than man's interpretation of the past is his ability to objectively comprehend changing events of his own lifetime. The study of contemporary society demands that both teacher and student acknowledge their myopic tendencies and actively seek new methods and materials for investigating shifts and alterations in present-day life. One potentially beneficial resource for analyzing the causes and effects of social change is the medium of popular music. If a social studies teacher is seeking to test his or her students' abilities in utilizing skills such as problem identification, information gathering, hypothesis formulating, and decisionmaking, then the use of popular music should provide a rich field for classroom experimentation.

Increasing use of audio materials need not require substantial capital investment for a high school or college. Even libraries deficient in audiovisual equipment can usually manage to supply a phonograph or a tape player to a teacher who requests one. Too frequently, however, the records utilized in social studies classes have been employed strictly as plastic earphones to the past, with little or no critical attention paid to the personal problems or social issues raised on the recordings. Edward R. Murrow's I Can Hear It Now series, for example, provides samples of 1920s commercials, cheers for Babe Ruth, and excerpts from speeches by Warren G. Harding, Calvin Coolidge, and Herbert

Hoover. Upon hearing the Murrow disc, students exhibit various responses: some are bored by the inherent antiquarianism of fifty-year-old clichés; others are happy for relief from the drudgery of textbook responsibilities for one day; and still others are befuddled by the kaleidoscopic array of historic names and events that pass too rapidly through the speakers. Only the extraordinarily bright student is able to comprehend the social and political issues of the 1920s—social conformity vs. civil liberty, governmental corruption, anti-immigrant, anti-Negro bigotry, and inflation/depression business cycles—by passively listening to a volume of the Murrow collection.

If social studies classrooms are to become forums for the reflective examination of the sources and results of social change, audiovisual presentations must provide relevant social illustrations for students. This goal can be most easily accomplished by requesting that students provide their own records for classroom scrutiny. For instance, rather than introducing a scratchy version of "John Henry" to a history class in an attempt to illustrate man vs. machine conflict, a teacher should challenge his or her students to uncover more contemporary examples of social and personal reactions to automation as they are depicted in the lyrics of current popular songs.

The initial task confronting social studies teachers who plan to employ this popular culture approach is for them to convince their students of the academic legitimacy of lyrical investigation. The argument can be made that just as former civilizations are studied by anthropologists through remnants of pottery and art, by historians through the texts of military plans and political addresses, and by English teachers through prose and poetry, so an analyst of contemporary society cannot afford to overlook the impact of the verbal imagery produced by the multimillion-dollar American music industry on the ideas of modern man. Although students may not be sophisticated enough to pursue genuinely systematic lyrical content analysis, they can recognize, define, and evaluate persistent themes and parallel idea patterns in popular music. Once such themes are identified, the social studies teacher may ask a class to evaluate the validity of a position taken on a specific issue by a particular singer, thus initiating a reflective examination of social change in problematic areas including religion, sex, war, alienation, poverty, and drugs.

The image of American society in contemporary lyrics is complex. While some songs, such as Merle Haggard's "Okie from Muskogee," praise patriotism, others, like Creedence Clearwater Revival's "Fortunate Son," condemn blind public support of military endeavors. A few songs, such as the Jefferson Airplane's "White Rabbit," seem to support the pleasures of drug use, while other tunes, like Steppenwolf's "The Pusher" and Canned Heat's "Amphetamine Annie," condemn the sale of narcotics and stress the deadly effects of speed and cocaine.

## WHERE CAN POPULAR MUSIC LYRIC RESOURCES BE OBTAINED?

The use of popular music in the classroom has received little educational commentary. Likewise, the ability of librarians to meet the needs of social studies teachers and students in terms of securing lyric resources and contemporary recordings has not been encouraging. The question that invariably arises during any discussion concerning the use of popular music is, "Where can the lyrics of contemporary songs be obtained?" This question is understandable. No social studies teacher should be expected to feel comfortable with a medium as unique and new as popular recordings. This initial insecurity, however, can be beneficial for stimulating professional growth and can also enable students to assume the role of experts by providing them nontraditional learning resources for classroom investigation. Teachers can still provide guidance in song selection, though, by becoming familiar with the lyric collections listed below:

Alan Aldridge, ed. *The Beatles Illustrated Lyrics*. New York: Delacorte, 1969.
_____. *The Beatles Illustrated Lyrics – 2*. New York: Delacorte, 1971.
Alan Aldridge and Mike Dempsey, eds. *Bernie Taupin – The One Who Writes the Words for Elton John: Complete Lyrics from 1968 to "Goodbye, Yellow Brick Road."* New York: Knopf, 1976.
Bob Atkinson, ed. *Songs of the Open Road: The Poetry of Folk Rock*. New York: New American Library, 1974.
Burt Bacharach and Hal David. *The Bacharach and David Song Book*. New York: Simon and Schuster, 1970.
*Chuck Berry – The Golden Decade*. New York: ARC Music Corporation, n.d.

*The Best of Popular Music: First Omnibus of Popular Songs.* Miami Beach: Hansen Publications, 1968.

Bruce L. Chipman, comp. *Hardening Rock: An Organic Anthology of the Adolescence of Rock 'n' Roll.* Boston: Little, Brown, 1972.

*The Judy Collins Songbook.* New York: Grosset and Dunlap, 1969.

John M. Conly, ed. *The Joan Baez Songbook.* New York: Ryerson Music Publishers, 1964.

David Dalton, ed. *The Rolling Stones: An Unauthorized Biography in Words, Photographs, and Music.* New York: Amsco Music Publishing Company, 1972.

Hal David. *What the World Needs Now and Other Love Lyrics.* New York: Trident Press, 1970.

Landon Gerald Dowdey, comp. *Journey to Freedom: A Casebook with Music.* Chicago: Swallow, 1969.

*Bob Dylan Song Book.* New York: M. Witmark, n.d.

Tom Glazer, ed. *Songs of Peace, Freedom, and Protest.* Greenwich, Conn.: Fawcett, 1970.

Richard Goldstein, ed. *The Poetry of Rock.* New York: Bantam, 1969.

Barbara Farris Graves and Donald J. McBain, eds. *Lyric Voices: Approaches to the Poetry of Contemporary Song.* New York: Wiley, 1972.

*The History of Rock Music.* New York: Charles Hansen Music and Books, n.d.

*Live at the Fillmore.* New York: Warner Brothers Publications, n.d.

David Morse, comp. *Grand Father Rock: The New Poetry and the Old.* New York: Dell, 1972.

*The Motown Era.* New York: Grosset and Dunlap, 1971.

A. X. Nicholas, ed. *The Poetry of Soul.* New York: Bantam, 1971.

_____. *Woke Up This Mornin': Poetry of the Blues.* New York: Bantam, 1973.

Phil Ochs. *The War Is Over.* New York: Collier, 1967.

Carol Offen, ed. *Country Music: The Poetry.* New York: Ballantine, 1977.

Milton Okum, comp. *Great Songs . . . of the Sixties.* Chicago: Quadrangle, 1970.

_____. *New York Times Country Music's Greatest Songs.* New York: Times Books, 1978.

_____. *New York Times Great Songs of the Seventies.* New York: Times Books, 1977.

_____. *Something to Sing About: The Personal Choices of America's Folk Singers.* New York: Macmillan, 1968.

*100 of the Greatest Rock and Roll Hits.* New York: Big 3 Music Corp. n.d.

*Paul Simon — Greatest Hits, Etc.* New York: Charing Cross Music, 1977.

Richard Peck, ed. *Sound and Silences: Poetry for Now.* New York: Dell, 1970.

David R. Pichaske, ed. *Beowulf to Beatles: Approaches to Poetry*. New York: Free Press, 1972.

*Progressive Rock Classics*. New York: Warner Brothers Publications, n.d.

Eric Sackheim, comp. *The Blues Line: A Collection of Blues Lyrics*. New York: Schirmer, 1969.

Louis M. Savary, ed. *Popular Song and Youth Today: Fifty Songs — Their Meaning and You*. New York: Association Press, 1971.

Irwin Silber, ed. *Songs America Voted By*. Harrisburg, Pa.: Stackpole Books, 1971.

Jerry Silverman, comp. *The Liberated Woman's Songbook*. New York: Collier, 1971.

*The Songs of Bob Dylan from 1966 through 1975*. New York: Knopf, 1976.

*The Songs of Paul Simon*. New York: Knopf, 1972.

Stephanie Spinner, ed. *Rock Is Beautiful: An Anthology of American Lyrics, 1953–1968*. New York: Dell, 1970.

*Steppenwolf Gold: Their Greatest Hits*. Los Angeles: West Coast Publications, n.d.

*Super Stars*. Los Angeles: West Coast Publications, n.d.

Jerry L. Walker, ed. *Favorite Pop/Rock Lyrics*. New York: Scholastic Book Service, 1969.

_____. *Pop/Rock Lyrics 2*. New York: Scholastic Book Service, 1970.

_____. *Pop/Rock Lyrics 3*. New York: Scholastic Book Service, 1971.

_____. *Pop/Rock Songs of the Earth*. New York: Scholastic Book Service, 1972.

*The Who Complete: A Complete Collection of the Best of the Who*. New York: Charles Hansen Music and Books, n.d.

Stevie Wonder. *Anthology — Stevie Wonder*, ed. Steve Francis. Miami: Screen Gems/Columbia Pictures, 1975.

## How Should a Social Studies Teacher Utilize Popular Music Resources?

Rather than continuing to outline the theory of using popular music in the social studies classroom, it is time to provide some specific teaching strategies that can be employed to motivate student interest. The following eleven lesson outlines illustrate several instructional approaches to issues of social, political, and personal concern through the use of words from popular songs. Each recommended instructional unit is thematically organized and headed by a specific question for reflective consideration, along with a set of six or more concepts directly related to each theme. They are also supported by two types of teaching resources — popular music recordings and textbook readings — which have been selected to illustrate each theme.

## Black History

*Question:*
What insights into the historical experiences of black Americans can be gained from the lyrics of songs performed by contemporary black singers?

*Concepts to investigate:*

| | | |
|---|---|---|
| slavery | ghetto life | educational opportunity |
| poverty | welfare system | job discrimination |
| segregation | racial pride | freedom |

*Approach:*
Have students listen to the lyrics of songs presented on black-oriented radio stations. Ask the class to list the central social and political issues verbalized by popular singers admired by black Americans. Ask students if the attitudes and values expressed by black singers are similar to or different from those voiced by contemporary white singers.

*Recommended songs:*
"Why I Sing the Blues"—B. B. King
"Ninety-Nine and A Half (Won't Do)"—Wilson Pickett
"Comment"—Les McCann
"Stormy Monday Blues"—Bobby Bland
"Trouble in Mind"—Nina Simone
"Masterpiece"—Temptations
"I'm Livin' in Shame"—Diana Ross and the Supremes
"I Wish"—Stevie Wonder
"Midnight Train to Georgia"—Gladys Knight and the Pips
"Back in the U.S.A."—Chuck Berry
"Express Yourself"—Charles Wright and the Watts 103rd Street
    Rhythm Band

"Stand" — Sly and the Family Stone
"Livin' in the Life" — Isley Brothers
"Papa Was a Rollin' Stone" — Temptations
"Compared to What" — Les McCann and Eddie Harris
"Tobacco Road" — Lou Rawls
"Living for the City" — Stevie Wonder

*Bibliography*

Garland, Phyl. *The Sound of Soul.* Chicago: Henry Regnery Company, 1969.
Hannerz, Ulf. "The Meaning of 'Soul.'" In *The Private Side of American History: Readings in Everyday Life,* ed. Thomas R. Frazier. New York: Harcourt Brace Jovanovich, 1975. Pp. 336–47.
Jones, LeRoi. *Blues People: Negro Music in White America.* New York: William Morrow, 1963.
Kofsky, Frank. *Black Nationalism and the Revolution in Music.* New York: Pathfinder Press, 1970.

## Religious Images

*Question:*

Why do popular singers and songwriters so frequently employ religious themes and images in the lyrics of their hit tunes?

*Concepts to investigate:*

| | | |
|---|---|---|
| predestination | faith | hymns |
| brotherhood | morality | ethics |
| gospel themes | ecumenicism | social gospel |

*Approach:*

Have each student construct a list of popular songs that have religious ideas, themes, or images in their lyrics. Invite two clergymen to speak to the class on the topic of "Social Concerns in Contemporary Religious Life." Have the ministers join the class in evaluating the varying religious meanings contained in the songs the students have compiled.

*Recommended songs:*

1. Traditional lyrics and images
   "Amazing Grace" — Judy Collins

"Oh Happy Day"—Edwin Hawkins Singers
"Turn, Turn, Turn"—Pete Seeger
"You'll Never Walk Alone"—Roy Hamilton
2. Salvation
"Operator"—Manhattan Transfer
"People Get Ready"—Impressions
"Spirit in the Sky"—Norman Greenbaum
"Are You Ready"—Pacific Gas and Electric
3. Brotherhood
"I'll Take You There"—Staple Singers
"Bridge over Troubled Water"—Simon and Garfunkel
"He Ain't Heavy . . . He's My Brother"—Hollies
4. Social criticism
"7 O'Clock News/Silent Night"—Simon and Garfunkel
"With God on Our Side"—Bob Dylan

*Bibliography:*
Cooper, B. Lee. "Rock Music and Religious Education: A Proposed Synthesis." *Religious Education* 70 (May-June 1975): 289–99.
Dowdey, Landon Gerald. *Journey to Freedom: A Casebook with Music.* Chicago: Swallow, 1969.
Heilbut, Tony. *The Gospel Sound: Good News and Bad Times.* New York: Simon and Schuster, 1971.
Rodnitsky, Jerome L. "The New Revivalism: American Protest Songs, 1945–1968." *South Atlantic Quarterly,* 70 (Winter, 1971): 13–21.

PROBLEMS OF YOUTH

*Question:*
How should young people respond to the conflicts in their lives?

*Concepts to investigate:*

| | | |
|---|---|---|
| maturation | independence | parental authority |
| responsibility | economic security | identity |
| *in loco parentis* | age discrimination | social pressure |

*Approach:*

Ask students to assemble several sets of popular song lyrics which accurately depict their feelings about personal problems and their observations about changing social values in contemporary American society.

*Recommended songs:*

1. Self-image
   "At Seventeen"—Janis Ian
   "All I Really Want to Do"—Bob Dylan
   "Makin' It"—David Naughton
   "Eighteen"—Alice Cooper
   "Almost Grown"—Chuck Berry
2. Parental authority
   "Me and Julio Down by the Schoolyard"—Paul Simon
   "Yakety Yak"—Coasters
   "Summertime Blues"—Eddie Cochran
   "Down on Me"—Big Brother and the Holding Company
   "Your Mama Don't Dance"—Loggins and Messina
3. Personal relationships
   "When You're in Love with a Beautiful Woman"—Dr. Hook
   "You're So Vain"—Carly Simon
   "Suspicious Minds"—Elvis Presley
   "Don't Think Twice, It's All Right"—Bob Dylan
   "Breaking Up Is Hard to Do"—Neil Sedaka
   "(I Can't Get No) Satisfaction"—Rolling Stones
   "Chuck E's in Love"—Rickie Lee Jones
   "Bridge over Troubled Water"—Linda Clifford
4. Social pressures
   "The Logical Song"—Supertramp
   "Society's Child"—Janis Ian
   "I Think We're Alone Now"—Tommy James and the Shondells
   "Town without Pity"—Gene Pitney
   "He's a Rebel"—Crystals
   "Sticks and Stones"—Ray Charles

*Bibliography:*

Cooper, B. Lee, and Larry S. Haverkos. "The Image of American Society in Popular Music: A Search for Identity and Values." *Social Studies* 64 (December 1973): 319–22.

Keniston, Kenneth. *The Uncommitted: Alienated Youth in American Society.* New York: Dell, 1965.

Roszak, Theodore. *The Making of A Counter Culture.* Garden City, N.Y.: Doubleday, 1969.

Wattenberg, William W. *The Adolescent Years* 2d. ed. New York: Harcourt Brace Jovanovich, 1973.

Wells, John. "Bent Out of Shape from Society's Pliers: A Sociological Study of the Grotesque in the Songs of Bob Dylan." *Popular Music and Society* 6 (1978): 27–38.

Yankelovich, Daniel. "The New Naturalism." In *The Changing Values on Campus.* New York: Pocket Books, 1972. Pp. 167–85.

## HISTORICAL IMAGES

*Question:*

How can historians use the statements, images and ideas from popular songs to enrich their understanding of particular actions or events of the past?

*Concepts to investigate:*

| | | |
|---|---|---|
| causation | interpretations | myths |
| facts | propaganda | images |
| determinism | stereotypes | chronology |
| fables | "great man" theory | parables |

*Approach:*

Have students discuss the oral history found in traditional ballads that praised the heroic deeds of Robin Hood and John Henry and in protest songs such as "Joe Hill" that condemned big business's hostility toward unionism in nineteenth-century America. Then ask the class to reflect on the historical images and attitudes depicted in each of the following songs.

*Recommended songs:*

| HISTORICAL TOPIC | POPULAR MUSIC RESOURCE |
|---|---|
| 1. The Battle of New Orleans | "The Battle of New Orleans"—Johnny Horton |
| 2. A Civil War incident | "The Night They Drove Old Dixie Down"—Joan Baez |
| 3. Labor problems in coal mining communities | "Sixteen Tons"—Tennessee Ernie Ford |
| 4. John F. Kennedy during World War II | "P.T. 109"—Jimmy Dean |
| 5. Assassination of Medgar Evers | "Only a Pawn in Their Game"—Bob Dylan |
| 6. Assassinations of Abraham Lincoln, Martin Luther King, Jr., and John F. Kennedy | "Abraham, Martin, and John"—Dion |
| 7. Assassination of John F. Kennedy | "Six White Horses"—Tommy Cash |
| 8. Valor of Vietnam soldiers | "The Ballad of the Green Berets"—Barry Sadler |
| 9. Antiwar movement during the Vietnam conflict | "With God on Our Side"—Bob Dylan |
| 10. Kent State incident | "Ohio"—Crosby, Stills, Nash, and Young |
| 11. Trial of the "Chicago 7" | "Chicago"—Crosby, Stills, Nash, and Young |
| 12. Death of George Jackson | "George Jackson"—Bob Dylan |
| 13. Imprisonment of Rubin Carter | "Hurricane'"—Bob Dylan |

*Bibliography:*

Cooper, B. Lee. "Folk History, Alternative History, and Future History." *Teaching History: A Journal of Methods* 2 (Spring 1977): 56–62.

Denisoff, R. Serge. *Sing a Song of Social Significance.* Bowling Green, Ohio: Bowling Green University Popular Press, 1972.

Eliot, Marc. *Death of a Rebel — Phil Ochs and a Small Circle of Friends.* Garden City, N.Y.: Anchor Books, 1979.

Friedburg, Harris. "Bob Dylan: Psycho-historian of a Generation." *Chronicle of Higher Education* 7 (January 28, 1974): 15–16.

Rosenstone, Richard A. "The Times They Are A-Changin': The Music of Protest." *Annals of the American Academy of Political and Social Science 382 (May 1969):* 131–44.

## LANGUAGE INNOVATIONS

*Question:*

How do contemporary singers and songwriters utilize slang terms and other nontraditional language structures in their lyrics?

*Concepts to investigate:*

| | | |
|---|---|---|
| jargon | poetic license | slang |
| second language | street talk | colloquialism |
| innovation | creativity | subculture |

*Approach:*

Have each student develop a list of nontraditional words, terms, phrases, and idea patterns from the lyrics of popular songs that illustrate the development of various linguistic subcultures. Invite an English instructor to speak to the class on the topic of flexibility and creativity in language usage (e.g., *Sputnik, A-OK, grok*).

*Recommended songs:*

1. Overview
   "I Dig Rock and Roll Music" — Peter, Paul, and Mary
2. Specific words, terms, and phrases
   "Jive Talkin' " — Bee Gees
   "Tell It Like It Is" — Aaron Neville
   "The Nitty Gritty" — Shirley Ellis
   "Please, Mrs. Henry" — Bob Dylan

"Superfly" — Curtis Mayfield
"Funky Broadway" — Wilson Pickett
"It's Your Thing" — Isley Brothers
3. Cultural phrasing and jargon
"Rock and Roll Music" — Chuck Berry
"Subterranean Homesick Blues" — Bob Dylan
"Put a Curse on You" — Melvin Van Peebles
"Pusherman" — Curtis Mayfield
"Fancy Dancer" — Commodores
"Tiny Montgomery" — Bob Dylan

*Bibliography:*

Brown, Claude. "The Language of Soul." In *Black America: Accommodation and Confrontation in the Twentieth Century*, ed. Richard Resh. (Lexington, Mass.: D.C. Heath, 1969). Pp. 244–49.

Charters, Samuel. *The Poetry of the Blues*. New York: Oak Publications, 1963.

Goldberg, Steven. "Bob Dylan and the Poetry of Salvation." *Saturday Review* (May 30, 1970): 43–46ff.

Graves, Barbara Farris, and Donald J. McBain, eds. *Lyric Voices: Approaches to the Poetry of Contemporary Song*. New York: Wiley, 1972.

Pichaske, David R., ed. *Beowulf to Beatles: Approaches to Poetry*. New York: Free Press, 1972.

Sarlin, Bob. "The First Songpoet — Bob Dylan." In *Turn It Up (I Can't Hear the Words): The Best of the New Singer/Songwriters*. New York: Simon and Schuster, 1973. Pp. 38–74.

## PERSONAL PROBLEMS

*Question:*

How should an individual react when he or she is a victim of social discrimination or public hypocrisy in American society?

*Concepts to investigate:*

| | | |
|---|---|---|
| prejudice | segregation | materialism |
| alienation | isolation | inequity |
| discrimination | powerlessness | hypocrisy |

*Approach:*

Develop a lyrical biography of a socially alienated, politically
powerless individual. Have students analyze this individual's situation,
provide suggestions about resolving his or her problems, and state
how they would respond to similar problems in their own lives.

*Recommended songs:*

1. Prejudice and social tyranny
   "Black Pearl"—Sonny Charles and the Checkmates, Ltd.
   "Society's Child"—Janis Ian
   "Blowin' in the Wind"—Bob Dylan
   "Why Can't We Live Together"—Timmy Thomas
   "Hickory Holler's Tramp"—O. C. Smith
   "Indian Reservation (The Lament of the Cherokee Reservation
        Indian)"—Raiders
   "Why I Sing the Blues"—B. B. King
   "I Am Woman"—Helen Reddy
   "Single Girl"—Sandy Posey
2. Personal alienation and public hypocrisy
   "Eleanor Rigby"—Beatles
   "Easy to Be Hard"—Three Dog Night
   "Joey"—Bob Dylan
   "A Most Peculiar Man"—Simon and Garfunkel
   "Nowhere Man"—Beatles
   "Won't Get Fooled Again"—Who
   "Who Killed Davey Moore?"—Bob Dylan
   "A Natural Man"—Lou Rawls
   "Games People Play"—Joe South and the Believers
   "Mr. Businessman"—Ray Stevens
   "Compared to What"—Les McCann and Eddie Harris
   "Elected"—Alice Cooper

*Bibliography:*

Bern, Eric. *Games People Play.* New York: Grove Press, 1964.
Cooper, B. Lee. "The Image of the Black Man: Contemporary Lyrics as Oral
        History." *Journal of the Interdenominational Theological Center,* 5 (Spring
        1978): 105–22.

_____. "The Image of the Outsider in Contemporary Lyrics." *Journal of Popular Culture* 12 (Summer 1978): 168–78.

de Beauvoir, Simone, and Betty Friedan. "Sex, Society, and the Female Dilemma." *Saturday Review* 2 (June 14, 1975): 10–20ff.

Eggan, Frederick Russell. *The American Indian: Perspectives for the Study of Social Change.* Chicago: Aldine, 1966.

Silberman, Charles E. *Crisis in Black and White.* New York: Random House, 1964.

## WOMEN'S LIBERATION

*Question:*

How do the lyrics of songs by contemporary female recording stars reflect the ideas and attitudes generated by the women's liberation movement in the United States?

*Concepts to investigate:*

| | | |
|---|---|---|
| sexism | affirmative action | E.R.A. |
| discrimination | equal opportunity | liberation |
| awareness | political influence | identity |

*Approach:*

Have the class construct a list of contemporary female singing stars. Assign teams of three students to investigate a female singer's personal background, the history of her recording success, and the social and political themes contained in her songs. In addition to the singers listed below, include Buffy Sainte-Marie, Peggy Lee, Carole King, Karen Carpenter, Bonnie Bramlett, Janis Joplin, Roberta Flack, Mary Travers, Toni Tennille, Marie Osmond, Bette Midler, and Natalie Cole.

*Recommended songs:*

1. Liberation
    "Different Drum" – Stone Poneys
    "I Am Woman" – Helen Reddy
    "It Ain't Me, Babe" – Joan Baez
    "Don't Rain on My Parade" – Barbra Streisand

2. Male chauvinism
   "When Will I Be Loved"—Linda Ronstadt
   "You're So Vain"—Carly Simon
   "Playboy"—Marvelettes
3. Social commentary
   "With God on Our Side"—Odetta
   "Big Yellow Taxi"—Joni Mitchell
   "We Shall Overcome"—Joan Baez
   "Blowin' in the Wind"—Jackie DeShannon
   "Masters of War"—Judy Collins
4. Sexual responsibility
   "Mr. Big Stuff"—Jean Knight
   "Love Child"—Diana Ross and the Supremes
   "Don't Touch Me"—Bettye Swann
5. Male-female relations
   "Me and Bobby McGee"—Janis Joplin
   "Respect"—Aretha Franklin
   "I Heard It through the Grapevine"—Gladys Knight and the Pips
   "All I Really Want to Do"—Cher

*Bibliography:*

Cooper, B. Lee. "Women's Studies and Popular Music: Using Audio Resources in Social Studies Instruction." *History and Social Science Teacher* 14 (Fall 1978): 29–40.

Coppage, Noel. "Joni Mitchell: Innocence on a Spree." *Stereo Review* (April 1976): 64–70.

———. "Country Music's Traipsin' Women." *Stereo Review* (December 1974): 84–89.

Olsin, James T. *Aretha Franklin.* Mankato, Minn.: Creative Educational Society, 1974.

Page, Earl, et al. "Diana: A Billboard Special Supplement." *Billboard* (March 20, 1976): 1–72.

Reinartz, Kay F. "The Paper Doll: Images of American Woman in Popular Songs." In *Women: A Feminist Perspective,* ed. Jo Freeman. Palo Alto, Calif.: Mayfield, 1975. Pp. 293–308.

Rodnitzky, Jerome L. "Songs of Sisterhood: The Music of Women's Liberation," *Popular Music and Society* 4 (1975): 77–85.

Sievert, William A. "For Every Bob Dylan, a Joni Mitchell," *Chronicle of Higher Education* (January 12, 1976): 17.

Silverman, Jerry, comp. *The Liberated Woman's Songbook*. New York: Collier, 1971.

Windeler, Robert. "Carole King: 'You Can Get to Know Me through My Music,' " *Stereo Review* 30 (May 1973): 76–77.

## Lyric Propaganda

*Question:*

How have songs been used throughout American history to directly influence public opinion on political issues?

*Concepts to investigate:*

| | | |
|---|---|---|
| propaganda | broadside ballads | image-making |
| slogans | folk songs | straw-man |
| influence | historical accuracy | stereotypes |

*Approach:*

Throughout American history, political campaigns and wars have stimulated the writing and performing of propagandistic songs. Students should be challenged to investigate the slanted perspectives presented in each of the following songs, with particular attention directed toward examining the propaganda devices utilized within the context of the lyrics.

*Recommended songs:*

1. Political issues
   "Chicago" – Crosby, Stills, Nash, and Young
   "Okie from Muskogee" – Merle Haggard
   "Only a Pawn in Their Game" – Bob Dylan
   "Won't Get Fooled Again" – Who
   "Elected" – Alice Cooper
   "Ohio" – Crosby, Stills, Nash, and Young
2. International conflicts
   "The Ballad of the Green Berets" – Barry Sadler
   "I Ain't Marching Anymore" – Phil Ochs
   "War" – Edwin Starr
   "The Fightin' Side of Me" – Merle Haggard

"Masters of War"—Bob Dylan
"The Battle Hymn of Lt. Calley"—Terry Nelson and C Company
"Draft Dodger Rag"—Phil Ochs
"The Battle of New Orleans"—Johnny Horton

*Bibliography:*
Cooper, B. Lee. "Social Change, Popular Music, and the Teacher." *Social Education* 37 (December 1973): 776–81ff.
Dane, Barbara, and Irwin Silber, eds. *The Vietnam Songbook.* New York: The Guardian, 1969.
Denisoff, R. Serge, and David Fandray. " 'Hey, Hey Woody Guthrie I Wrote You a Song': The Political Side of Bob Dylan." *Popular Music and Society* (1977): 31–42.
Glazer, Tom, ed. *Songs of Peace, Freedom, and Protest.* Greenwich, Conn.: Fawcett, 1970.
Ochs, Phil. *The War Is Over.* New York: Collier, 1967.
Reid, Robert. "Music and Social Problems—A Poster Series." Portland, Maine: J. Weston Walch, 1971.
Seidman, Laurence I. " 'Get on the Raft with Taft'; and Other Musical Treats." *Social Education* 40 (October 1976): 436–37.
_____. "Teaching about the American Revolution through Its Folk Songs." *Social Education* 37 (November 1973): 653–64.

## SOCIAL MOBILITY

*Question:*
How do the lyrics of popular songs depict routes toward upward mobility and personal independence for young Americans?

*Concepts to investigate:*

| | | |
|---|---|---|
| social mobility | education | success |
| equal opportunity | materialism | access |
| Horatio Alger myth | myth of the self-made man | democracy |

*Approach:*
Explain the rags-to-riches Horatio Alger theme that dominated the social thought of upwardly mobile Americans during the late nineteenth and early twentieth centuries. Then have students consider the

different types of personal goals and aspirations that are depicted in the lyrics of contemporary songs. Finally, have the members of the class compare the materialistic goals of the self-made man myth with the more idealistic objectives set forth by most contemporary singers.

*Recommended songs:*
"Makin' It"—David Naughton
"Dead End Street"—Lou Rawls
"Take This Job and Shove It"—Johnny Paycheck
"Johnny B. Goode"—Church Berry
"Keep On Pushin' "—Impressions
"I Am Woman"—Helen Reddy
"My Way"—Frank Sinatra
"I Got a Name"—Jim Croce
"People Gotta Be Free"—Rascals
"I've Got To Be Me"—Sammy Davis, Jr.
"A Natural Man"—Lou Rawls
"You Can Make It If You Try"—Sly and the Family Stone
"Movin' Out (Anthony's Song)"—Billy Joel

*Bibliography:*
"Ray Charles—Playboy Interview." *Playboy* (March 1970): 67–82.
Garland, Phyl. "Roberta Flack: New Musical Messenger." *Ebony* (January 1971): 54–62.
Glazier, Steven. "Richie Havens: From Brooklyn to the Other Side of the Universe." In *The Rolling Stone Rock 'N' Roll Reader*, ed. Ben Fong-Torres. New York: Bantam, 1974. Pp. 282–84.
Morse, David. *Motown and the Arrival of Black Music.* New York: Collier, 1971.
Rodnitzky, Jerome L. "Bob Dylan: Beyond Left and Right." In *Minstrels of the Dawn: The Folk-Protest Singer as a Cultural Hero.* Chicago: Nelson-Hall, 1976. Pp. 101–34.

## SOCIAL COMMENTARY

*Question:*
What are some of the controversial social and political topics that are repeatedly emphasized in the lyrics of popular songs?

*Concepts to investigate:*

| | | |
|---|---|---|
| muckraking | ecology | propaganda |
| race relations | ideology | political cynicism |
| social criticism | media influence | |

*Approach:*

Have each student assemble a list of four to six songs which illustrate varying points of view on a significant social or political issue. Discuss the assumptions that undergird the arguments presented by each singer toward a selected topic. Then have the class decide which of the lyrical arguments is the most forceful on a particular issue.

*Recommended songs:*

1. Drug abuse
   "The Pusher"—Steppenwolf
   "White Rabbit"—Jefferson Airplane
   "Mr. Tambourine Man"—Bob Dylan
   "Amphetamine Annie"—Canned Heat
   "Along Comes Mary"—Association
   "Kicks"—Paul Revere and the Raiders
   'Purple Haze"—Jimi Hendrix Experience
   "Mother's Little Helper"—Rolling Stones
2. Environmental protection
   "Mercy, Mercy Me (The Ecology)"—Marvin Gaye
   "Pleasant Valley Sunday"—Monkees
   "The Family of Man"—Three Dog Night
   "A Hard Rain's A Gonna Fall"—Bob Dylan
   "Whose Garden Was This?"—Tom Paxton
   "Where Do the Children Play?"—Cat Stevens
   "Big Yellow Taxi"—Joni Mitchell
   "Pollution"—Tom Lehrer
   "Ecology Song"—Steven Stills
3. Race relations
   "In the Ghetto"—Elvis Presley
   "Say It Loud—I'm Black and I'm Proud"—James Brown
   "Southern Man"—Neil Young
   "Oxford Town"—Bob Dylan
   "Choice of Colors"—Impressions

"Mighty Mighty, Spade and Whitey" — Curtis Mayfield
"Don't Call Me Nigger, Whitey" — Sly and the Family Stone
"Brown Sugar" — Rolling Stones
4. War
    "2 + 2 = ?" — Bob Seger System
    "I-Feel-Like-I'm-Fixin'-To-Die Rag" — Country Joe and the Fish
    "Masters of War" — Bob Dylan
    "Ballad of the Green Berets" — Barry Sadler
    "War" — Edwin Starr
    "I Ain't Marching Anymore" — Phil Ochs
    "Give Peace a Chance" — Leon Russell
    "Fightin' Side of Me" — Merle Haggard

*Bibliography:*
"Children of Bobby Dylan: Boom in Protest Songs with a Rock Beat." *Life* (November 5, 1965): 43–50.
Cooper, B. Lee. "Bob Dylan, Isaac Asimov, and Social Problems: Materials for Reflective Teaching." *International Journal of Instructional Media* 4 (1976–77): 105–15.
Denisoff, R. Serge. "Folk-Rock: Folk Music, Protest, or Commercialism?" *Journal of Popular Culture,* 3 (Fall 1969): 214–30.
———. "Kent State, Muskogee, and the White House." *Broadside* 108 (July 1970): 2–4.
Eisen, Jonathan, ed. *The Age of Rock: Sound of the American Cultural Revolution.* New York: Vintage Books, 1969.
———. *The Age of Rock – 2: Sights and Sounds of the Cultural Revolution.* New York: Vintage Books, 1970.
Rodnitzky, Jerome L. "The New Revivalism: American Protest Songs Since 1945." In *American Vistas, 1877 to the Present,* 2d ed., ed. Leonard Dinnerstein and Kenneth T. Jackson. New York: Oxford University Press, 1975. Pp. 323–31.

FUTURE CONCERNS

*Question:*
According to the lyrical commentaries of contemporary singers and songwriters, what are the dominant social and political issues Americans must face during the final two decades of the twentieth century?

*Concepts/issues to investigate:*

| | | |
|---|---|---|
| future shock | prediction | prophecy |
| planning | population | social change |
| energy | automation | international conflict |

*Approach:*

Have each student select a popular recording containing lyrics that deal with an unresolved social or political issue that is likely to have an impact on future society. After listening to the record, discuss the specific topic, evaluate the significance of the issue, and place it on a rank-ordered scale of concern with items identified by the other members of the class.

*Recommended songs:*

1. Race relations
    "Black and White"—Three Dog Night
    "Oxford Town"—Bob Dylan
    "Why Can't We Live Together"—Timmy Thomas
2. Social change
    "A Change Is Gonna Come"—Sam Cooke
    "The Times They Are A-Changin' "—Bob Dylan
    "Shape of Things to Come"—Max Frost and the Troopers
3. Political hypocrisy
    "Eve of Destruction"—Barry McGuire
    "Only a Pawn in Their Game"—Bob Dylan
    "Monster"—Steppenwolf
4. War
    "War"—Edwin Starr
    "Masters of War"—Bob Dylan
    "Universal Soldier"—Buffy Sainte-Marie
5. Fear of a police state
    "Mad Dog"—Lee Michaels
    "For What It's Worth"—Buffalo Springfield
    "My Crime"—Canned Heat
6. Automation and alienation
    "Ball of Confusion"—Temptations
    "Subterranean Homesick Blues"—Bob Dylan
    "In the Year 2525"—Zager and Evans

*Bibliography:*

Cooper, B. Lee. "Images of the Future in Popular Music: Lyrical Comments on Tomorrow." *Social Education* (May 1975): 276–85.

Dunstan, M. J., and P. Garland. *Worlds in the Making: Probes for Students of the Future.* Englewood Cliffs, N.J.: Prentice-Hall, 1970.

Theobald, Robert. *Futures Conditional.* Indianapolis: Bobbs-Merrill, Inc., 1972.

Toffler, Alvin. *Future Shock.* New York: Bantam, 1970.

———, ed. *The Futurists.* New York: Random House, 1972.

# TWO

# Challenging Sexism through Popular Music

Recently I observed, "A new wind is blowing through American class-rooms. This stiff breeze is dislodging the blinding cobwebs of male chauvinism, scattering the dusty female stereotypes of past days, and blowing closed forever the pages of sexist textbooks."[1]

Today, however, instructors must strive to do more than merely heighten attention to women's studies. The study of the role of the American woman must be enlightening to *both* sexes if such knowledge is to have future social impact.

The fundamental challenge facing social studies teachers who wish to alter long-standing sexist biases in American society is to reform traditional educational practices which have dulled the sensitivities of male *and* female students to the complex roles of women in contemporary social and political life. Students must be encouraged to reflect upon the full range of life-styles, occupations, and attitudes available to both sexes. Still, it is the female image that demands initial attention in order to make such parallel comparisons possible. Anne Firor Scott, noting the stereotypic images that have traditionally dominated historical studies, speculates,

> In some ideal world there would be no such thing as women's history since social historians would recognize that male *and* female make up society, create mores, pattern the culture; economic historians would be aware that women have always been part of the labour force and

have contributed to economic choices; legal historians would know that case law and to some degree statute law have been shaped by the needs and demands of women; political historians would be aware of the people who organized the precincts as well as the people who met at the summit.[2]

I believe the social studies classroom can become an active arena for exposing and attacking the monolithic stereotype of the submissive female. I also feel that through the use of audio resources, students can be encouraged to examine and to compare the multiplicity of behaviors exhibited by men and women in a pluralistic society. Since the lyrics of popular songs contain rich social and personal commentary, they should be introduced as instructional materials for critical classroom investigation.

All effective teaching approaches are directed by clearly articulated objectives. Although no single set of goals can encompass the total responsibility for teaching a realistic view of American women, the following list of objectives underpin my position:

1. To examine the stereotypes and social myths that shroud the behavioral patterns of women in contemporary society.
2. To illustrate the professional activities and avocational pursuits in which women currently participate.
3. To introduce a variety of male and female models which can be used as focal points for student investigation and reflection.
4. To examine selected written and oral resources on the images of women in American society.
5. To improve the self-image of female students while enhancing the understanding of male students concerning the social circumstances of contemporary women.

These objectives are geared toward defining identity/self-image, emphasizing social reality, promoting change in both thought and action, and pursuing a realistic, balanced view of contemporary women.

Noted author James Baldwin has written, "People are trapped in history and history is trapped in them."[3] This perceptive comment should challenge social studies teachers to explore the extent to which their students have been "trapped" into a restricted view of women in society. One particularly productive approach for adding a new dimension to a unit on women's studies is to utilize the lyrics from contemporary songs to illustrate the pluralistic nature of male and female relationships. This technique can be introduced by selecting a series of personal and social themes for classroom study.

Outlines of several proposed lesson plans that might be used by social studies teachers to generate a more balanced view of the feminist position are presented on the following pages. These lesson plans—organized in a male/female lyrical dichotomy—can be expanded or combined to illustrate specific points of interpersonal, social, political, or economic concern. For instance, the male attitude toward the institution of marriage, which is traditionally defined as ambivalent at best, has its counterpart in the female mind. This fact can be demonstrated to students by playing antithetical recordings by Linda Ronstadt and the Stone Poneys ("Different Drum"—Capitol 2004) and Dinah Shore ("Love and Marriage"—RCA 6266). One strength of utilizing this teaching approach is its flexibility. An instructor can examine a universal social concept, such as "marriage," from a variety of perspectives, depending upon the specific recordings employed. Once a central theme has been identified, though, several members of the class will inevitably attempt to outdo the teacher by assembling their own audio references to support other positions or to illustrate still different values. Thus, the original two-song illustration on the topic of marriage may be expanded through student suggestions to include "Worst That Could Happen" (Buddah 75) by the Brooklyn Bridge, "I'm Gonna Get Married" (ABC 10032) by Lloyd Price, "It's Too Soon to Know" (Argo 5402) by Etta James, and "Someone Saved My Life Tonight" (MCA 40421) by Elton John. Although this open-ended, student-initiated audio debate may disrupt other preplanned class presentations, the enthusiasm and new ideas generated within the class will more than compensate for occasional problems created by expanding the time assigned for a specific topic.

Assembled below are several lesson plans illustrating the technique of using contemporary song lyrics to examine the images and roles of women in contemporary American society. It is my opinion that without the introduction of such innovative classroom resourses, many students—male and female—will continue to be "trapped" in history.

## SUBMISSIVE INDIVIDUALS

*Question:*
Why do some persons seem compelled to submit to demands made by members of the opposite sex?

*Concepts to investigate:*

| | |
|---|---|
| dependence | submission |
| alienation | selflessness |

*Songs and performers:*

FEMALE IMAGES
"Good-Hearted Woman" (RCA 10529) — Waylon and Willie
"Chain of Fools" (Atlantic 2464) — Aretha Franklin
"Oh Me Oh My (I'm a Fool for You Baby)" (Atco 6722) — Lulu
"Piece of My Heart" (Shout 221) — Erma Franklin
"Help Me Make It through the Night" (Mega 615-0015) — Sammi Smith
"Midnight Train to Georgia" (Buddah 383) — Gladys Knight and the Pips
"Angel of the Morning" (Bell 705) — Merilee Rush
"Where You Lead" (Columbia 45414) — Barbra Streisand

MALE IMAGES
"Love Me" (RCA EPA 992) — Elvis Presley
"Carpet Man" (Soul City 762) — Fifth Dimension
"When a Man Loves a Woman" (Atlantic 2326) — Percy Sledge
"If You Don't Come Back" (Atlantic 2201) — Drifters
"Snap Your Fingers" (Todd 1072) — Joe Henderson
"Since I Met You Baby" (Atlantic 1111) — Ivory Joe Hunter
"I'm Your Puppet" (Bell 648) — James and Bobby Purify
"Under Your Spell Again" (Imperial 66144) — Johnny Rivers

## DOMINANT INDIVIDUALS

*Question:*
How do some persons achieve positions of physical or emotional dominance over others?

*Concepts to investigate:*

| | |
|---|---|
| domination | fear |
| courage | power |

*Songs and performers:*

FEMALE IMAGES

"Lucretia MacEvil" (Columbia 45235) — Blood, Sweat, and Tears

"Polk Salad Annie" (Monument 1104) — Tony Joe White

"Swamp Witch" (MGM 14496) — Jim Stafford

"Lady Marmalade" (Epic 50048) — LaBelle

"Mother-In-Law" (Minit 623) — Ernie K-Doe

"Man or Mouse" (Duke 413) — Junior Parker

"Don't Mess with Bill" (Tamla 54126) — Marvelettes

"Honky Tonk Woman" (London 910) — Rolling Stones

"Mary Lou" (Roulette 4177) — Ronnie Hawkins

MALE IMAGES

"You Don't Mess Around with Jim" (ABC 11328) — Jim Croce

"Seventh Son" (Imperial 6612) — Johnny Rivers

"Hard to Handle" (Atco 6592) — Otis Redding

"Brown-Eyed Handsome Man" (Chess 1635) — Chuck Berry

"Steamroller Blues" (RCA 74-0910) — Elvis Presley

"Sixteen Tons" (Atlantic 3323) — Don Harrison Band

"A Man and a Half" (Atlantic 2575) — Wilson Pickett

"Goldfinger" (United Artists 790) — Shirley Bassey

"Secret Agent Man" (Imperial 66159) — Johnny Rivers

## NEGATIVE SELF-IMAGE

*Question:*

Why do some persons feel that they are incapable of controlling their own lives?

*Concepts to investigate:*

| | |
|---|---|
| sexism | prejudice |
| paternalism | loneliness |
| stereotypes | powerlessness |

*Songs and performers:*

FEMALE IMAGES

"I'm Livin' in Shame" (Motown 1139)—Diana Ross and the Supremes

"Born a Woman" (MGM 13501)—Sandy Posey

"Dreams of the Everyday Housewife" (Capitol 2224)—Glen Campbell

"Down on Me" (Mainstream 662)—Big Brother and the Holding Company

"When Will I Be Loved" (Capitol 4050)—Linda Ronstadt

"Half Breed" (MCA 40102)—Cher

"Society's Child (Baby, I've Been Thinking)" (Verve Forecast 5027)—Janis Ian

"Single Girl: (MGM 13612)—Sandy Posey

"Mother's Little Helper" (London 902)—Rolling Stones

MALE IMAGES

"Angel of Mercy" (Stax 0121)—Albert King

"Hard-Time Losin' Man" (ABC 11405)—Jim Croce

"Small Sad Sam" (Versative 107)—Phil McLean

"Carpet Man" (Soul City 762)—Fifth Dimension

"That Lucky Old Sun" (ABC 10509)—Ray Charles

"Why I Sing the Blues" (Bluesway 61024)—B. B. King

"(I Can't Get No) Satisfaction" (London 9766)—Rolling Stones

"Born under a Bad Sign" (Stax 217)—Albert King

"Eighteen" (Warner Brothers 7449)—Alice Cooper

POSITIVE SELF-IMAGE

*Question:*

How do persons express the confidence that they can control their own destinies?"

*Concepts to investigate:*

confidence                      individualism

pride                           success

*Songs and performers:*
FEMALE IMAGES
"These Boots Are Made for Walkin' " (Reprise 0532) — Nancy Sinatra
"You're So Vain" (Elektra 45824) — Carly Simon
"Don't Rain on My Parade" (Columbia 33161) — Barbra Streisand
"I Am Woman" (Capitol 3350) — Helen Reddy
"Mr. Big Stuff (Stax 0088) — Jean Knight
"Fancy" (Capitol 2675) — Bobbie Gentry
"I'm a Woman" (Reprise 1319) — Maria Muldaur
"How Does That Grab You, Darlin' " (Reprise 0461) — Nancy Sinatra
MALE IMAGES
"My Life" (Columbia 10853) — Billy Joel
"I Got a Name" (ABC 11389) — Jim Croce
"My Way" (Reprise 0817) — Frank Sinatra
"A Natural Man" (MGM 14262) — Lou Rawls
"Dead End Street" (Capitol 5869) — Lou Rawls
"I'm a Man" (Checker 814) — Bo Diddley
"Steamroller Blues" (Warner Brothers 7144) — James Taylor
"I'm a Happy Man" (United Artists 853) — Jive Five


## PERSONAL INDEPENDENCE AND MUTUAL RESPECT

*Question:*
Can a person maintain personal principles and exercise independent judgment — and still receive respect from others who hold different opinions?

*Concepts to investigate:*

| | |
|---|---|
| ethics | independence |
| freedom | principles |
| respect | individualism |

*Songs and performers:*
FEMALE IMAGES
"Respect" (Atlantic 2403) — Aretha Franklin
"Don't Make Me Over" (Specter 1239) — Dionne Warwick
"Different Drum" (Capitol 2004) — Stone Poneys

"Think" (Atlantic 2528)—Aretha Franklin
"It's Your Thing" (T Neck 901)—Isley Brothers
"Don't Touch Me" (Capitol 2382)—Bettye Swann
MALE IMAGES
"Respect" (Volt 128)—Otis Redding
"Ninety-Nine and A Half (Won't Do)" (Atlantic 2334)—Wilson Pick-
ett
"Satisfied Mind" (Philips 40400)—Bobby Hebb
"I've Got to Be Me" (Reprise 0779)—Sammy Davis, Jr.
"Stand!" (Epic 10450)—Sly and the Family Stone
"Gentle on My Mind" (Capitol 5939)—Glen Campbell

## REBELS AND OUTCASTS

*Question:*
What physical characteristics, actions, or ideas earn a person the label
of "rebel" in contemporary American society?

*Concepts to investigate:*
aggression                          ostracism
rebellion                           crime

*Songs and performers:*
FEMALE IMAGES
"Mean Woman Blues" (Monument 824)—Roy Orbison
"Rag Doll" (Philips 40211)—Four Seasons
"Suzanne" (Reprise 0615)—Noel Harrison
"Evil Ways" (Columbia 45069)—Santana
"Lady Godiva" (Capitol 5740)—Peter and Gordon
"Swamp Witch" (MGM 14496)—Jim Stafford
"Mississippi Queen" (Windfall 532)—Mountain
"Harper Valley PTA" (Plantation 3)—Jeannie C. Riley
"Sweet Cream Ladies, Forward March" (Mala 12035)—Box Tops
"Witchy Woman" (Asylum 11008)—Eagles
MALE IMAGES
"Born to Be Wild" (Dunhill 4138)—Steppenwolf
"Ramblin' Man" (Capricorn 0027)—Allman Brothers Band

"Big Bad John" (Columbia 42175)—Johnny Dean
"Ramblin' Gamblin' Man" (Capitol 2297)—Bob Seger System
"Trouble Man" (Talma 54218)—Marvin Gaye
"Outlaw Man" (Asylum 11025)—Eagles
"Papa Was a Rollin' Stone" (Gordy 7121)—Temptations
"Ringo" (RCA 8444)—Lorne Greene
"Big Boy Pete" (Arvee 595)—Olympics
"The Snake" (Soul City 767)—Al Wilson

## BIBLIOGRAPHY

The following books and articles suggest various instructional approaches designed to help students overcome sexist attitudes and to aid them in developing healthy self-images.

Alpern, Mildred. "Images of Women in European History." *Social Education* 42 (March 1978):220–24.

Bell, Susan G. "Discovering Women's History through Art in the Classroom." *History Teacher* 6 (August 1973):503–10.

Brown, Richard C. "Postage Stamps and American Women: Stamping Out Discrimination in the Mails." *Social Education* 38 (January 1974):20–23.

Cooper, B. Lee. "The Traditional and Beyond: Resources for Teaching Women's Studies." *Audiovisual Instruction* 22 (December 1977):14–18ff.

Domann, Cathy, and Mary Lee Wright. "Teaching the Big Ideas: What Is Liberation? A Closer Look at the Women's Equal Rights Amendment." In *Teaching American History: The Quest for Relevancy*, ed. Allan O. Kownslar. Washington, D.C.: National Council for the Social Studies, 1974. Pp. 57–79.

Grambs, Jean D. "Sex Stereotypes in Instructional Materials, Literature, and Language: A Survey of Research." *Women's Studies Abstracts* 1 (December 1972):1–4, 91–94.

_____, ed. *Teaching about Women in the Social Studies: Concepts, Methods, and Materials.* Washington, D.C.: National Council for the Social Studies, 1976.

Hoffert, Sylvia D. "Some Techniques in Teaching Women's History." *Teaching History* 1 (Spring 1976):25–27.

Jeffrey, Kirk, and Diane Cirksema. "Women's History in the High School Survey: An Integrationist Approach," *History Teacher* 11 (November 1977):39–46.

Lerner, Gerda. "New Approaches to the Study of Women in American History." *Journal of Social History* 3 (1970):53–62.

_____. "Teaching Women's History." *AHA Newsletter* 14 (May/June 1976):3–6.

Morgan, Robin, ed. *Sisterhood Is Powerful: An Anthology of Writings from the Women's Liberation Movement.* New York: Random House, 1970.

Riley, Glenda. "Is Clio Still Sexist? Women's History in Recent American History Texts." *Teaching History* 1 (Spring 1976):15–24.

Scott, Anne Firor. "Women in American Life." In *The Reinterpretation of American History and Culture,* eds. William H. Cartwright and Richard L. Watson. Washington, D.C.: National Council for the Social Studies, 1973. Pp. 151–63.

Sochen, June. *Herstory: A Woman's View of American History.* New York: Alfred Pub. Co., 1974.

Trecker, Janice Law. "Teaching the Role of Women in American History." In *Teaching Ethnic Studies,* ed. James A. Banks. Washington, D.C.: National Council for the Social Studies, 1973. Pp. 279–92.

_____. "Women in U.S. History High School Textbooks." *Social Education* 35 (March 1971): 249–61ff.

# THREE

# Popular Music and Religious Education

Sing unto Him a new song; play skillfully with a loud noise.
— Psalms 33:3

For the present . . . music remains the religion of the young. It is a
religion which plays upon the themes of the mystery of the universe and
man himself, the problem of good and evil, the importance of magic and
ritual, the possibility of divine intervention, and the potential for both
personal and cosmic transformation.
— Edward F. Heenan and H. Rosanne Falkenstein

The relationship between religion and popular music has yet to be
clearly defined. While some writers have denounced rock and roll as
Satan's tool to debase the moral character of America's youth,[1] others
have asserted that fundamental tenets of Christian religious doctrine
and social gospel evangelism are inherent in the lyrics of numerous
popular songs.[2] Despite the public acclaim for religiously oriented
musical productions such as *Jesus Christ Superstar* and *Godspell*, individuals hostile to contemporary music have continued to reject all pro-
posals for detente in the holy war between church choirs and rock
bands. One result of this uncompromising criticism of popular music as
antireligious has been the alienation of youth from church choir tradi-
tionalism and a conscious drifting among some young people toward a
new religiosity founded on a cult of drugs and psychedelic music.[3]
Although the following discussion may not permanently resolve the

continuing war between religious purists who hate rock music and rock
fanatics who openly disdain all facets of organized religion, I hope that
it will suggest a reasonable technique for adapting the lyrics of popular
songs to church school education.

During the past decade church membership rolls have declined and
Sunday school attendance has dwindled. This latter trend is most
visible among youth classes and young adult sections. One reason for
this phenomenon seems obvious: the teaching materials employed in
most religious education classes bear little relation to the personal
concerns of individuals between the ages of sixteen and thirty. The
recognition of this fact, however, is not enough to halt declining church
school attendance. Unless church leaders are content to see Sunday
school classes become either baby-sitting services for preadolescents or
social hours for senior citizens, positive steps must be taken to revitalize
educational efforts in youth areas. Initially, clear objectives that have
the potential to jar religious education from its current state of atrophy
must be adopted. Among these principles, the following goals seem
paramount: (1) to identify socially relevant biblical ideas, ideals, and
imperatives; (2) to define indigenous personal and social concerns
among various groups within the church; (3) to foster active debate,
investigation, and cooperation among young people and adults in the
church in discussing significant problems; and (4) to urge each church
member to undertake an introspective analysis of his or her own
personal value structure. Although a variety of curricular materials
might be utilized to foster this type of dynamic educational experience,
the leaders of religious education classes would be hard pressed to find a
better source of textual motivation than the lyrics of popular songs.
These lyrics, when creatively combined with selected biblical references and thought-provoking questions, demonstrate genuine promise
of producing problem-centered discussion and social action that have
not been present in most Sunday school classes.

In a recent essay appearing in the Methodist *Christian Home* magazine, William E. Wolfe asserts that ". . . pop music has become people
music with no age brackets applicable. At times the [Top 40] charts
have looked like the table of contents in a hymnbook with a message
for everyone."[4] Judging from the acceptance of guitar-accompanied

folk masses in the Catholic Church, the presentation of popular songs
by youth choirs during Protestant services, the initiation of interdenominational, church-sponsored tours to view productions such as
*Jesus Christ Superstar,* and the citation of Bob Dylan, Paul Simon, and
Carole King lyrics by ministers and priests alike, one would be tempted
to think that Wolfe's statement accurately depicts a dominant attitude
in religious thought and practice throughout the United States. Unfortunately, this is not the case. In fact, the failure of a majority of
ministers and lay Sunday school teachers to recognize the potentially
powerful connection between the themes developed in the lyrics of
popular songs and Christian doctrinal teaching has retarded attempts to
introduce this type of material into church school classes.

The key to successfully introducing popular music in religious education lies in the selection of appropriate themes and lyrics for study. In
pursuing these elements, tendencies toward tokenism and didacticism
in lyrical analysis must be squelched. Too often in the past, church
school teachers who have attempted to utilize contemporary songs in
their classes have chosen a single popular tune and then subjected it to a
tedious, hour-long exegesis. Predictably, boredom rather than intellectual stimulation was the result. Just as an overdose of biblical analysis
tends to stupify rather than instruct the laity, so too the overinterpreta-
tion of a single song kills interest and stifles diversity of thought. A
multiple song approach, developed along identifiable thematic lines and
stressing a problematic basis for individual analysis, is required to stimulate class interest and to increase the level of personal involvement. By
selecting a potent theme that clearly combines elements of Christian
philosophy with contemporary social issues, a teacher can be assured
that the members of a religious education class will be forced to adopt a
reflective stance toward the lyrical material being presented.

What themes should be employed in church school classes? The
options are endless. Questions that may be fruitfully confronted include: What is the extent of human freedom in society? Why do people
have problems relating openly to each other? Who are the prophets of
our time—and what are they saying? What is "religious music" in our
time? Why are so many people alienated in our society? Although at
first glance these topics may sound quite elementary, one must not
forget that the most fundamental Christian concepts such as "love" and

"brotherhood" have remained the most difficult to understand and to achieve.

Once a theme for study has been selected, the church school instructor is faced with three interrelated tasks. First, appropriate biblical passages that clearly establish the theological basis for the problem under investigation must be assembled. This chore is somewhat eased by the existence of a thematic concordance in most Bibles. Next, a list of open-ended questions must be prepared to help spark discussion in the class. One must guard against making these questions too specific or factual since the role of the questions is to initiate introspection and personal evaluation of the lyrics being presented, rather than to foster a scientifically objective analysis.[5] Finally, the teacher must select specific songs, photocopy the lyrics for class distribution, and tape the recordings that are to be employed in the classroom presentation. This final set of activities, particularly the responsibility for reproducing lyrics, is simultaneously the most stimulating and most frustrating aspect of this teaching technique. Many traditionally trained church school instructors will simply throw their hands up in dismay, declaring, "Where in the world can I be expected to find the lyrics to popular tunes?" Fortunately, this question is relatively easy to answer. Several recording companies and singing groups have published song books containing the lyrics of their hit recordings. In addition to this, monthly and bimonthly song hit magazines and teenage fan books containing endless lists of lyrics are readily available at local newsstands and supermarkets. In some cases, lyrics may be found accompanying record albums, either on the back of an album cover, on a record's dust cover, or on a song sheet included separately within the album case. Finally, there are several excellent anthologies of popular music lyrics, some of which are already arranged in thematic patterns and slanted toward religious topics, available in paperback editions at most bookstores.[6] These published sources, together with the availability of several young people who already "know" pop lyrics and would be glad to share their "understanding" with a harried adult teacher, should enable any church school instructor to assemble a variety of rock, blues, folk, and country music lyrics.

A serious question must be raised at this point concerning the applicability to religious education of reflective thought, which stresses the critical examination of all positions. Churches, it might be argued, have a vested interest in propagating singular points of view. It hardly seems appropriate for Sunday school classes to serve as forums for the exploration of value conflicts. Of course, one must acknowledge that this position may be true for extremely fundamentalistic religious sects; in such churches it is doubtful that popular music would even be permitted in Sunday school classes under any circumstances. In most churches, though, the acceptance of social involvement through normal mission and outreach channels has precipitated a genuine thirst among the laity for defining interpersonal, social responsibilities. Through skillful application of this popular music teaching technique, traditional Christian values that are generally discussed only at the abstract level (e.g., equality, brotherhood, justice, and freedom) can be exposed to the sharp focus of preachment/practice discontinuity. At this point, where doubt is engendered between the arenas of theory and practice, reflective thinking is fostered and the moral needle provided in folk songs, the trenchant social criticism of the blues, and the open attacks of rock singers on American society's hypocritical value structures become the vehicles for creating such doubts. Among the specific questions that may be posed by an instructor are:

Is Father McKenzie in the Beatles' "Eleanor Rigby" typical of most priests and ministers who write sermons "that no one will hear" or understand?

Is Neil Diamond's "Solitary Man" pursuing personal fidelity from a moral position of strength or weakness?

Do churches have unwritten "signs" (Five Man Electrical Band's "Signs") that alienate young people?

Do church members ignore local community problems in favor of serving "the bleedin' crowd" (Three Dog Night's "Easy To Be Hard") in Africa and India?

Are the ritualistic observation of religious holidays and casual social attendance at church each Sunday examples of "the games people play" (Joe South's "Games People Play")?

Should church members demonstrate more overt concern over black problems of ghetto flats, poor health, malnutrition, poverty, miseducation, welfare inequities, and other notions mentioned by B. B. King ("Why I Sing the Blues"), Lou Rawls ("Dead End Street"), and Albert King ("Angel of Mercy")?

Is Les McCann preaching about the misdirection of social commitment to "unreal values" in the pattern of the ancient biblical prophets in the song "Compared to What"?

Through the use of popular music, a religious education class will probably discover a more fertile basis for group interaction than was ever possible through the rereading of the Sermon on the Mount. But just as Socrates has his critics, so too the Sunday school teacher who dares to combine the use of contemporary songs with the application of reflective thought toward social issues may find a cup of fundamentalist hemlock waiting for him or her in the narthex. Some ministers and lay leaders may object to the use of the popular music in the church parlor because of the frequent tendency for slang phrases or profanity to appear in lyrical context; other critics, feeling that true aesthetic standards are being shirked, may argue that only classical music or traditional hymns should be played, sung, or studied in Sunday school; and yet another disenchanted group may condemn the teaching approach itself as antireligious because it is conflict-oriented and therefore at odds with their views of Christian love and cooperation. More humorously, there is also a segment of the church membership who will cast their vote solely upon the quantitative dimension of Sunday school attendance. Low attendance dictates disapproval; high attendance indicates merit in the educational technique, and thus support. But regardless of the nature of the praise or condemnation, no teacher who is genuinely seeking to motivate his religious education class could utilize a more universally available or appropriate source of social commentary than the lyrics of contemporary songs.

Clearly, the ultimate objective of employing popular music in religious education is to produce behavioral as well as attitudinal change. Church members should be motivated to social action by their education experiences.[7] Although there are many social evils such as ecological imbalance, racial discrimination, poverty, and war cited in the lyrics of popular songs, the lyricist/singer seldom suggests any organizational means for resolving the problems identified. As Jerome L. Rodnitzky has correctly observed, "The protest songs of the sixties are generally low-keyed and detached. They continually and creatively describe evils without suggesting solutions. The stress is on recognition rather than eradication of social injustice."[8] Any religious education worthy of the name must serve as a catalyst for action. First, it must illustrate and illuminate social concerns; and second, it must initiate creative forces that attempt to resolve the problems that were uncovered.

The serious study of popular music should not be limited to sociologists, psychologists, and other academics. Young people and adults in Sunday school classes can gain valuable insights into the nature of their religious commitments through the examination of selected lyrics from contemporary songs. In the broadest sense, there are few forms of social, political, or religious commentary that are more readily adaptable to educational endeavors. And if religious education is to become more dynamic, then instructors must consider the possibility that Thoreau's different drummer might be Ringo Starr rather than Billy Graham.

The following lesson plans conclude this brief chapter. Rather than ending consideration of this approach, however, it is hoped that reading them will mark the beginning of a period of extended educational experimentation.

## Religious Values, Social Issues, and Popular Music

### A Six-Week Course Outline

| Weekly Theme | Scriptural Quotations | Class Questions | Lyric Resources |
|---|---|---|---|
| 1. Popular music and social issues in American society | None | Do the lyrics of contemporary songs reflect the social problems or personal concerns of people in present-day American society? | (Although no lyrics are employed during this first session Wolfe's article from the *Christian Home* had been assigned to each class participant.) |

| | | | |
|---|---|---|---|
| 2. Alienation and loneliness | Nehemiah 2:2<br>Psalms 43:5<br>Jonah 2:7 | What is the source of alienation or loneliness in the song you are studying?<br><br>How could *you* – as a concerned individual and Christian – help the person in the song to resolve the problem(s) that seems to be troubling him or her? | A. "Eleanor Rigby" – Beatles<br>B. "Indian Reservation" – Raiders<br>C. "Solitary Man" – Neil Diamond<br>D. "One" – Three Dog Night<br>E. "Signs" – Five Man Electrical Band<br>F. "Rainy Days and Mondays" – Carpenters |
| 3. Problems of relating to others | Matthew 25:40<br>Romans 14:7 | According to the lyrics of the song that you are analyzing, what is the source of friction that is prohibiting the establishment of an open, firm, honest relationship? | A. "Easy to Be Hard" – Three Dog Night<br>B. "Games People Play" – Joe South and the Believers<br>C. "The Dangling Conversation" – Paul Simon and Art Garfunkel<br>D. "Walk a Mile in My Shoes" – Joe South and the Believers<br>E. "Society's Child" – Janis Ian |
| 4. Contemporary prophets: Lyrics of social analysis and prediction | Matthew 11:9<br>Matthew 12:39<br>Luke 7:16<br>Luke 24:19<br>John 9:17<br>Acts 3:22-23 | What are the characteristics – physical, social, and philosophical – that you would expect of a "prophet" who would appear in the 1980s? | A. "Won't Get Fooled Again" – Who<br>B. "America, Communicate with Me" – Ray Stevens<br>C. "Eve of Destruction" – Barry McGuire<br>D. "Shape of Things to Come" – Max Frost and the Troopers |

|   |   |   |   | E. "For What It's Worth"—Buffalo Springfield |
|---|---|---|---|---|
|   |   |   |   | F. "In the Year 2525"—Zager and Evans |
|   |   |   |   | G. "The Times They Are A-Changin' "—Odetta |
|   |   |   |   | H. "Blowin' in the Wind"—Peter, Paul and Mary |
| 5. Black and blue music: The personal and social problems depicted in songs by black artists | Jeremiah 5:21 Psalms 82:5 Proverbs 23:9 Hosea 4:14 | A. What are the specific personal or social problems depicted in the song you are examining?<br><br>B. Are the problems in this song peculiar to black Americans only?<br><br>C. Is there any constructive way in which the members of this church could help to alleviate the problems described in this song? | A. "Why I Sing the Blues"—B. B. King<br>B. "Angel of Mercy"—Albert King<br>C. "Compared to What"—Les McCann and Eddie Harris<br>D. "Dead End Street"—Lou Rawls<br>E. "Sticks and Stones"—Ray Charles<br>F. "I Don't Want You Cutting Off Your Hair"—B. B. King |
| 6. Religious themes in contemporary music | Psalms 77:6 Psalms 33:3 Psalms 137:4 Isaiah 42:10 | A. Which of these songs do you regard as "religious"? Why?<br><br>B. Which songs are nonreligious, or even antireligious? Why? | A. "Bridge over Troubled Water"—Simon and Garfunkel<br>B. "Jesus Is a Soul Man"—Johnny Rivers<br>C. "Let It Be"—Beatles |

C. How can "religious music" be defined?

D. Why do so many contemporary musicians and singing stars employ religious themes and images in their songs?

D. "7 O'Clock News/Silent Night"—Simon and Garfunkel

E. "Kyrie Eleison"—Electric Prunes

F. "Turn Turn Turn"—Judy Collins

G. "Spirit in the Sky"—Norman Greenbaum

H. "Amazing Grace"—Judy Collins

I. "People Get Ready"—Impressions

J. "Are You Ready?"—Pacific Gas and Electric

K. "I Don't Know How to Love Him"—Helen Reddy

L. "Put Your Hand in the Hand"—Ocean

M. "Oh Happy Day"—Edwin Hawkins Singers

N. "He's Got the Whole World in His Hands"—Laurie London

O. "With God on Our Side"—Joan Baez

# FOUR

# The Black Experience as Illustrated in Popular Music

Black music has been the vanguard reflection of black feeling and the continuous repository of black consciousness.

—Ron Wellburn[1]

Everybody wants to know why I sing the blues. . . . Well, I've been around a long time, I really have paid my dues.

—B. B. King[2]

The ability of a teacher to stimulate reflection on issues of significance to young blacks is clearly dependent upon his or her skill in identifying universal concerns among members of the American black community. One instructional resource that can help a history instructor accomplish this goal is popular music. Traditionally, the lyrics of black singers have rarely been introduced in classrooms. The tendency of academicians, particularly historians, to rely solely upon *written* sources—newspaper articles and editorials; official records from state legislatures and both houses of Congress; books and essays by abolitionists, slaves, politicians, and ministers; as well as other standard literary works—has rendered black history "speechless." In only a few instances has the rich oral tradition of the black man even been considered, let alone thoroughly investigated, by American historians. The following pages will present several instructional approaches that could be introduced to portray more accurately the concerns of black Americans and to translate contemporary black history into a more dynamic oral and literary process.

The significance of the oral tradition in the heritage of the contemporary black American has been frequently expressed and thoroughly documented.[3] For more than three centuries black culture in America has dramatically chronicled its ideas, attitudes, and events in ballad form. Still, most educators continue to rely solely upon written texts, which deaden the minstrel's personal appeal and dull the spiritual force of his or her message. The lyrics of artists such as Isaac Hayes, B. B. King, Aretha Franklin, Smokey Robinson, Roberta Flack, Ray Charles, and Curtis Mayfield, which provide significant insights into the past, present, and future of black America, must be utilized to help foster a living classroom experience. Even at a time when historians and teachers of history are more actively utilizing the written commentaries of previously neglected voices—women, minorities, politically powerless people—to enrich perspectives on the American past, they continue to overlook the significant oral contributions of musical artists in the rich Afro-American tradition. It is even more difficult to understand why most serious scholars of black history have ignored the dramatic emergence of popular music as a major business enterprise,[4] as a source of social criticism,[5] and as a means of national and international cultural exchange.[6]

One very productive approach for adding voices to the heretofore mute texts of Afro-American history involves selecting several significant themes for classroom study. Once identified, these themes can be employed to provide a framework for students to arrange recorded commentaries in a manner that will reveal the texture and pluralism of black culture. Ideally, the interplay of ideas within each thematic structure will encourage each class member to develop a personal position on the central issues.

This thematic structure can be easily expanded to illustrate specific points of social, political, or economic concern. For instance, the black man's ambivalent attitude toward material goods can be dramatically demonstrated to students by contrasting Barret Strong's assertion, "Gimme money! That's all I want!" ("Money"—Anna 11101) with the lyrical warning of the O'Jays, "Money can drive some people out of their minds!" ("For the Love of Money"—CBS 3544). Student contributions to this theme will invariably expand the discussion to include "Busted" (ABC 10481) by Ray Charles, "Money Honey" (Atlantic

1006) by the Drifters, "Spanish Harlem" (ATCO 6185) by Ben E. King, "Patches" (Atlantic 2748) by Clarence Carter, "Payin' the Cost to Be the Boss" (Bluesway 61015) by B. B. King, and more.

The following topical outlines are designed to illustrate this social theme approach. Each section is thematically organized and directed toward the examination of a set of at least six concepts which are directly related to each theme. The topics are supported by popular music recordings and literary resources which have been selected to support the central theme.

## MAJORITY RULE AND MINORITY RIGHTS

*Question:*
Does black music reflect that minority's hope to achieve social and personal goals through participation in a political system which is designed to respond to majoritarian pressures?

*Concepts to investigate:*

| | | |
|---|---|---|
| political process | representation | black power |
| majority rule | social change | revolution |
| minority rights | voting | political parties |
| propaganda | government | elections |

*Songs and performers:*
"Ball of Confusion" (Gordy 7099) — Temptations
"The Declaration" (Bell 860) — Fifth Dimension
"(For God's Sake) Give More Power to the People" (Brunswick 55450) — Chi-Lites
"You're the Man" (Tamia 54221) — Marvin Gaye
"A Change Is Gonna Come" (RCA 8486) — Sam Cooke
"Smiling Faces Sometimes" (Gordy 7108) — Undisputed Truth

*Bibliography*

Carawan, Guy, and Condie Carawan, comps. *We Shall Overcome! Songs of the Southern Freedom Movement.* New York: Oak Publications, 1963.

Franklin, John Hope. *From Slavery to Freedom: A History of Negro Americans.* 4th ed. New York: Knopf, 1974. Pp. 463–511.

Kofsky, Frank. *Black Nationalism and the Revolution in Music.* New York: Pathfinder Press, 1970.

Miller, Lloyd, and James K. Skipper, Jr. "Sounds of Black Protest in Avant-Garde Jazz." In *The Sounds of Social Change: Studies in Popular Culture.* Chicago: Rand McNally, 1972. Pp. 26–37.

## VIOLENCE IN THE BLACK COMMUNITY

*Question:*

Does the high level of physical violence that occurs within many urban black communities indicate feelings of personal frustration and anxiety caused by social discrimination and political isolation?

*Concepts to investigate:*

| | | |
|---|---|---|
| aggression | rape | alienation |
| vandalism | homicide | hostility |
| arson | assassination | anxiety |

*Songs and performers:*

"Big Boy Pete" (Arvee 595)—Olympics
"Hi-Heel Sneakers" (Checker 1067)—Tommy Tucker
"Trouble Man" (Tamla 54228)—Marvin Gaye
"Stagger Lee" (ABC 9972)—Lloyd Price
"I'm Ready" (Chess 1579)—Muddy Waters
"Smokey Joe's Cafe" (ATCO 6059)—Robins

*Bibliography*

Grier, William H., and Price M. Cobbs. *Black Rage.* New York: Bantam, 1968.

Kerner, Otto, chairman. *Report of the National Advisory Commission on Civil Disorders.* New York: Bantam, 1968.

Lipsky, Michael, and David J. Olson. *Riot Commission Politics: The Processing of Racial Crisis in America.* New Brunswick, N.J.: Transaction Books, 1974.

## RELIGIOUS COMMITMENTS

*Question:*

Does the image of religion in black popular music illustrate the hope for social integration and spiritual brotherhood?

*Concepts to investigate:*

| | | |
|---|---|---|
| predestination | segregation | integration |
| brotherhood | faith | ethics |
| gospel songs | morality | ecumenicism |

*Songs and performers:*

"Oh Happy Day" (Pavilion 20001)—Edwin Hawkins Singers
"People Get Ready" (ABC 10622)—Impressions
"I'll Take You There" (Stax 0125)—Staple Singers
"The Weight" (Atlantic 2603)—Aretha Franklin
"You'll Never Walk Alone" (Epic 9015)—Roy Hamilton
"Superstition" (Tamla 54226)—Stevie Wonder

*Bibliography:*

Dowdey, Landon Gerald. comp. *Journey to Freedom: A Casebook with Music.* Chicago: Swallow, 1969.
Heilbut, Tony. *The Gospel Sound: Good News and Bad Times.* New York: Simon and Schuster, 1971.
Jackson, Mahalia. *Movin' On Up.* New York: Hawthorn Books, 1966.
Work, John W., ed. *American Negro Songs and Spirituals.* New York: Bonanza, 1940.

## RACIAL PRIDE

*Question:*

How does black music attempt to generate pride in the black heritage and to illustrate the achievements of the black man and woman in American culture?

*Concepts to investigate:*

| | | |
|---|---|---|
| personal identity | racial pride | Afro-American history |
| black heritage | segregation | behavior models |
| courage | dignity | self-respect |

*Songs and performers:*

"We're a Winner" (Curtom 1966) – Curtis Mayfield
"Say It Loud – I'm Black and I'm Proud (King 6187) – James Brown
"We're Rolling On" (ABC 11071) – Impressions
"To Be Young, Gifted and Black (RCA 0269) – Nina Simone
"I've Got to Be Me" (Reprise 0779) – Sammy Davis, Jr.
"Stand!" (Epic 10450) – Sly and the Family Stone
"This Is My Country" (Curtom 1934) – Impressions

*Bibliography:*

Brown, Claude. "The Language of Soul." In *Black America: Accommodation and Confrontation in the Twentieth Century*, ed. Richard Resh. Lexington, Mass.: D. C. Heath, 1969. Pp. 244–49.

Hannerz, Ulf. "The Meaning of 'Soul.'" In *The Private Side of American History: Readings in Everyday Life*, vol. 2, ed. Thomas R. Frazier. New York: Harcourt Brace Jovanovich, 1975. Pp. 336–47.

Jones, LeRoi. *Black Music.* New York: William Morrow, 1968.

McCutcheon, Lynn. "Unsung Heroes Who Also Sang," *Negro History Bulletin* 36 (January 1973): 9–11.

## BLACK WOMEN

*Question:*

How are black women depicted in the lyrics of contemporary songs?

*Concepts to Investigate:*

| | | |
|---|---|---|
| sexism | racism | liberation |
| equal opportunity | discrimination | male chauvinism |
| prostitution | affirmative action | self-respect |

*Songs and performers:*
"Lady Marmalade" (Epic 50048)—LaBelle
"Mr. Big Stuff" (Stax 0088)—Jean Knight
"A Natural Woman" (Atlantic 2441)—Aretha Franklin
"Love Child" (Motown 1135)—Diana Ross and the Supremes
"Don't Make Me Over" (Scepter 1239)—Dionne Warwick
"Think" (Atlantic 2518)—Aretha Franklin
"Mama Didn't Lie" (Chess 1845)—Jan Bradley
"Black Pearl" (A & M 1053)—Sonny Charles and the Checkmates, Ltd.

*Bibliography:*

Beal, Francis M. "Double Jeopardy: To Be Black and Female." In *Sisterhood Is Powerful: An Anthology of Writings from the Women's Liberation Movement,* ed. Robin Morgan. New York: Vintage Books, 1970. Pp. 340–53.

Cade, Toni, ed. *The Black Woman: An Anthology.* New York: New American Library, 1970.

Chisholm, Shirley. *Unbought and Unbossed,* 2d ed. New York: Avon, 1972.

Lerner, Gerda, ed. *Black Women in White America: A Documentary History.* New York: Vintage Books, 1972.

Morse, Charles, and Ann Morse. *Roberta Flack.* Mankato, Minn.: Creative Educational Society, 1974.

Olsen, James T. *Aretha Franklin.* Mankato, Minn.: Creative Educational Society, 1974.

Washington, Mary Ellen, ed. *Black-Eyed Susans: Classic Stories By and About Black Women.* Garden City, N.Y.: Doubleday, 1975.

## URBAN LIFE

*Question:*
What does the quality of life experienced by most urban blacks illustrate about city living in the United States?

*Concepts to investigate:*

| | | |
|---|---|---|
| ghetto | street wisdom | population density |
| discrimination | urban renewal | law enforcement |
| poverty | public transportation | block busting |
| | unemployment | |

*Songs and performers:*
"Ain't No Love in the Heart of the City" (Dunhill 15003)—Bobby Bland
"Living for the City" (Tamla 54242)—Stevie Wonder
"Inner City Blues (Make Me Wanna Holler)" (Tamla 54209)—Marvin Gaye
"Masterpiece" (Gordy 7126)—Temptations
"Dead End Street" (Capitol 5869)—Lou Rawls
"Bright Lights, Big City" (Vee Jay 398)—Jimmy Reed
"Spanish Harlem" (Atco 6185)—Ben E. King

*Bibliography:*

Ehrlich, Paul R., Ann H. Ehrlich, and John P. Holdren. *Human Ecology: Problems and Solutions.* San Francisco: W. H. Freeman, 1973.

Keil, Charles. *Urban Blues.* Chicago: University of Chicago Press, 1966.

Ornstein, Allan O. *Urban Education: Student Unrest, Teacher Behaviors, and Black Power.* Columbus, Ohio: Charles E. Merrill, 1972.

Silverberg, Robert. "Black is Beautiful." In *The Year 2000: An Anthology,* ed. Harry Harrison. New York: Berkley Pub. Co., 1970. Pp. 155–70.

Southern, Eileen. *The Music of Black Americans: A History.* New York: W. W. Norton, 1971.

## THE BLUES HERITAGE

*Question:*
How do the lyrics of popular songs illustrate the historical images and experiences of the black man or woman in America?

*Concepts to investigate:*

| | | |
|---|---|---|
| slavery | ghetto life | educational opportunity |
| poverty | welfare programs | job discrimination |
| segregation | racial pride | prison life |

*Songs and performers:*
"Why I Sing the Blues" (Bluesway 61024)—B. B. King
"Trouble in Mind" (Colpix 175)—Nina Simone
"Stormy Monday Blues" (Duke 355)—Bobby Bland
"Ninety-Nine and a Half (Won't Do)" (Atlantic 2334)—Wilson Pickett

"The World Is a Ghetto" (United Artists 50975)—WAR
"Nobody Knows You (When You're Down and Out)" (United Artists
255)—Bobby Womack
"Chain Gang" (RCA 7783)—Sam Cooke
"Busted" (ABC 10481)—Ray Charles
"Compared to What" (Atlantic 2694)—Les McCann and Eddie Harris
"War" (Gordy 7101)—Edwin Starr
"Ball of Confusion" (Gordy 7099)—Temptations

*Bibliography:*

Charters, Samuel. *The Bluesmen.* New York: Oak Publications, 1967.
DuBois, W. E. B. "Of the Sorrow Song." In *The Black Aesthetic,* ed. Addison
    Gayle, Jr. Garden City, N.Y.: Doubleday, 1972. Pp. 92–103.
Ferris, William R., Jr., "Racial Repertoires among Blues Performers." *Ethno-
    musicology* 14 (September 1970): 439–49.
Jones, LeRoi. *Blues People: Negro Music in White America.* New York: William
    Morrow, 1963.
Levine, Lawrence W. *Black Culture and Black Consciousness: Afro-American
    Folk Thought from Slavery to Freedom.* New York: Oxford University
    Press, 1977.
Moore, Carmen. *Somebody's Angel Child: The Story of Bessie Smith.* New York:
    Crowell, 1969.
Neff, Robert, and Anthony Conner, comps. *Blues.* Boston: Godine, 1975.
Oliver, Paul. *Aspects of the Blues Tradition.* New York: Oak Publications, 1970.
Oliver, Paul. *The Meaning of the Blues.* New York: Collier, 1972.
Shirley, Kay, and Frank Driggs, eds. *The Book of the Blues.* New York: Crown,
    1963.
Stewart-Baxter, Derrick. *Ma Rainey and the Classic Blues Singers.* New York:
    Stein and Day, 1970.

Several years ago an eloquent student of black culture declared,

> . . . It seems to me that if the Negro represents, or is symbolic of,
> something in and about the nature of American culture, this certainly
> should be revealed by his characteristic music. In other words, I am
> saying that if the music of the Negro in America, in all its permutations,
> is subjected to a socio-anthropological as well as musical scrutiny, some-
> thing about the essential nature of the Negro's existence in this country

ought to be revealed, as well as something about the essential nature of this country, i.e., society as a whole.[7]

This observation is still relevant, and until the formal scholarship and the informal oral tradition of the black man are synthesized in the classroom, the value of black history will never be realized. This essay suggests only one innovative instructional approach — the lyrical investigation of social themes — as a model for classroom study. The ability of history teachers to adopt nontraditional (though popular) oral resources remains a question mark. It is my opinion that without the introduction of such innovative instructional techniques, the majority of black and white students will continue to question the validity of black history in their lives.

# FIVE

# Biographical Study and Popular Music

Social studies instructors should exploit existing student interest in contemporary musicians to teach the techniques of biographical construction. Although the political impact of performers such as Bob Dylan and Ray Charles may not approach that of Theodore Roosevelt and Woodrow Wilson, the methodology involved in exploring the facts of their lives is identical. In addition, there are several unique advantages to examining the lives of popular music figures. Not only are numerous written interview resources readily available, but also some unique oral history artifacts—song lyrics and spoken commentary from 33⅓ and 45 r.p.m. recordings—can be employed in assembling modern biographies. Of course, the introduction of such nontraditional subject matter might create initial unrest among parents, school administrators, and other teachers; still, it is worth the risk of criticism if such innovative classroom practices can foster intellectual growth and historical understanding.

The lives of great men—Socrates, Julius Caesar, Jesus Christ, Napoleon Bonaparte, and Abraham Lincoln—have fascinated scholars and students alike for decades. For this reason social studies teachers have frequently employed biographical studies to illustrate the political activities, social events, and scientific achievements of particular periods of history. This instructional approach is both interesting and effective. However, it should not be limited to studying "great men" of the past. Social studies students should be encouraged to do more than simply absorb written commentaries about celebrated world leaders. They should become actively involved in the progress of gathering oral and written evidence, ordering events chronologically, assessing the significance of specific activities, and making evaluations about the overall contributions of individuals to the political, intellectual, social, cultural, and economic life of their society.

Scholarly literature published during the past decade on the value of oral history materials as instructional tools amply attests to their success as classroom resources.[1] These reports have convinced many historians that nonprint educational resources can be beneficial learning tools. Accordingly, rapidly expanding collections of oral history materials may be found in the libraries of schools and colleges throughout the United States. Commercial companies such as the Center for Cassette Studies in Hollywood, California, have been instrumental in meeting the instructional needs of history teachers and their students through the distribution of taped discussions and debates. Despite the success of these taped interviews with contemporary journalists, politicians, scholars, and other public figures, there is one nontraditional oral resource that remains largely unexploited for academic purposes: the lyrics of popular songs—jazz, rhythm and blues, bluegrass, country, rock, blues, and folk. Educational theorists and history teachers should recognize that contemporary singers and songwriters have exerted great influence through the medium of popular music on the ideas, attitudes, and values of millions of Americans. Tunes sung by Curtis Mayfield, Carole King, Nina Simone, Cat Stevens, Stevie Wonder, Lou Rawls, Joni Mitchell, and Marvin Gaye provide substantial sources of oral evidence and social commentary for serious students of contemporary United States history.

Lyrics created by contemporary performers often contain suggestive autobiographical and sociological overtones. Undeniably, the accumulation of reliable historical evidence in the genre of oral/lyrical presentations poses several unique problems. What criteria can be employed to establish a popular music figure's credibility as a historical resource? In response to this question, one might consider items such as career longevity, the universal applicability of lyrical commentary, the ability of a particular singer to inspire new performing styles, and the distinctive poetic style or musical expression contained in specific songs. Though several studies of the lyrical works of Chuck Berry,[2] Ray

Charles,[3] James Brown,[4] and Aretha Franklin[5] have attempted to establish benchmarks for the scholarly analysis of popular music, written reports describing efforts to utilize the lyrical materials of these four singers for social investigation in the classroom are nonexistent.

Perhaps a brief review of the life of one contemporary performer will serve to illustrate the rich potential for biographical analysis. As a jazz artist, organist-singer-songwriter Les McCann has gained increasing public exposure during the past decade via the international jazz concert circuit and the image-building promotional activities of the Atlantic Recording Corporation. Since 1969, McCann has served as a major lyrical spokesman for many black Americans. His historical portrait of America and his viewpoints on contemporary events tend to mirror William Lloyd Garrison's commitment to the uncompromising nature of social truth; not unexpectedly, McCann also shares Garrison's flair for hyperbole and political propaganda. This personal idiosyncrasy for absolute judgment has added to public interest in his utterances. For a social studies teacher concerned with investigating contemporary social and intellectual thought, the attitudes and impressions articulated by McCann provide numerous illustrations that are certain to stimulate students to reflect on the meaning of American life.[6]

In several songs McCann declares his personal, spiritual allegiance to the underprivileged. In 1969, for example, he joined saxophonist Eddie Harris at the Montreaux Jazz Festival in Switzerland to produce the brilliant and controversial tune "Compared to What." This song of social criticism directly attacks a variety of current social practices as being based on hypocritically "unreal values." McCann sings of the "crass distortion" between the myth of social equality and the reality of economic depravation in the highly stratified American society. On July 8, 1972, at the Newport Jazz Festival in Yankee Stadium, McCann brought his audience to their feet with his rendition of "The Price You Got to Pay to Be Free." His insertion of a few strains from the "black national anthem" ("Lift Every Voice and Sing") in the final chorus reveals McCann's impish genius for blending a gentle civil rights refrain with his own vitriolic commentary. The defiant phrase—"Then you're gonna call me a militant—God damn, you got your nerve!"—inserted in the song also reflects his sympathy for the general frustration experienced by many blacks. In a 1972 album, McCann thematically combines the Marvin Gaye tune "What's Going On" with his own song "Talk to the People" to foster support for the mutual benefits of communal cooperation instead of the more traditional political-legalistic associations. His observations on this subject, though undeniably idealistic, echo the theories of numerous radical social scientists on the nature of interpersonal relationships.

But the genius of any artistic endeavor, whether literary, verbal, or visual, does not lie solely in either the accuracy or the intensity of its social commentary. Les McCann bares his romantic soul in a variety of vocal and instrumental numbers that are interspersed among the sociopolitical indictments on his albums. In "Comment" McCann calls for all men to be brothers; in "Seems So Long" he speaks passionately of the man-woman relationship and the sadness of lost love. Most historians, of course, would not attempt to analyze areas of affective, nonverbal communication.[7] Nevertheless, one cannot deny that touching the hearts of men through song adds yet another dimension to McCann's pleas for social justice.

In addition to the process of analyzing lyrical commentaries as outlined above, a social studies teacher may wish to examine the biographical background of a popular music figure. An examination of Les McCann's social/psychological development from childhood to jazz stardom,[8] for example, presents several fascinating challenges. Among the periods of his life that could be examined historically by combining audio, literary, and interview resources are: (1) his public school education; (2) his experiences in church choirs and with several secular preprofessional musical groups; (3) early family and peer influences, which shaped his ideological/sociological commitments to racial pride, individual independence, human dignity, and community; and (4) his financial transition from amateur musical status to professional performances as an acknowledged jazz great. Other areas of classroom interest might include his penchant for discovering and encouraging other talented individuals (Roberta Flack) and for adapting lyrics of his contemporaries (Eddie Harris, Gene McDaniels, Marvin Gaye, and Stevie Wonder) to transmit his own social philosophy; his international reputation gained during numerous jazz festival performances at Antibes, Montreaux, and Newport; and his image of the black man's historical experience and future goals.

Study of the music and life of Les McCann can shed valuable light on the nature and meaning of the black experience in America during the past decade.[9] His recordings provide a rich resource for a social studies teacher. McCann's songs contain revealing anecdotes, internalized images and stereotypes, observations about personal and social conflict, confessions of weakness and declarations of strength, and illustrations of distinctive speech patterns and phrases.[10] His lyrics are vivid and highly image-laden. The modern instructor should learn to use tools like McCann's music and ideas to broaden the comprehension of students about American society.

Although biographical analysis has long been recognized as a useful technique to unfold the personal panorama of American history, it can be a difficult method to introduce in an instructional setting. The following pages provide lists of resource materials for social studies teachers who want to experiment with the popular culture biography approach recommended above. The material is constructed around the lives and songs of nine well-known popular music artists. In each case, the performer's name is followed by three types of historical evidence: (1) recent books and articles, (2) lyric anthologies, and (3) several record albums containing the most popular tunes performed by the artist. These literary and audio resources should enable any teacher to initiate biographical study in his or her classroom. Obviously, the objective of utilizing both written and oral resources is not only to broaden the base of historical investigation about prominent musical figures but also to spark additional student interest, imagination, and creativity.

## JOAN BAEZ

*Books and articles*

Baez, Joan. *Daybreak*. New York: Avon, 1969.

DeTurk, David A., and Poulin, A., Jr. "Joan Baez—An Interview." In *The American Folk Scene: Dimensions of the Folksong Revival*. New York: Dell, 1967. Pp. 231–49.

Farina, Richard. "Baez and Dylan: A Generation Singing Out." In *The Age of Rock: Sounds of the American Cultural Revolution*, ed. Jonathan Eisen. New York: Bantam Books, 1974. Pp. 1–8.

Grissim, John, Jr. "Joan Baez." In *The Rolling Stone Rock 'N' Roll Reader*, ed. Ben Fong-Torres. New York: Bantam Books, 1974. Pp. 1–8.

Hentoff, Nat. "The *Playboy* Interview: Joan Baez," *Playboy* 17 (July 1970):54–62ff.

Rodnitzky, Jerome. "A Pacifist St. Joan–The Odyssey of Joan Baez." In *Heroes of Popular Culture*, ed. Ray B. Browne, Marshall Fishwick, and Michael T. Marsden. Bowling Green, Ohio: Bowling Green University Popular Press, 1972. Pp. 138–56.

"Sibyl with Guitar." *Time* (November 23, 1962):54–56.

*Lyric anthology*

Conly, John M., comp. *The Joan Baez Songbook*. New York: Ryerson Music Publishers, Inc., 1964.

*Records*

Baez, Joan, *The Joan Baez Ballad Book* (VDS 41/42). New York: Vanguard Records, 1972.

Baez, Joan. *Where Are You Now My Son?* (SP 4390) New York: A & M Records, Inc., 1973.

Baez, Joan. *From Every Stage* (SP 3704). New York: A & M Records, Inc., 1976.

## BEATLES

*Books and articles*

Belz, Carl. "The English Scene: The Beatles." In *The Story of Rock*, 2d ed. New York: Harper and Row, 1972. Pp. 126–49.

Bird, Donald Allport, Stephen C. Holder, and Diane Sears. "Walrus Is Greek for Corpse: Rumor and the Death of Paul McCartney." *Journal of Popular Culture* 10 (Summer 1976):110–21.

Carr, Roy, and Tony Tyler. *The Beatles Illustrated Record*. New York: Harmony Books, 1975.

Castleman, Harry, and Walter J. Podrazik, comps. *All Together Now: The First Complete Beatles Discography, 1961–1975*. New York: Ballantine, 1975.

Castleman, Harry, and Walter J. Podrazik, comps. *The Beatles Again!* Ann Arbor, Mich.: Pierian Press, 1977.

Cohn, Nik. "The Beatles." In *Rock: From the Beginning*. New York: Pocket Books, 1969. Pp. 114–30.

DiLello, Richard. *The Longest Cocktail Party*. Chicago: Playboy, 1972.

Fawcett, Anthony. *John Lennon – One Day at a Time: A Personal Biography of the Seventies*. New York: Grove Press, 1976.

Fong-Torres, Ben. "George Harrison: Lumbering in the Material World." In

*What's That Sound? The Contemporary Music Scene from the Pages of "Rolling Stone,"* ed. Ben Fong-Torres. Garden City, N.Y.: Doubleday/Anchor Books, 1976. Pp. 35–54.

Friedman, Rick. *The Beatles: Words without Music.* New York: Grosset and Dunlap, 1968.

Hamill, Pete. "John Lennon: Long Night's Journey into Day." In *What's That Sound? The Contemporary Music Scene from the Pages of "Rolling Stone,"* ed. Ben Fong-Torres. Garden City, N.Y.: Doubleday/Anchor Books, 1976. Pp. 55–70.

McCabe, Peter, and Robert D. Schonfeld. *Apple to the Core: The Unmaking of the Beatles.* New York: Pocket Books, 1972.

Marcus, Greil. "The Beatles." In *The Rolling Stone Illustrated History of Rock and Roll,* ed. Jim Miller. New York: Random House, 1976. Pp. 172–81.

Martynova, A. "Beatles as Cinderella: A Soviet Fairy Tale." In *The Age of Rock / 2: Sights and Sounds of the American Cultural Revolution,* ed. Jonathan Eisen. New York: Vintage Books, 1970. Pp. 214–18.

Mellers, Wilfrid. *Twilight of the Gods: The Music of the Beatles.* New York: Schirmer, 1973.

Morris, James. "Beatle Culture." In *The History of Popular Culture since 1815,* ed. Norman F. Cantor and Michael S. Werthman. New York: Macmillan, 1968. Pp. 372–74.

"Nine Ways of Looking at the Beatles." *Stereo Review* 30 (February 1973):56–63.

Poirier, Richard. "Learning from the Beatles." *Partisan Review* 34 (Fall 1967):526–46.

Szwed, John F. "On Tour with the Beatles." In *The Rock Giants,* ed. Pauline Rivelli and Robert Levin. New York: World, 1970. Pp. 46–49.

Tremlett, George. *The Paul McCartney Story.* New York: Popular Library, 1977.

*Lyric anthologies*

Aldridge, Alan, ed. *The Beatles Illustrated Lyrics.* New York: Delacorte, 1969.
_____. *The Beatles Illustrated Lyrics – 2.* New York: Delacorte, 1971.

Okun, Milton, ed. *Great Songs of Lennon and McCartney.* New York: Quadrangle, 1973.


*Records*

Beatles. *The Beatles / 1962–1966* (SKBO 3403). New York: Apple Records, 1973.

Beatles. *The Beatles / 1967–1970* (SKBO 3404). New York: Apple Records, 1973.

Beatles. *The Beatles at the Hollywood Bowl* (SMAS 11638). Hollywood, Calif.: Capitol Records, 1977.

*The Beatles' Story: A Narrative and Musical Biography of Beatlemania* (STBO 2222). Hollywood, Calif.: Capitol Records, n.d.

Beatles. *Rarities* (SHAL 12060). Hollywood, Calif.: Capitol Records, 1980.

Beatles. *Rock 'N' Roll Music* (SKBO 11537). Hollywood, Calif.: Capitol Records, 1976.

Beatles. *Sgt. Pepper's Lonely Hearts Club Band* (MAS 2653). Hollywood, Calif.: Capitol Records, 1967.

## CHUCK BERRY

*Books and articles*

Belz, Carl. "Chuck Berry: Folk Poet of the Fifties." In *The Story of Rock*, 2d ed. New York: Harper and Row, 1972. Pp. 61–66.

Brown, Geoff. "Chuck Berry." In *Rock Life*, ed. Gavin Petrie. New York: Hamlyn Publishing Group, 1974. Pp. 47–51.

Christgau, Robert. "Chuck Berry: Eternal Rock and Roller." In *Any Old Way You Choose It: Rock and Other Pop Music, 1967–1973*. Baltimore: Penguin, 1973. Pp. 140–48.

Cooper, B. Lee. "Review of Chuck Berry's Golden Decade. . . ." *History Teacher* 8 (February 1975):300–301.

Daly, Mike. "Back at It Again as Always: Chuck Berry's Golden Decade." In *Rock and Roll Will Stand*, ed. Greil Marcus. Boston: Beacon Press, 1969. Pp. 28–36.

Guralnick, Peter. "Chess Records: Before the Fall." In *Feel Like Going Home: Portraits in Blues and Rock 'N' Roll*. New York: Outerbridge and Dienstfrey, 1971. Pp. 180–202.

Knobler, Peter. "Chuck Berry: 'Sweet Sixteen Is Thirty-Two,' " *Crawdaddy* (April 16, 1972):25–27.

Lydon, Michael. "Chuck Berry Lives!" *Ramparts* 8 (December 1969):47–56.

Marcus, Greil. "Chuck Berry." In *The Rolling Stone Interviews, Volume I*, ed. Jann Wenner et al. New York: Paperback Library, 1971. Pp. 173–87.

Newman, Ralph M. "The Chuck Berry Story: Long Lives Rock and Roll," *Time Barrier Express*, No. 27 (April–May 1980):34–46.

Salvo, Patrick William. "A Conversation with Chuck Berry," *Rolling Stone* (November 23, 1972):35–42.

*Lyric anthology*
*Chuck Berry – The Golden Decade.* New York: Arc Music Corporation,
   n.d.

*Records*
Berry, Chuck. *Chuck Berry – The Golden Decade* (CH 1514). New York:
   Chess/Janus Records, 1972.
Berry, Chuck. *Chuck Berry's Golden Decade – Volume 2.* (CH 60023)
   New York: Chess/Janus Records, 1972.
Berry, Chuck. *The London Chuck Berry Sessions* (CH 60020). New
   York: Chess/Janus Records, 1972.

## BOB DYLAN

*Books and articles*
Belz, Carl. "Bob Dylan." In *The Story of Rock,* 2d ed. New York: Harper and
   Row, 1972. Pp. 157–68.
Campbell, Greg M. "Bob Dylan and the Pastoral Apocalypse." *Journal of
   Popular Culture* 8 (Spring 1975):696–707.
Cohn, Nik. "Bob Dylan." In *Rock: From the Beginning.* New York: Pocket
   Books, 1969. Pp. 148–53.
Ephron, Nora, and Susan Edmiston. "Bob Dylan Interview." In *The Age of
   Rock / 2: Sights and Sounds of the American Cultural Revolution,* ed.
   Jonathan Eisen. New York: Vintage Books, 1970. Pp. 63–71.
Fong-Torres, Ben, et al. *Knockin' on Dylan's Door: On the Road in '74.* New
   York: Pocket Books, 1974.
Friedberg, Harris. "Bob Dylan: Psycho-historian of a Generation," *Chronicle of
   Higher Education* 8 (January 28, 1974):15–16.
Gleason, Ralph J. "Bob Dylan: 'What Do You Want Me to Say?' " In *The
   "Rolling Stone" Interviews – Volume 2,* ed. Ben Fong-Torres. New York:
   Warner Paperback Library, 1973. Pp. 11–29.
Gleason, Ralph J. "The Times They Are A-Changin'," *Ramparts* (April
   1965):36–48.
Goldberg, Steven. "Bob Dylan and the Poetry of Salvation." In *Boy Dylan: A
   Retrospective,* ed. Craig Mc Gregor. New York: William Morrow, 1972.
   Pp. 364–77.
Gray, Michael. *Song and Dance Man: The Art of Bob Dylan.* New York: E. P.
   Dutton, 1972.
Hentoff, Nat. "Bob Dylan: The Rolling Thunder Review." In *What's That
   Sound? The Pages of "Rolling Stone."* Garden City, N.Y.: Doubleday/
   Anchor Books, 1976. Pp. 169–88.

Kermode, Frank. Stephen Spender, and Art Kane. "Bob Dylan: The Metaphor at the End of the Funnel." *Esquire* (May 1972):109–18ff.

Landau, Jon. "John Wesley Harding." In *The Age of Rock: Sounds of the American Cultural Revolution,* ed. Jonathan Eisen. New York: Vintage Books, 1969. Pp. 214–29.

McGregor, Craig, ed. *Bob Dylan: A Retrospective.* New York: William Morrow, 1972.

Nash, Roderick. "Bob Dylan." In *From These Beginnings: A Biographical Approach to American History.* New York: Harper and Row, 1973. Pp. 512–41.

Nelson, Paul. "Bob Dylan." In *The Rolling Stone Illustrated History of Rock and Roll,* ed. Jim Miller. New York: Random House, 1976. Pp. 206–13.

Ribakove, Sy, and Barbara Ribakove. *Folk Rock: The Bob Dylan Story.* New York: Dell, 1966.

Rodnitzky, Jerome L. "Bob Dylan: Beyond Left and Right." In *Minstrels of the Dawn: The Folk-Protest Singer as a Cultural Hero.* Chicago: Nelson-Hall, 1976. Pp. 101–34.

Sarlin, Bob. "The First Songpoet—Bob Dylan." In *Turn It Up (I Can't Hear the Words): The Best of the New Singer/Songwriters.* New York: Simon and Schuster, 1973. Pp. 38–74.

Scaduto, Anthony. *Dylan: An Intimate Biography.* New York: New American Library, 1973.

Vassal, Jacques. "Dylan." In *Electric Children: Roots and Branches of Modern Folkrock.* New York: Taplinger, 1976. Pp. 116–48.

Watts, Michael. "Bob Dylan." In *Rock Life,* ed. Gavin Petrie. New York: Hamlyn Publishing Group, 1974.

Williams, Paul. *Dylan—What Happened?* Glen Ellen, Calif.: Entwhistle Books, 1980.

Willis, Ellen. "The Sound of Dylan." *Commentary* (November 1967):71–78.

*Lyric anthology*
*The Bob Dylan Song Book.* New York: Witmark, n.d.
*The Songs of Bob Dylan from 1966 through 1975.* New York: Knopf, 1978.

*Records*
Dylan, Bob. *Bob Dylan's Greatest Hits* (PC 9463). New York: Columbia Records/CBS, n.d.

Dylan, Bob. *Bob Dylan's Greatest Hits—Volume II* (PG 31120). New York: Columbia Records/CBS, 1971.

Dylan, Bob. *Slow Train Coming* (FC 36120). New York: Columbia Records/CBS, 1979.

## BUDDY HOLLY

*Books and articles*

Cott, Jonathan. "Buddy Holly." In *The Rolling Stone Illustrated History of Rock and Roll*, ed. Jim Miller. New York: Random House, 1976. Pp. 78–81.

Dean, Maury. "Wo-Uh-Ho Peggy Sue: Exploring a Teenage Queen Linguistically," *Popular Music and Society* 2 (Spring 1973):244–54.

Emerson, Ken. "Review of Buddy Holly/The Crickets – 20 Golden Greats." *High Fidelity* (August 1978):116–18.

Goldrosen, John. *Buddy Holly: His Life and Music*. New York: Quick Fox, 1979.

Laing, Dave. *Buddy Holly*. New York: Macmillan, 1971.

Smith, Clyde, comp. "Buddy Holly Singles." *Record Exchanger* 1 (November-December 1970):9.


*Lyric anthology*

Peer, Ralph, II, and Elizabeth Peer, comps. *Buddy Holly . . . A Biography in Words, Photographs, and Music*. New York: Peer International Corporation, 1972.

*Records*

Busey, Gary. *The Buddy Holly Story* (SE 35412). New York: Epic Records, 1978.

Holly, Buddy. *Buddy Holly Showcase* (CRL 57450). New York: Coral Records, n.d.

Holly, Buddy. *Legend* (CDMSP 802). Middlesex, England: MCA Coral, n.d.

Holly, Buddy. *The Nashville Sessions* (CDLM 8038). Middlesex, Eng.: MCA Coral, 1975.

Holly, Buddy, and the Crickets. *The Buddy Holly Story* (CRL 57279). New York: Coral Records, n.d.

Holly, Buddy, and the Crickets. *Buddy Holly Lives: 20 Golden Greats* (MCA 3040). Universal City, California: MCA Records, 1978.

Holly, Buddy, and Bob Montgomery. *Western and Bop* (CDLM 8055). Middlesex, Eng.: MCA Coral, n.d.


## ROLLING STONES

*Books and articles*

Abrams, Robert. "Everybody's Children." In *Twenty-Minute Fandangos and Forever Changes: A Rock Bazaar*, ed. Jonathan Eisen. New York: Vintage Books, 1971. Pp. 148–54.

Beckett, Alan, and Merton, Richard. "Stones/Comment." In *The Age of Rock:*

*Sounds of the American Cultural Revolution*, edited by Jonathan Eisen. New York: Vintage Books, 1969. Pp. 109–17.

Carr, Roy. *The Rolling Stones: An Illustrated Record.* New York: Harmony Books, 1976.

Christgau, Robert. "The Rolling Stones." In *The Rolling Stone Illustrated History of Rock and Roll*, ed. Jim Miller. New York: Random House, 1976. Pp. 182–89.

Cohn, Nik. "The Rolling Stones." In *Rock: From the Beginning.* New York: Pocket Books, 1969. Pp. 131–41.

Coppage, Noel. "The Rolling Stones." *Stereo Review* (January 1975):84–85.

Cott, Jonathan, and Cox, Sue. "An Interview with Mick Jagger." In *Rolling Stones: An Unauthorized Biography in Words, Photographs, and Music*, ed. David Dalton. New York: Amsco Music Pub. Co., 1972. Pp. 98–109.

Greenfield, Robert. *S.T.P.: A Journey through America with the Rolling Stones.* New York: E. P. Dutton, 1974.

Hellman, John M., Jr. " 'I'm a Monkey': The Influence of the Black American Blues Argot on the Rolling Stones," *Journal of American Folklore* 86 (October-December 1973):367–73.

Kofsky, Frank. "The Rolling Stones' Their Satanic Majesties Request: An Exegesis." In *The Rock Giants*, edited by Pauline Rivelli and Robert Levin. New York: World, 1970. Pp. 50–57.

Landau, Jon. "The Rolling Stones: What Can a Poor Boy Do?" In *What's That Sound? The Contemporary Music Scene from the Pages of "Rolling Stone,"* ed. Ben Fong-Torres. Garden City, N.Y.: Doubleday/Anchor Books, 1976. Pp. 136–41.

Lydon, Michael. "The Rolling Stones—A Play in the Apocalypse." *Ramparts* (March 1970):28–53.

Marks, J. *Mick Jagger: The Singer, Not the Song.* New York: Curtis, 1973.

Tremlett, George. *The Rolling Stones.* New York: Warner, 1974.

Watts, Michael. "Rolling Stones." In *Rock Life*, ed. Gavin Petrie. New York: Hamlyn Publishing Group, 1974. Pp. 4–9.

*Lyric anthology*

Dalton, David, comp. *Rolling Stones: An Unauthorized Biography in Words, Photographs, and Music.* New York: Amsco Music Pub. Co., 1972.

*Records*

Rolling Stones, *Hot Rocks, 1964–1971* (London 2PS 606/7). New York: ADKCO (London) Records, 1972.

Rolling Stones, *Made in the Shade* (COC 79102). New York: Rolling Stones Records, 1975.

Rolling Stones, *Out of Our Heads* (PS 429). New York: London Records, n.d.

## PAUL SIMON

*Books and articles*

Ames, Morgan. "Simon and Garfunkel in Action." *High Fidelity* (November 1967):62–66.

Landau, Jon. "Paul Simon: The *Rolling Stone* Interview." In *What's That Sound? The Contemporary Music Scene from the Pages of "Rolling Stone,"* ed. Ben Fong-Torres. Garden City, N.Y.: Doubleday/Anchor Books, 1976. Pp. 200–220.

Leigh Spencer. *Paul Simon: Now and Then.* Liverpool: Raven Books, 1973.

Pollock, Bruce. "Paul Simon: Survivor from the Sixties." *Saturday Review* 3 (June 12, 1976):43–44ff.

Simels, Steve. "Simon and Garfunkel, Soloists." *Stereo Review* 36 (February 1976):88.

White, Timothy. "Public Pitches and Stolen Moments with Pinin' Simon." *Crawdaddy* (February 1976):45–51.

*Lyric anthology*

*The Songs of Paul Simon.* New York: Knopf, 1972.

Simon, Paul. *Greatest Hits, Etc.* New York: Charing Cross Music, 1977.

*Records*

Simon, Paul. *Greatest Hits, Etc.* (JC 35032). New York: Columbia Records/ CBS, 1977.

Simon, Paul. *Live Rhymin': Paul Simon in Concert* (PC 32855). New York: Columbia Records/BCS, 1974.

Simon, Paul. *Still Crazy after All These Years* (PC 33540). New York: Columbia Records/CBS, 1975.

Simon and Garfunkel, *Bookends* (PC 9529). New York: Columbia Records/ CBS, 1968.

Simon and Garfunkel, *Bridge over Troubled Water* (KCS 9914). New York: Columbia Records/CBS, n.d.

Simon and Garfunkel, *Sounds of Silence* (CS 9269). New York: Columbia Records, 1965.

## THE WHO

*Books and articles*

Cohn, Nik. "The Who." In *Rock: From the Beginning.* New York: Pocket Books, 1969. Pp. 202–7.

Herman, Gary. *The Who*. New York: Collier, 1972.

Marsh, Dave. "The Who." In *The Rolling Stone Illustrated History of Rock and Roll*, ed. Jim Miller. New York: Random House, 1976. Pp. 266–71.

Pollock, Bruce. "Peter Townshend." In *In Their Own Words: Twenty Successful Song Writers Tell How They Write Their Songs*. New York: Collier, 1975). Pp. 78–90.

Wenner, Jann. "The Who: Pete Townshend." In *What's That Sound? The Contemporary Music Scene from the Pages of "Rolling Stone,"* edited by Ben Fong-Torres. Garden City, N.Y.: Doubleday/Anchor Books, 1976. Pp. 71–95.

*Lyric anthology*
*The Who Complete: A Complete Collection of the Best of the Who*. New York: Charles Hansen Music and Books, n.d.

*Records*
Who. *The Kids Are Alright* (MCA 2-11005). Universal City, Calif.: MCA Records, 1979.

Who. *Meaty Beaty Big and Bouncy* (DL 79184). Universal City, Calif.: MCA Records, 1971.

Who. *Tommy* (MCA 2-10005). Universal City, Calif.: MCA Records, 1973.

Who. *Who Are You* (MCA 3050). Universal City, Calif.: MCA Records, 1978.

## STEVIE WONDER

*Books and articles*
Albertson, Chris. "The Extraordinary Stevie Wonder." *Stereo Review* (January 1977):94.

Alterman, Louise. "Stevie Wonder and John Denver – A Study in Contrasts." *New York Times* (August 25, 1974):22.

"Black, Blind and on Top of Pop." *Time* (April 8, 1974):51–52.

Christgau, Robert. "Little Stevie Grows Older." In *Any Old Way You Choose It: Rock and Other Pop Music, 1967–1973*. Baltimore: Penguin, 1973. Pp. 299–303.

Dragonwagon, C. *Stevie Wonder*. New York: Flash, 1977.

Fong-Torres, Ben. "Stevie Wonder: 'I Want to Get into as Much Weird Stuff as Possible.'" In *What's That Sound? The Contemporary Music Scene from the Pages of "Rolling Stone."* Garden City, N.Y.: Doubleday/Anchor Books, 1976. Pp. 304–18.

Hasegawa, Sam. *Stevie Wonder.* Mankato, Minn.: Creative Educational Society, 1974.

Orth, Maureen. "Stevie, the Wonder Man." *Newsweek* (October 28, 1974):59–65.

Rockwell, John. "Stevie Wonder." In *The Rolling Stone Illustrated History of Rock and Roll,* ed. Jim Miller. New York: Random House, 1976. Pp. 338–39.

Underwood, Lee. "Boy Wonder Grows Up." *down beat* (September 12, 1974):14–15ff.

Vance, Joel. "Stevie Wonder." *Stereo Review* (August 1973):60–62.

*Lyric anthology*

Francis, Steve, comp. *Anthology – Stevie Wonder.* Miami: Screen Gems/Columbia Publications, 1975.

*Records*

Wonder, Stevie. *Fulfillingness' First Finale* (T 6332 S1). Hollywood, Calif.: Motown Record Corporation, 1974.

Wonder, Stevie. *Innervisions* (T6326 S1). Hollywood, Calif.: Motown Record Corporation, 1973.

Wonder, Stevie. *Journey Through the Secret Life of Plants* (T13-371 C2). Hollywood, Calif.: Motown Record Corporation, 1979.

Wonder, Stevie. *Looking Back* (M 804 LP 3). Hollywood, Calif.: Motown Record Corporation, n.d.

Wonder, Stevie. *Songs in the Key of Life* (T 13340 C2). Hollywood, Calif.: Motown Record Corporation, 1976.

Wonder, Stevie. *Talking Book* (T 6319 S1). Hollywood, Calif.: Motown Record Corporation, 1972.

## A BIBLIOGRAPHY OF GENERAL BIOGRAPHICAL RESOURCES ON CONTEMPORARY MUSIC PERFORMERS

Case, Brian, and Stan Britt, eds. *The Illustrated Encyclopedia of Jazz.* New York: Harmony Books, 1978.

Dellar, Fred, Roy Thompson, and Douglas B. Green, comps. *The Illustrated Encyclopedia of Country Music.* New York: Harmony Books, 1977.

Feather, Leonard, comp. *The New Edition of The Encyclopedia of Jazz.* New York: Bonanza, 1967.

Gentry, Linnell, comp. *A History and Encyclopedia of Country, Western, and Gospel Music,* 2d ed. Nashville: Clairmont Corporation, 1969.

Logan, Nick, and Bob Woffinden, comps. *The Illustrated Encyclopedia of Rock.* New York: Harmony Books, 1976.

Logan, Nick, with Bob Woffinden, eds. *The New Musical Express Book of Rock – No. 2.* London: Star Books, 1973.

Marchbank, Pearce, and Barry Miles, comps. *The Illustrated Rock Almanac.* New York: Paddington Press, 1977.

Naha, Ed, comp. *Lillian Roxon's Rock Encyclopedia,* rev. ed. New York: Grosset and Dunlap, 1978.

Nite, Norm N., comp. *Rock On: The Encyclopedia of Rock N' Roll.* New York: Crowell, 1974.

Nite, Norm N., comp. *Rock On – Volume II: The Illustrated Encyclopedia of Rock N' Roll – The Modern Years, 1964 to the Present.* New York: Crowell, 1978.

Roxon, Lillian, comp. *Lillian Roxon's Rock Encyclopedia.* New York: Grosset and Dunlap, 1969.

Shestack, Melvin, comp. *Lillian Roxon's Rock Encyclopedia.* New York: Crowell, 1974.

Stambler, Irwin, comp. *Encyclopedia of Pop, Rock, and Soul.* New York: St. Martin's Press, 1974.

Stambler, Irwin, comp. *Encyclopedia of Popular Music.* New York: St. Martin's Press, 1965.

Stambler, Irwin, and Grelun Landon, comps. *Encyclopedia of Folk, Country, and Western Music.* New York: St. Martin's Press, 1969.

PART TWO

# Popular Music
# as a Mirror
# of American Society

# SIX

# The Outsider
# in Popular Music

Beyond the boundaries of tradition and the barriers of law lies the territory of the outsider. The success of the contemporary rebel in capturing the public mind in the United States defies simple explanation. Perhaps the activities of outsiders provide necessary psychological relief to a modern public confronted by bureaucratic complexity, social stratification, political insensitivity, and personal feelings of inadequacy, anxiety, and apathy. The following study suggests that the lyricized behavior of outsiders in popular songs serves as an emotional outlet enabling individuals vicariously to overcome the frustrations of living in an alienating, repressive society.

Violent, antisocial behavior has frequently aroused public interest in America. Popular fascination with acts of physical coercion and torture is as old as the tales of vigilante tar-and-feather parties for British tax collectors. Likewise, the Boston Tea Party, described as an act of "civil disobedience" by Martin Luther King, Jr., was clearly an incident of overt violence and law-breaking in colonial Massachusetts.[1] Many traditional American heroes of history and fiction — Wyatt Earp, Billy the Kid, Jesse James, Mike Fink, John Dillinger, and Paul Bunyan — were antisocial men.[2] In recent times television and motion picture directors have spawned a new breed of hostile heroes. Billy Jack, Bullit, and "Dirty Harry" Calahan have joined forces with a seemingly endless variety of roughnecks portrayed by such virile actors as Paul Newman, Steve McQueen, Robert Redford, and Marlon Brando to titillate and intrigue the viewing public.[3] Even the rise in popularity of professional football in what had been America's "baseball paradise" can be related to the emergence of individually identifiable renegades of the Mean Joe Green/Dick Butkus mold. It is not surprising, then, that the field of popular music should also contribute to the veneration of violent men.

Songs depicting the exploits of exceptional men are as traditional as the balladeer's trade. Prominence of the folk ethic in contemporary music has served to highlight the growing popularity of biographical themes. Tales of extreme courage are common. In contrast to the ancient hymns of valor, however, most of the characters described in modern lyrics are unattractive, unheroic, and unimaginatively violent in their expressions of hostility toward society. The audio image of the exceptional man is that of an outsider—a confused, arrogant, unstable individual with an established reputation for generating a particular style of mayhem and surviving through a combination of charisma, luck, and brute force.

Why do records expounding the exploits of these undisciplined beings enjoy such success? What does public interest in songs that depict aggressive, antisocial behavior indicate about the American psyche? These questions are extremely difficult—if not impossible—to answer. Psychologists do not agree upon the root causes of violent behavior. If a consensus can be established among behavioral theorists on issues related to human aggression, it may be found in the following generalizations: (1) hostility is generated by situations which create pain, boredom, or fear in the mind of the aggressor, (2) the major catalyst for violent actions is frustration, and (3) a frequent source of frustration is social and economic deprivation.[4] The tendency for aggression to result from relative rather than absolute deprivation is an almost universally acknowledged phenomenon.[5]

One obvious question that arises from this situation is: How can the aggressive energies spawned in persons by social frustration be harmlessly discharged? Direct action—which may include lashing out at, hitting, or even killing the source of frustration—is socially unacceptable. A more positive alternative is to attempt to substitute some brand of physical activity—running, jumping, punching a bag—as a release for pent-up psychic energy. A final choice in attempting to deal with hostile feelings might be found in the cathartic effects of engaging in some form of fantasy aggression—dreaming of slugging an enemy, viewing a violent motion picture, or listening to a tale of malevolent action on the radio. Of course, none of these activities will totally resolve the basic problem. One psychologist has noted, "Research has shown over and over again that the only solution is to find ways of reducing violence as we continue to reduce the injustice that produces the frustrations that frequently erupt in violent aggression.[6]

The term *outsider* was selected for this study specifically because it does not conform to any specific sociological characterization or psychological definition. In terms of behavioral patterns, the central figures being examined in this essay display uneven combinations of the following traits or tendencies:

- They are front-runners in socially unacceptable practices and illegal activities.
- They are notoriously individualistic and egotistically arrogant about their personal reputations.
- They rarely take time to "sing the blues," to rationalize their plight, or to philosophize about their actions—instead, they are invariably action-oriented and habituated to the practices of physical violence.
- They may be black or white, rich or poor, young or old, married or single, or from rural or urban areas—but they are invariably prone to exhibitionism in such areas as dress, dance, and sexual behavior.
- They are accustomed to dealing in drugs (using and pushing) and alcohol (consuming, brewing, and distributing) and pursuing various forms of gambling as keys to their physical well-being and economic existence.
- They are hostile to all forms of authority—from dictatorial high school principals to nagging wives—but reserve a special loathing for police officers.
- They reject all conventional forms of social courtesy, legal sanction, intimate relationships.

This listing of general characteristics to identify the outsider must be supplemented with more specific information. Several verbal cues can warn the listening audience that the individual being portrayed in a popular song is an outsider—a rugged beast prone to antisocial activities. Sometimes the title of the song reveals the character of the man in question. For instance, one would hardly expect songs entitled "Big Bad John," "Big Boy Pete," or "Bad, Bad Leroy Brown" to be sung by the Mormon Tabernacle Choir. But this system of judgment is not fool-proof: songs such as "A Boy Named Sue" (Johnny Cash) or "Sunshine" (Jonathan Edwards) might mislead a novice who is attempting to spot lyric violence. Rather than relying strictly upon song title descriptions as keys to identifying aggressive behavior, I have developed a specific list of "tough guy" indicators that delineates physical, behavioral, and attitudinal signs of rebellion against established social norms and legal sanctions. Although lyrical interpretation does constitute the backbone of this study, no attempt has been made to construct a rigid content analysis frame for the songs being investigated.[7] The qualities of personality selected to define an outsider are:

| | |
|---|---|
| Physical supremacy | Good/bad facial features |
| | Strength |
| | Size or stature |
| | Peculiar physical traits (scars, amputated limbs, etc.) |
| Sexual prowess | Potency and productivity |
| | Endurance during intercourse |
| | Experience with different females |
| | Reputation among companions |
| Courage | Fearlessness |
| | Contentiousness |
| | Arrogance among peers or in the face of enemies |
| Vices | Sexual promiscuity or rape |
| | Alcoholism |
| | Gambling (cards, pool, dice) |
| | Drug abuse |
| | Profane language |
| Weapons | Guns |
| | Knives or razors |
| | Fists, feet, teeth |

| Companions | Motorcycle gang |
| --- | --- |
| | Gambling buddies |
| | Outlaw band |
| | None (loner) |
| Source of reputation | Public media |
| | Companions |
| | Victims or enemies |
| | Police |
| Personal effects | Clothing |
| | Accessories (rings, jewelry) |
| | Automobiles |
| | Home or apartment furnishings |
| Nicknames | Among friends |
| | Among enemies |
| | To self |
| Defiance of authority and assertion of personal independence | Unpatterned life-style |
| | Hostility to law |
| | Failure to take orders |
| Assertion of frustration with the existing social or political system | Attacks on social stratification |
| | Hatred of police |
| | Cynicism toward politicians |

The preceding outline of characteristics provides a skeleton to which the flesh of lyrical description can be added. For example, the area of physical supremacy is graphically depicted in phrases such as "stronger than a country horse" (Jim Croce's "You Don't Mess Around with Jim"), "bulldog mouth" (Carole King's "Smackwater Jack"), "scar on his cheek and his evil eye" (Johnny Cash's "A Boy Named Sue"), and "muscle and blood and skin and bone" (Ernie Ford's "Sixteen Tons").

The area of weapons is amply described lyrically by references to guns ("Stagger Lee," by Lloyd Price; "Smackwater Jack," by Carole King; and "Outlaw Man," by the Eagles), Knives ("A Boy Named Sue," by Johnny Cash; "Smokey Joe's Cafe," by the Robins; and "Mack the Knife," by Bobby Darin), and razors ("Bad, Bad Leroy Brown" by Jim Croce, and "High Heel Sneakers," by Jerry Lee Lewis).

Retaining the same sequence of indicators developed in the preceding section, specific records listed in the following chart illustrate the scope of the outsider image over two decades.

## The Image of the Outsider in Contemporary Lyrics, 1956–1976

*Physical supremacy*
"A Boy Named Sue"—Johnny Cash (Columbia 44944)
"You Don't Mess Around with Jim"—Jim Croce (ABC 11328)
"Big Bad John"—Jimmy Dean (Columbia 42175)
"Sixteen Tons"—Tennessee Ernie Ford (Capitol 3262)
"Amos Moses"—Jerry Reed (RCA 9904)
"Ramblin' Gamblin' Man"—Bob Seger System (Capitol 2297)

*Sexual prowess*
"Medicine Man"—Buchanan Brothers (Event 3302)
"Sixty Minute Man"—Clarence Carter (Fame 250)
"Light My Fire"—Jose Feliciano (RCA 9950)
"Superman"—Ides of March (Warner Brothers 7403)
"Steamroller Blues"—Elvis Presley (RCA 74-0910)
"Hard to Handle"—Otis Redding (ATCO 6592)

*Courage*
"Trouble Man"—Marvin Gaye (Talma 54228)
"Saturday Night's Alright for Fighting"—Elton John (MCA 40105)
"Big Boy Pete"—Olympics (Arvee 595)
"A Man and a Half"—Wilson Pickett (Atlantic 2575)
"Big Iron"—Marty Robbins (Columbia 41589)
"Jumpin' Jack Flash"—Rolling Stones (London 908)

*Vices*
"Folsom Prison Blues"—Johnny Cash (Columbia 44513)
"Desperado"—Alice Cooper (Warner Brothers 7529)
"Superfly"—Curtis Mayfield (Curtom 1978)
"The Ballad of Thunder Road"—Robert Mitchum (Capitol 3986)
"(I Washed My Hands in) Muddy Water"—Johnny Rivers (Imperial 66175)
"Papa Was a Rollin' Stone"—Temptations (Gordy 712)

*Weapons*
"Mack the Knife" – Bobby Darin (ATCO 6147)
"Outlaw Man" – Eagles (Asylum 11025)
"Smackwater Jack" – Carole King
"High Heel Sneakers" – Jerry Lee Lewis (Smash 1930)
"Stagger Lee" – Lloyd Price (ABC 9972)
"Big Iron" – Marty Robbins (Columbia 41589)

*Companions*
"I Get Around" – Beach Boys (Capitol 5174)
"Saturday Night's Alright for Fighting" – Elton John (MCA 40105)
"Stag-O-Lee" – Wilson Pickett (Atlantic 2448)
"Street Fightin' Man" – Rolling Stones (London 909)
"Leader of the Pack" – Shangri-Las (Red Bird 10-014)

*Source of reputation*
"Goldfinger" – Shirley Bassey (United Artists 790)
"The Ballad of Bonnie and Clyde" – Georgie Fame (Epic 10283)
"Ringo" – Lorne Greene (RCA 8444)
"Theme from Shaft" – Isaac Hayes (Enterprise 9083)
"The Man Who Shot Liberty Valance" – Gene Pitney (Musicor 1020)
"Soul Man" – Sam and Dave (Stax 231)

*Personal effects*
"Bad, Bad Leroy Brown" – Jim Croce (ABC 11359)
"Dead Man's Curve" – Jan and Dean (Liberty 55672)
"The Ballad of Thunder Road" – Robert Mitchum (Capitol 3986)
"Big Boy Pete" – Olympics (Arvee 595)
"Stagger Lee" – Tommy Roe (ABC 11307)
"Hi-Heel Sneakers" – Tommy Tucker (Checker 1067)

*Nicknames*
"Super Bad" – James Brown (King 6329)
"Trouble Man" – Marvin Gaye (Talma 54228)
"Secret Agent Man" – Johnny Rivers (Imperial 66159)
"Seventh Son" – Johnny Rivers (Imperial 66112)
"Agent Double-O-Soul" – Edwin Starr (Ric-Tic 103)
"Sixty Minute Man" – Trammps (Buddah 321)

*Defiance of authority and assertion of personal independence*
"Ramblin' Man" — Allman Brothers (Capricorn 0027)
"Midnight Rider" — Joe Cocker (A & M 1370)
"George Jackson" — Bob Dylan (Columbia 45516)
"Sunshine" — Jonathan Edwards (Capricorn 8021)
"A Natural Man" — Lou Rawls (MGM 14262)
"Born To Be Wild" — Steppenwolf (Dunhill 4138)

*Assertion of frustration with the existing social or political system*
"Eighteen" — Alice Cooper (Warner Brothers 1971)
"Ninety-Nine and a Half (Won't Do)" — Wilson Pickett (Atlantic 2334)
"Indian Reservation (The Lament of the Cherokee Reservation
    Indian)" — Raiders (Columbia 45332)
"Dead End Street" — Lou Rawls (Capitol 5869)
"Big Boss Man" — Jimmy Reed (Vee Jay 380)
"Get Off My Cloud" — Rolling Stones (London 9792)

Several singers have achieved recording fame and fortune in eulogiz-
ing the activities of "tough, mean bastards." Mick Jagger and the Rolling
Stones, both before and since the terror and violence at Altamont,[8]
have fostered the rebellious image of "Jumpin' Jack Flash" and the
"Street Fightin' Man." Alice Cooper's theatrical perversions are punctu-
ated by songs of violent men, particularly "Killer" and "Desperado." The
most skillful cultivator of the outsider image was the late Jim Croce.
His villians paraded almost laughingly across a variety of discs — and
found their way regularly to the top of the *Billboard* charts. In addition
to his 45 r.p.m. hits featuring Big Jim Walker ("You Don't Mess
Around with Jim") and "Bad, Bad Leroy Brown," Croce added to his
menagerie of malefactors through album descriptions of an ex-Marine
bouncer named Gil ("Top Hat Bar and Grille") and a freewheeling stock
car driver called "Rapid Boy." Other popular singers who have frequently projected the image of rebellion in the lyrics of their songs
include Johnny Rivers ("Secret Agent Man," "Seventh Son," and "I
Washed My Hands in Muddy Water"), Wilson Pickett ("A Man and a
Half," and "I'm a Midnight Mover"), and Jerry Reed ("Amos Moses").

The audience that appreciates the simplistic, individualistic vigilan-
tism of the motion pictures *Death Wish, Lipstick,* and *Taxi Driver* is also
likely to be impressed with the easy solutions to complex problems

offered by Marvin Gaye's "Trouble Man" and Isaac Hayes' "Shaft." The power of personal presence compels public attention.[9] Action overrides contemplation; books and poetry give way to the fury of fists; suicide is rejected in favor of murder; the quest for being ceases to be mental and becomes the overt search for self through the humiliation or destruction of others. Through all of this dynamic action, the outsider emerges as an ultimately free man. He is uninhibited by law, custom, circumstance, or fear. He faces a society that demands his allegiance and compels his obedience; but he rises above the dehumanizing social order to shun all forms of authority and to denounce the humility of passive citizenship. Unfortunately, he also rejects all of the tender elements of Rousseau's uncivilized state of nature and turns his turf into a Hobbesian nightmare, sans Leviathan, sans justice. Self writ large dominates the scene. The outsider is at the center of the stage in a tragic drama that has only one logical or possible conclusion—his death.

In the context of popular music, as in other forms of mass media, the outlaw emerges as the purest statement of the audience's alter ego. Just as Aristotle noted that bad citizens were often good men trapped in an unjust society, so the universal dilemma of social entrapment is depicted in folk style through the actions of Stagger Lee, John Shaft, Willie McCoy, and the Trouble Man. Of course, few of the outsiders display Aristotelian nobility. In fact, while some of the renegades are simply expressing a nonrational response to their surroundings (Smackwater Jack), others are positively motivated by precisely the same negative social objectives that are repulsive to a "just" outlaw. In these latter cases, expressions of sexual dominance, attempts to amass material goods, or the wild pursuit of random thrill-seeking compel many of the rakes, rogues, and ruffians to openly defy a social system they cannot penetrate by legal means. But all of the outsiders—from Aristotle's "just" rebels to the most amoral (if not immoral) outlaws—exist as active, self-motivated, functioning beings. Therein lies their public appeal.

The contemporary listening audience is saddled with a technologically assisted, passive existence. Despite the momentary catharsis provided by football games, detective films, or frantic dancing, the listener is willingly swept up in the strength of the audio rebel's inner-directed dynamism. More than that, the audience revels in his quest for being, even when reality overtakes the badman, either in the form of legal vengeance (the rope or the policeman's bullet) or in the currency of antisocietal authority (gang vengeance or murder).[10]

This explanation is neither startling nor particularly unique. What is significant, though, is the vast reserve of recorded violence available to the public as a vicarious substitute for the real thing. One scholar recently speculated that the use of drugs and the loud playing of rock music created a kind of isolated shell of security in a world that alienates, represses, and is essentially unresponsive to individual needs and desires;[11] similarly, the prominence of the outsider in contemporary music signals the public's search for nonpassive images. A listener counteracts his or her own lack of personal authority by mentally associating with a violent character who responds to *every* frustrating situation openly and with force. From the depths of personal isolation, frustration, and failure, the Walter Mittyish audience can revel in the virility and power of an audio actor.[12]

What specific images of contemporary American society cross the mind of the listener? The cruel world of the outsider is not totally fictional. It is based upon an Orwellian extension of reality. The listeners crystallize and translate the disc world into their own terms. They accept the image of lovers in sexual competition—without joy, sensitivity, privacy, intimacy, or warmth; they note that law enforcement officers are isolated souls, driven by unspoken hatreds or unarticulated envy for the freedom of the outsider; they accept the violent man as a hero—an independent being who is frustrated by social complexity, technological change, universal materialism, and personal anxiety or betrayal. The human desires for honesty, integrity, warmth, and other tender goals that make civilized life worth living are rarely considered or discussed. Typically, the outsider bears the marks of his environmental trap like the stripes of a jailed criminal. He may be able to rise above the pit of apathy long enough to make his name known momentarily, but his independence and self-motivation are inevitably compromised by his emotional responses and his failure to comprehend the complexity of his plight. Like Butch Cassidy and the Sundance Kid, he chooses freedom in the end; but that choice of freedom leads to death, not life.[13]

If popular music is serving a therapeutic function with respect to easing the social tensions in American life, why don't public officials praise this aspect of the audio media? The reason is obvious. It would be politically blasphemous to declare that contemporary society needs the charades of outsiders to pacify the public. To admit openly that frustration, isolation, and immobilization have been the result of technological advancement and social change in the United States would be sacrilegious in a progress-oriented, technocratic society.[14] The pariah label was publicly thrust upon those singers in the 1960s who chose to attack directly representatives of the military-industrial complex for warmongering in Vietnam. Bob Dylan, Phil Ochs, Joan Baez, and the other protest singers who articulately challenged "the system" were openly denounced. It should be noted, however, that the feelings of personal frustration noted in this essay are rarely grounded in unresolved national problems. The image of the world scene with respect to civil rights, war and peace, pollution, and other public concerns is inevitably structured as a secondary concern within each person's mind. The true silent majority consists of listeners and observers who rarely reflect upon concerns that are related to any issue beyond their personal security and welfare. Contemporary society has taught these people that the search for authentic heroes is universally frustrating, while the search for self is unrewarding. In the mid-1950s the balladeer of the outsider stepped into this vacuum. As stated earlier, the tale of a man bigger than life is not new. The mass availability of popular songs praising the life of outsiders, however, has created a new barometer for measuring the magnitude of alienation. The outsider has emerged as a mythical force to challenge that which the listener feels helpless to defeat — organized society, the system.

# SEVEN

# Popular Music
# and the Computer

The curricula at many liberal arts colleges are expanding to include a variety of popular-culture topics. It is not surprising that contemporary literature, modern music, experimental films, and numerous other nontraditional subjects have attracted scholarly attention during the 1960s and 1970s. Liberal arts educators cannot ignore powerful new artistic trends. What is strange, though, is the disdain most college teachers have demonstrated toward modern technology. Unfortunately, this attitude pervades most liberal arts campuses. Faculty disinterest in, or hostility toward, the use of computer facilities is incomprehensible. Even more disheartening, though, is the fact that there are so few examples of academic adaptations of computers in social science and humanities courses. In fact, when written inquiries were addressed by one liberal arts college dean to twelve nearby institutions about their experiences in using computers for teaching liberal arts subjects, *no* responses were returned. This essay suggests several ways in which computer technology can be applied to the investigation of historical, sociological, and artistic issues related to contemporary music.

During the past decade numerous liberal arts colleges have acquired small computers or have gained access to more complex computer facilities located at nearby state universities. Almost invariably, however, the use patterns of these computer resources have developed according to administrative rather than academic needs: admissions offices place their entire student applicant pools in the computer for cross-indexing; development and alumni offices secure special discs to hold the names and addresses of all graduates in quick retrievable storage; registrars, more cautious than most administrative officers, reluctantly acknowledge that construction of class schedules and even more complex registration processes might be simplified through programming on the computer facility; and, finally, business offices, ever watchful of their vast store of confidential salary information, admit that the computer might be useful in several types of budget-related operations. While this administrative activity goes on, the academic dean and most department chairpersons sit back, watching in silence.

Liberal arts college faculties should become leaders rather than observers in the utilization of computer technology. Academicians must begin to harness the power of this new teaching and learning device. It is unconscionable to hide behind the nineteenth-century clichés of Henry David Thoreau and Henry Adams, behaving as if more simple, traditional ways will somehow sustain moral purity or halt the erosion of contemporary society away from human reason and toward technological ruin. Apart from a few venturesome, career-oriented souls in business administration and mathematics, most liberal arts instructors view the availability of a computer terminal in the same way they would greet the presence of a fine stud horse grazing on the campus lawn. Potential value may be present, but there is little reason to expect anything of academic merit to result from it. This attitude must change. Indeed, if classroom teachers in the humanities, social sciences, and natural sciences do not explore the strengths—and limitations—of computers, contemporary education will become technologically blind. Limited vision has always been anathema to the liberal arts tradition. It is time to liberate the computer from administrative captivity and to encourage faculty members to explore the vast array of teaching possibilities that exist through this new medium.

Newberry College, a small liberal arts institution with a student population of eight hundred, is located in the Piedmont area of South Carolina and is supported by the Lutheran Church in America. This institution secured on-campus placement of a Digital PDP 11/40 Computer in 1975 through a Title III Grant from the Department of Health, Education, and Welfare. The administratively dominated use pattern outlined above has prevailed during the past four years despite temporary inroads by one mathematician and one economist who are attempting to promote new courses centered on the available computer resource.

During the spring of 1977, two Newberry faculty members with no previous computer training launched a research project that sought to identify new academic outlets for the computer. Initially, a professor of foreign languages began to tinker with a computer terminal housed in the registrar's office. He gained some programming tips in the faculty lounge from a mathematics instructor and then returned to the terminal to investigate the secrets of a new symbol-based language system. He eventually learned, through the trial-and-error method, to make the machine respond to his programming wishes.

At the same time, a professor of history with a hardy interest in the study of popular culture was researching a series of problems in a traditional note-card-shuffling fashion. While reading in the field of contemporary music,[1] he had unearthed several hypotheses that begged testing. Specifically, two issues seemed conducive to statistical examination. First, did the so-called British invasion of the American popular music field during the 1964–66 period come about because English singing groups were able to introduce a raft of new songs that had never before been heard in the United States? Second, do popular recording artists rise to prominence and maintain their fame primarily because they are constantly able to create new songs to support their distinctive identities? The pursuit of reasonable, statistically valid answers to these two questions brought the foreign language teacher and the historian together. And the Newberry College computer became a means to an end in their research quest.

The historian, using a variety of authoritative print resources,[2] developed a set of note-cards containing the titles, artists, recording companies, and release years for more than 1,200 popular songs that had been issued from 1950 to 1976. He selected only those songs that were listed on *Billboard*'s "Top 100" or "Rhythm-and-Blues Charts" at least *twice* during the past quarter century. Once assembled, the linguist placed this data package in the campus computer. He later developed a series of programs that would permit the research resources to be reorganized and communicated in chronological or alphabetical order by song, by artist, or by recording company. The programming problem was difficult but not too complex for any undergraduate student taking an introductory course in computer programs. The two New-berry faculty members found that they had to rely upon their own mental acuity rather than the information-packed computer to decide the proper questions ("functions") that had to be asked ("developed") in order to resolve the two issues of research concern. They also found that the intellectual task of formulating a logical research framework in respect to examining a problem is even *more* demanding with a computer present. Instead of replacing human knowledge, they discovered that the computer remains a passive servant to the creativity of the human mind.

The foreign language expert and the historian finally determined the appropriate computer-assisted approaches to resolving each of the questions they were attempting to answer. The pursuit of the first question concerning the uniqueness of the songs performed by British musicians during the mid-1960s presented a unique research problem for the two Newberry academicians. Using three encyclopedias of popular music,[3] the researchers identified ten of the most popular and productive British singing groups of the 1964–66 period: the Beatles, the Rolling Stones, Herman's Hermits, Gerry and the Pacemakers, the Dave Clark Five, Chad and Jeremy, Peter and Gordon, the Searchers, the Bachelors, and Eric Burdon and the Animals. Taking all of the *Billboard* hits that these English singing groups produced during the designated three-year period, they programmed the computer to iden-tify any of their songs that had previously been recorded and released by American artists between 1950–63. The results, as shown in Table 7.1, demonstrated that British performers relied heavily on traditional American pop tunes for their hit recordings. Of course, it would also be valuable to study the tremendous post-1966 influence of these *same* European rock groups on emerging American singers by noting the number of *their* original hit recordings that have been revived by American performers since 1967.

A liberal arts instructor might wish to engage students in a broader quest designed to probe the cultural connections between the United States and Great Britain *prior* to the arrival of the Beatles. How did American music of the pre-1964 period gain such widespread influence in England? Why did so many record-buying Americans apparently fail

TABLE 7.1

THE RELIANCE OF BRITISH SINGING GROUPS BETWEEN 1964 AND 1966 ON HIT SONGS PREVIOUSLY RECORDED BY AMERICAN POPULAR MUSIC PERFORMERS FROM 1950 TO 1963

| BRITISH GROUP | TOTAL NUMBER OF SONGS BY BRITISH SINGERS ACHIEVING *BILLBOARD* LISTING, 1964–66 | SONGS REVIVED BY BRITISH GROUPS, WITH THE NAMES OF AMERICAN ARTISTS WHO ORIGINALLY RECORDED THEM, 1950–63 | PERCENTAGE OF SONGS REVIVED BY BRITISH GROUPS, 1964–66 |
|---|---|---|---|
| The Bachelors | 8 | "Diana" (Paul Anka – 1957)<br>"In the Chapel in the Moonlight" (Kitty Kallen – 1954)<br>"Love Me with All Your Heart" (Ray Charles Singers – 1964)<br>"Marie" (Four Tunes – 1953)<br>"No Arms Can Ever Hold You" (Gaylords – 1955) | 63 |
| The Beatles | 46 | "Act Naturally" (Buck Owens – 1963)<br>"Ann (Go to Him)" (Arthur Alexander – 1962)<br>"Boys" (Shirelles – 1960)<br>"Chains" (Cookies – 1962)<br>"Matchbox" (Carl Perkins – 1957)<br>"Please Mr. Postman" (Marvelettes – 1961)<br>"Roll Over Beethoven" (Chuck Berry – 1956)<br>"Slow Down" (Larry Williams – 1958)<br>"Twist and Shout" (Isley Brothers – 1962) | 20 |

| Artist | | Song | |
|---|---|---|---|
| Eric Burdon and the Animals | 33 | "Boom Boom" (John Lee Hooker – 1962) | 12 |
| | | "Bring It on Home to Me" (Sam Cooke – 1962) | |
| | | "C. C. Rider" (Chuck Willis – 1957) | |
| | | "House of Rising Sun" (Bob Dylan – 1962) | |
| Chad and Jeremy | 18 | "Before and After" (Fleetwoods – 1964) | 11 |
| | | "Early Mornin' Rain" (Peter, Paul, and Mary – 1965) | |
| Dave Clark Five | 39 | "Do You Love Me?" (Contours – 1962) | 18 |
| | | "I Like It Like That" (Chris Kenner – 1961) | |
| | | "A Little Bit Now" (Majors – 1962) | |
| | | "Over and Over" (Bobby Day – 1959) | |
| | | "Reelin' and Rockin'" (Chuck Berry – 1958) | |
| | | "You Got What It Takes" (Marv Johnson – 1959) | |
| | | "You Must Have Been a Beautiful Baby" (Bobby Darin – 1961) | |
| Gerry and the Pacemakers | 18 | "I'll Be There" (Damita Jo – 1961) | 11 |
| | | "You'll Never Walk Alone" (Roy Hamilton – 1954) | |
| Herman's Hermits | 15 | "Silhouettes" (Rays – 1957) | 13 |
| | | "Wonderful World" (Sam Cooke – 1960) | |
| Peter and Gordon | 17 | "To Know Him Is to Love Him" (Teddy Bears – 1958) | 12 |
| | | "Woman" (Johnny Desmond – 1953) | |
| Rolling Stones | 13 | "Not Fade Away" (Buddy Holly – 1957) | 15 |
| | | "Tell Me" (Dick and Dee Dee – 1962) | |
| The Searchers | 15 | "Bumble Bee" (LaVern Baker – 1960) | 13 |
| | | "Love Potion No. 9" (Clovers – 1959) | |

to recognize the frequent use of "old" American hits by new British groups? What particular kinds of American music influenced the Rolling Stones and the Beatles prior to their conquest of the American popular music scene? What were the economic consequences of the 1964 musical "invasion" of the United States by British singing groups?

The second question, concerning the unique repertoires of popular recording artists, is extremely difficult to assess, even with the assistance of a computer. The task of examining the recording careers of *each* recording artist who had managed to place a tune on the *Billboard* charts would be too time consuming, so the researchers restricted themselves to an identifiable sample of stars. Using a variety of encyclopedia resources[4] to identify the top recording artists according to the number of criteria, a representative list of "superstars" was developed. The five performers selected for this survey were Pat Boone, Glen Campbell, Aretha Franklin, Wilson Pickett, and Elvis Presley. For each of these artists the researchers programmed the computer to check the number of revival songs these stars performed successfully during their lengthy careers. Table 7.2 reflects this information.

Table 7.2 reveals that the most potent hitmakers in the popular music industry, though generally accepted as creative and innovative forces, are also major contributors to reviving rock music standards. That is, they skillfully mix their releases by producing original numbers *along with* traditional hits to launching a career (Donny Osmond and Leif Garret) or to provide a necessary respite between creative surges (Linda Ronstadt and Johnny Rivers). This type of study could parallel the traditional studies of liberal arts teachers who examine personal production trends in painting styles or classical music endeavors.

It should be clear from this essay that a computer can function as a valuable tool for stimulating academic pursuits. Untrained academic personnel can manipulate it with a minimum of coaching, and they can use it as an adjunct to student and faculty thinking in a variety of problematical circumstances. The use of a computer is not a threat to the liberal arts tradition. Just the opposite: as an academic ally, it can help to foster reflective thinking by diminishing the drudgery so often required in research card-shuffling.

An undergraduate liberal arts education should increase one's ability

TABLE 7.2

NUMBER OF HIT SONGS BY SELECTED SUPERSTARS WHICH ORIGINALLY ACHIEVED BILLBOARD LISTING BY ANOTHER POPULAR ARTIST, 1950–1977

| NAME OF PERFORMER | NUMBER OF REVIVED SONG HITS BY THE ARTIST | SELECTED ILLUSTRATION OF SPECIFIC REVIVED SONGS (WITH ORIGINAL ARTIST AND INITIAL DATE OF RELEASE) |
|---|---|---|
| Pat Boone | 12 | "I Almost Lost My Mind" (Ivory Joe Hunter – 1950) |
| | | "I'll Be Home" (Flamingos – 1956) |
| | | "It's Too Soon to Know" (Orioles – 1948) |
| | | "Long Tall Sally" (Little Richard – 1956) |
| | | "Tutti Frutti" (Little Richard – 1955) |
| Glen Campbell | 6 | "All I Have to Do Is Dream" (Everly Brothers – 1958) |
| | | "Dream Baby (How Long Must I Dream)" (Roy Orbison – 1962) |
| | | "Hey Little One" (Dorsey Burnette – 1960) |
| | | "It's Only Make Believe" (Conway Twitty – 1958) |
| | | "Oh Happy Day" (Edwin Hawkins Singers – 1969) |
| Aretha Franklin | 22 | "Bridge over Troubled Water" (Simon and Garfunkel – 1970) |
| | | "Eleanor Rigby" (Beatles – 1966) |
| | | "Spanish Harlem" (Ben E. King – 1961) |
| | | "The Weight" (Jackie DeShannon – 1968) |
| | | "You Send Me" (Sam Cooke – 1957) |
| Wilson Pickett | 10 | "Born to Be Wild" (Steppenwolf – 1968) |
| | | "Hey Jude" (Beatles – 1968) |
| | | "Mama Told Me (Not to Come)" (Three Dog Night – 1970) |
| | | "Stagger Lee" (Lloyd Price – 1958) |
| | | "You Keep Me Hangin' On" (Supremes – 1966) |
| Elvis Presley | 18 | "Big Boss Man" (Jimmy Reed – 1961) |
| | | "Crying in the Chapel" (Orioles – 1953) |
| | | "The Promised Land" (Chuck Berry – 1964) |
| | | "Steamroller Blues" (James Taylor – 1970) |
| | | "What'd I Say" (Ray Charles – 1959) |

to reflect upon problems of personal and social significance. A computer cannot do this. The computer can produce errorless data lists at a dazzling rate of speed; it can sort and find, alphabetize, and place in chronological order seemingly endless amounts of information. Yet it remains a programmed tool. The fact that most liberal arts colleges hide their computers in the basements of science buildings and place terminals in obscure cubbyholes demonstrates that most teachers have failed to appreciate the value of the instrument in respect to contemporary academic speculations. Perhaps George Orwell has indoctrinated our generation too thoroughly. Liberal arts instructors should not let business managers, admissions recruiters, and financial aid officers control this tremendous learning vehicle merely because they are unwilling to admit that they must—like Prometheus—learn about new technology in order to bring light to others.

# EIGHT

# Urban Life
# in Popular Music

During the mid-fifties, in virtually every urban civilization in the world, adolescents staked out their freedom in the cities, inspired and reassured by the Rock and Roll beat. Rock and Roll was perhaps the first form of popular culture to celebrate without reservation characteristics of city life that had been among the most criticized. In Rock and Roll, the strident, repetitive sounds of the city life were, in effect, reproduced as melody and rhythm.

—Charlie Gillett[1]

Sociologist Charlie Gillett contends that contemporary music became the dictionary, barometer, microscope, gyroscope, and source of social etiquette for American youth in the 1950s.[2] If the city was a confusing, mechanized jungle, the translation of the life forces of survival and success were often found in the lyrics and rhythms provided on record albums, over radios, and on jukeboxes. The following pages will expand upon and update Gillett's observations. By utilizing the personalized perspectives provided in song lyrics, the author will demonstrate how modern singers and songwriters assemble pluralistic attitudes, ideas, events, and values that often help to form the concept of "urban existence" in the minds of young Americans.

Media analysts tend to believe that television is a fine barometer of public opinion. Karl E. Meyer focused on prime-time programming between 1958 and 1975 to demonstrate the "urbanized thinking" of 1979 Americans: whereas frontier sagas such as "Gunsmoke," "Wagon

Train," "Have Gun, Will Travel," "Rifleman," "Maverick," "Wells Fargo," "Wyatt Earp," and "Cheyenne" dominated evening TV ratings during the late fifties, the urban situation comedy reigned in the nighttime spotlight two decades later. The top-rated shows of 1975 included "All in the Family," "Laverne and Shirley," "Sanford and Son," "Rhoda," "Welcome Back, Kotter," "Kojak," and "Mary Tyler Moore." Meyer observed:

> Sooner or later, Americans had to come to terms with a reality we have sought to deny or ignore—that we are in essence a nation of city slickers, that the urban way of life is the norm, that far more of us live in apartment houses than in clapboards in Stockbridge or on peanut farms in Plains. . . . No longer invisible on prime time, the big city is ubiquitous. Not only do the most popular sitcoms have a clearly defined urban setting, but their themes reflect urban concerns: racial friction, single living, changing sex roles, office politics, generalization conflict, and so forth. For the first time since its inception, television is presenting a recognizable cross-section of big-city denizens: blue collar and white collar, ethnic and unwhite, doctor, lawyer, beggarman, and shrink.[3]

Although Meyer may be correct, the signs of social change occurred in another medium much earlier. In fact, popular music anticipated television's urban-theme commitment by two decades. As a mirror of city life in the fifties, sixties, and seventies, song lyrics were more attentive to urban issues both because of their originators and their audience. One clear illustration of the urban perspective that undergirds popular music may be noted in the titles of books examining the singers, songs, composers, rhythmic styles, and record companies in contemporary music:

*Chicago Breakdown* (1975) by Mike Rowe
*Jazz Style in Kansas City and the Southwest* (1971) by Ross Russell
*The Jefferson Airplane and the San Francisco Sound* (1969) by Ralph J.
    Gleason
*Motown and the Arrival of Black Music* (1971) by David Morse
*The Nashville Sound: Bright Lights and Country Music* (1970) by Paul
    Hemphill
*The New Haven Sound, 1946–1976* (1977) by Paul Lepri

*The Sound of the City: The Rise of Rock and Roll* (1971) by Charlie Gillett

*The Sound of Philadelphia* (1975) by Tony Cummings

*They All Sang on the Corner: New York City's Rhythm and Blues Vocal Groups of the 1950s* (1973) by Philip Groia

*Uptown — The Story of Harlem's Apollo Theatre* (1971) by Jack Schiffman

*Urban Blues* (1966) by Charles Keil

*Walking to New Orleans: The Story of New Orleans Rhythm and Blues* (1964) by John Broven

Beyond scholarly titles, though, the relationship between American popular music and metropolitan population centers can be documented through the familiar linkages of city names with distinctive singing styles. Thus one commonly associates New Orleans and Kansas City with jazz, St. Louis and Chicago with the blues, Nashville with country music, New York with rhythm and blues, Detroit with the "Motown sound," and Memphis with soul sounds. The all-pervasive disco tempo, according to one music critic, ". . . suggests the heartbeat of modern urban life."[4]

What has not been widely acknowledged, though, is the fact that contemporary tunes can be utilized as a rich source of social commentary as well as a bundle of danceable rhythmic patterns. The realm of popular music is much more complex than the relatively narrow television programming schedule. Although courtship themes may dominate contemporary lyrics quantitatively,[5] examples of urban-related social and political commentaries in the music of the past thirty years abound. These metropolitan life-style observations can be found in all major forms of modern music — pop, soul, and country. Although certain singers have become associated with pro-urban or anti-urban tunes, this ideological connotation is neither consistent nor necessarily intentional. It would be as unfair to attribute universal anti-city feelings to John Denver ("Thank God I'm a Country Boy") and Glen Campbell ("Country Boy (You Got Your Feet in L.A.)") as it would to ascribe totally pro-urban attitudes to Chuck Berry ("Back in the U.S.A."). In order to be instructive rather than propagandistic, one must utilize a variety of songs and artists to illustrate the multiplicity of images of urban life in American popular music from 1950 and 1979.

Suggesting that contemporary lyrics be utilized in high school and college classrooms is hardly original.[6] However, few teachers have employed the rich potential for studying urban life in America that can be provided through pop records. The use of lyrics combines varying descriptive elements of biography, fantasy, memory, illusion, fact, and folklore. Such a strange mixture of resources may not please traditionally trained historians, statistically oriented sociologists, or other scholars who currently instruct classes in urban society; initial hostility may be overcome if critics accept the fundamental pedagogical principle that student motivation ("recognition of personal problems or social conflict situations") is an absolute prerequisite to serious reflective thought on any subject. The specific teaching approach I am advocating is outlined below. It is designed to create questions, uncertainty, cognitive dissonance, conflict, and controversy within students' minds by presenting at least two different lyrical positions.

## THE CHANGING IMAGE OF THE METROPOLIS

*Question:*
How has the image of American city life changed during the past three decades?

*Concepts to investigate:*

| | | |
|---|---|---|
| population density | ghetto | ethnic groups |
| cultural opportunities | suburbia | urban renewal |
| labor unions | ecology | industrial growth |

*Songs and performers:*
1950–59
   "Chicago" (Capitol 3793) – Frank Sinatra
   "New York's My Home" (Decca 30111) – Sammy Davis, Jr.
   "Mack the Knife" (Atco 6147) – Bobby Darin
   "Back in the U.S.A." (Chess 1729) – Chuck Berry
   "Kansas City" (Fury 1023) – Wilbert Harrison
1959–69
   "Detroit City" (RCA Victor 47-8183) – Bobby Bare
   "Twelve Thirty" (Dunhill 4099) – Mamas and the Papas
   "San Franciscan Nights" (MGM 13769) – Animals

"Subterranean Homesick Blues" (Columbia 43242)—Bob Dylan
"Summer in the City" (Kama Sutra 250)—Lovin' Spoonful
1970–79
    "Bright Lights, Big City" (Capitol 3114)—Sonny James
    "Stayin' Alive" (RSO 885)—Bee Gees
    "Hot Child in the City" (Chrysalis 2226)—Nick Gilder
    "In the Ghetto" (Fame 91000)—Candi Staton

## URBAN DECADENCE AND SOCIAL DECLINE

*Question:*
Why do many people claim that the increasing urban population has
produced a general decline in the quality of American life?

*Concepts to investigate:*

| | | |
|---|---|---|
| pollution | racism | political repression |
| alienation | materialism | moral decay |
| poverty | violence | artificiality |
| bigotry | unemployment | prostitution |

*Songs and performers:*
"For the Love of Money" (Philadelphia International 3544)—O'Jay's
"Freddie's Dead" (Curtom 1975)—Curtis Mayfield
"Masterpiece" (Gordy 7126)—Temptations
"I'm Gonna Move to the Outskirts of Town" (Impulse 202)—Ray
Charles
"Runaway Child, Running Wild" (Gordy 7084)—Temptations
"Takin' It to the Streets" (Warner Brothers 8196)—Doobie Brothers
"Lido Shuffle" (Columbia 10491)—Boz Scaggs
"Life in the Fast Lane" (Asylum 45403)—Eagles
"Hey Big Brother" (Rare Earth 5038)—Rare Earth
"Baker Street" (United Artists 1192)—Gerry Rafferty
"Mr. Businessman" (Monument 1083)—Ray Stevens
"Movin' Out (Anthony's Song)" (Columbia 10708)—Billy Joel
"Ball of Confusion" (Gordy 7099)—Temptations
"In the Ghetto" (Fame 91000)—Candi Staton
"People Are Strange" (Elektra 45621)—Doors
"American Woman" (RCA 74-0325)—Guess Who

"Mrs. Robinson" (Columbia 44511)—Simon and Garfunkel
"Monster" (Dunhill 4221)—Steppenwolf

## Urban Civilization as Cultural Pinnacle

*Question:*
How do supporters of city life justify their claims that the contemporary urban environment in America is a superior style of existence?

*Concepts to investigate:*

| | | |
|---|---|---|
| companionship | upward mobility | tolerance |
| flexibility | social change | opportunity |
| excitement | personal growth | pride |
| | culture | |

*Songs and performers:*
"San Francisco (Be Sure to Wear Some Flowers in Your Hair)" (Ode 103)—Scott McKenzie
"San Franciscan Nights" (MGM 13769)—Animals
"Promised Land" (RCA 10074)—Elvis Presley
"I Left My Heart in San Francisco" (Columbia 42332)—Tony Bennett
"Downtown" (Warner Brothers 5495)—Petula Clark
"Back in the U.S.A." (Asylum 45519)—Linda Ronstadt
"Kansas City" (Reprise 20236)—Trini Lopez
"A Natural Man" (MGM 14262)—Lou Rawls
"Night Life" (Tamla 54268)—Miracles
"Hollywood City" (Columbia 42405)—Carl Perkins
"Sweet Little Sixteen" (Chess 1683)—Chuck Berry
"Dancing in the Street" (Gordy 7033)—Martha and the Vandellas
"Boy from New York City" (Blue Cat 102)—Ad Libs

## City Life and the Black American

*Question:*
How has the urban environment affected the social, political, and economic development of black men and women in modern America?

*Concepts to investigate:*

| | | |
|---|---|---|
| racism | social mobility | equal opportunity |
| ghetto | political involvement | affirmative action |
| education | economic incentive | |

*Songs and performers:*
"On Broadway" (Atlantic 2182)—Drifters
"Johnny B. Goode" (Chess 1691)—Chuck Berry
"Uptown" (Philles 102)—Crystals
"Bright Lights, Big City" (Vee-Jay 398)—Jimmy Reed
"You Haven't Done Nothin' " (Tamla 54252)—Stevie Wonder
"Promised Land" (Chess 1916)—Chuck Berry
"Superfly" (Curtom 1978)—Curtis Mayfield
"For the Love of Money" (Philadelphia International 3544)—O'Jays
"Down and Out in New York City" (Polydor 14168)—James Brown
"Masterpiece" (Gordy 7126)—Temptations
"A Natural Man" (MGM 14262)—Lou Rawls
"Freddie's Dead" (Curtom 1975)—Curtis Mayfield
"Inner City Blues (Make Me Wanna Holler)" (Tamla 54209)—Marvin Gaye
"Almost Grown" (Chess 1722)—Chuck Berry
"Money Honey" (Atlantic 1006)—Drifters
"Dead End Street" (Capitol 5869)—Lou Rawls
"The Ghetto" (Atco 6719)—Donny Hathaway

## IMAGES OF SPECIFIC CITIES

*Question:*
Why do particular cities in the United States seem to have images which make them unique in the public mind?

*Concepts to investigate:*

| | | |
|---|---|---|
| stereotypes | chamber of commerce | tourism |
| industrialism | historical heritage | images |
| publicity | urban sociology | crime |
| "fun city" | political corruption | culture |

*Songs and performers:*
New York
  "I Guess the Lord Must Be in New York City" (RCA 74-0261)—
  Nilsson
  "New York City" (E.M.I. America 8005)—Zwol
  "New York, You Got Me Dancing" (Buddah 564)—Andrea True
  Connection
  "Native New Yorker" (RCA 11129)—Odyssey
  "Another Rainy Day in New York City" (Columbia 10360)—Chi-
  cago
Chicago
  "Chicago" (Atlantic 2804)—Graham Nash
  "The Night Chicago Died" (Mercury 73492)—Paper Lace
  "Chicago" (Capitol 3793)—Frank Sinatra
  "Deadend Street" (Capitol 5869)—Lou Rawls
  "Bad, Bad Leroy Brown" (ABC 11359)—Jim Croce
Los Angeles
  "Hollywood City" (Columbia 42405)—Carl Perkins
  "Country Boy (You Got Your Feet in L.A.)" (Capitol 4155)—Glen
  Campbell
  "L.A. Freeway" (MCA 40054)—Jerry Jeff Walker
  "L.A. International Airport" (Capitol 3035)—Susan Raye
  "Hollywood Nights" (Capitol 4618)—Bob Seger
San Francisco
  "(Sittin' on) The Dock of the Bay" (Volt 157)—Otis Redding
  "San Francisco is a Lonely Town" (Sound Stage 72641)—Joe Simon
  "I Left My Heart in San Francisco" (Columbia 42332)—Tony Ben-
  nett
  "San Franciscan Nights" (MGM 13769)—Animals
  "San Francisco (Be Sure to Wear Flowers in Your Hair)" (Ode
  103)—Scott McKenzie

## The Urban Female

*Question:*
What is the popular image of the urban female?

*Concepts to investigate:*

liberation     prostitution     independence
equality     security     affirmative action
discrimination     sexism     domination
submission     chauvinism     integration

*Songs and performers:*
"Lady Marmalade" (Epic 50048)—LaBelle
"Ghetto Woman" (ABC 11310)—B. B. King
"Black Pearl" (A & M 1053)—Sonny Charles and the Checkmates, Ltd.
"Nadine" (Chess 1883)—Chuck Berry
"I'm Livin' in Shame" (Motown 1139)—Diana Ross and the Supremes
"The Witch Queen of New Orleans" (Epic 10749)—Redbone
"Native New Yorker" (RCA 11129)—Odyssey
"Poor, Poor Pitiful Me" (Asylum 45462)—Linda Ronstadt
"That Evil Child" (Kent 4542)—B. B. King
"Hot Child in the City" (Chrysalis 2226)—Nick Gilder
"Sweet City Woman" (Bell 45-120)—Stampeders
"Big City Miss Ruth Ann" (Sussex 248)—Gallery
"Mrs. Robinson" (Columbia 44511)—Simon and Garfunkel
"Second Hand Rose" (Columbia 43469)—Barbra Streisand
"Twelve Thirty" (Dunhill 4099)—Mamas and the Papas
"Don't Go City Girl on Me" (Dot 17697)—Tommy Overstreet
"New Orleans Ladies" (Capitol 4586)—Louisiana's Le Roux

## THE URBAN MALE

*Question:*
Is the popular image of the urban male positive or negative?

*Concepts to investigate:*

self-motivation     character     intimidation
authority     violence     materialism
dignity     honesty     perseverance
chauvinism                    power

*Songs and performers:*
"Movin' Out (Anthony's Song)" (Columbia 10708) — Billy Joel
"You Don't Mess Around with Jim" (ABC 11328) — Jim Croce
"Mack the Knife" (Atco 6147) — Bobby Darin
"Take a Letter Maria" (Atco 6714) — R. B. Greaves
"Boy from New York City" (Blue Cat 102) — Ad Libs
"Mr. Businessman" (Monument 1083) — Ray Stevens
"Bad, Bad Leroy Brown" (ABC 11359) — Jim Croce
"Taxi" (Elektra 45770) — Harry Chapin
"Big Boy Pete" (Arvee 595) — Olympics
"Workin' in the Car Wash Blues" (ABC 11447) — Jim Croce
"Trouble Man" (Tamla 54228) — Marvin Gaye
"Theme from *Shaft*" (Enterprise 9038) — Isaac Hayes
"Kansas City Star" (Smash 1965) — Roger Miller
"My Life" (Columbia 10853) — Billy Joel
"Rhinestone Cowboy" (Capitol 4095) — Glen Campbell

## THE URBAN TROUBADOR

*Question:*
Why do some contemporary singers and songwriters seem to focus their lyrical attention on the nature and meaning of urban life?

*Concepts to investigate:*

| | | |
|---|---|---|
| autobiography | experience | biography |
| nostalgia | folk song | reflection |
| troubadour | individualism | balladeer |

*Songs and performers:*
Billy Joel
   "Movin' Out (Anthony's Song)" (Columbia 10708)
   "My Life" (Columbia 10853)
   "Piano Man" (Columbia 45963)
   "The Entertainer" Columbia 10064)
Bob Dylan
   "Rainy Day Women #12 & 35" (Columbia 43592)
   "Positively 4th Street" (Columbia 43389)

"Like a Rolling Stone" (Columbia 43346)
"Subterranean Homesick Blues" (Columbia 43242)
Paul Simon
"Still Crazy after All These Years" (Columbia 10332)
"Kodachrome" (Columbia 45859)
"Me and Julio Down by the Schoolyard" (Columbia 45585)
"America" (Columbia 45663)—with Art Garfunkel
"Mrs. Robinson" (Columbia 44511)—with Art Garfunkel
Chuck Berry
"School Day" (Chess 1653)
"Sweet Little Sixteen" (Chess 1683)
"Johnny B. Goode" (Chess 1691)
"Back in the U.S.A." (Chess 1729)
"You Never Can Tell" (Chess 1906)
"Promised Land" (Chess 1916)
Jim Croce
"You Don't Mess Around with Jim" (ABC 11328)
"Operator (That's Not the Way It Feels)" (ABC 11335)
"Bad, Bad Leroy Brown" (ABC 11359)
"I Got a Name" (ABC 11389)
"Workin' at the Car Wash Blues" (ABC 11447)
Stevie Wonder
"You Haven't Done Nothin' " (Tamla 54252)
"Living for the City" (Tamla 54242)
"Superstition" (Tamla 54226)
"Heaven Help Us All" (Tamla 54200)
Curtis Mayfield
"Future Shock" (Curtom 1987)
"Superfly" (Curtom 1978)
"Freddie's Dead" (Curtom 1975)
"Choice of Colors" (Curtom 1943)
"We're a Winner" (ABC 11022)

Is Chicago the happy-go-lucky, "toddlin' town" described by Frank
Sinatra, or is it a center for political repression as Graham Nash asserts?
And if State Street is really such a great street, what does Jim Croce
mean when he calls the South Side of Chicago "the baddest part of

town"? Does the death of Richard Daley and the recent ascendance of Jane Byrne meet the Chi-Lites' request for a redistribution of political power? Do young blacks in Chicago still believe, as Lou Rawls does, that it is possible to escape from the ghetto? There are no correct answers to these questions, but any teacher should recognize the value of asking his or her students to address them.

Translating the eight themes outlined above into active classroom discussions will depend upon the particular pedagogical approach, but certain fundamental understandings must be established between the teacher and students before they undertake lyrical analysis. First, the songs should not be randomly chosen but must be carefully selected to illustrate particular urban-related ideas. Second, the values and ideas expressed in a song must be open for critical examination by the class. Neither the singer nor the songwriter should be biographically "interpreted" – only the context of the lyric should be reviewed and discussed. Third, an open atmosphere must prevail during the discussion stage, or the technique of utilizing popular culture resources will become as deadening as using a traditional textbook. Students should be encouraged to challenge each other's ideas and be permitted to introduce other songs to enhance, contradict, or broaden a particular theme.

To demonstrate the expansive characteristic of this instructional approach, let me report the response of one of my classes. My goal was to illustrate to a group of college freshmen the hypothesis that the city has replaced the frontier in the minds of many twentieth-century Americans as the place where freedom, fame, and fortune could be readily attained. The inhibiting factors of rural life – fewer job opportunities, limited capital, lack of positive response to creative ideas or outlets for untried schemes, and little diversity in thinking and life-styles – could more likely be overcome by moving to the big city. The songs I selected to depict the increasing opportunities for social mobility through metropolitan relocation were: Dave Loggins' "Please Come to Boston," Chuck Berry's "Johnny B. Goode," Elvis Presley's "Promised Land."

No sooner had I played these songs and launched the "small-town narrowness vs. big-city opportunity" theme than my students hit me with three different positions. First, one group claimed I was ignoring the small-town virtues of love, individual concern, time for experimentation, human understanding, and simplicity of life. Among the recordings offered to illustrate these characteristics were John Denver's "Thank God I'm a Country Boy" and Merle Haggard's "Okie from Muskogee." Other students maintained that urban life often crushes the spirit of a talented individual because it lacks sensitivity, tends to produce loneliness and isolation, and creates a fear of failure. The songs suggested to illustrate this position were: Bobby Bare's "Detroit City," Jim Croce's "Working in the Car Wash Blues," Gladys Knight and the Pips' "Midnight Train to Georgia," and the Spinners' "I'm Comin' Home." A third group built their case on the suggestions of the second. These students argued that more people were leaving urban situations to find personal gratification (Canned Heat's "Goin' Up the Country" and Crosby, Stills, Nash, and Young's "Woodstock"), to escape the pressures of urban existence (Mac Davis' "Stop and Smell the Roses" and Ray Stevens' "Mr. Businessman"), or just to return to more friendly, more familiar surroundings (Don Williams' "Tulsa Time" and Roger Miller's "Kansas City Star").

Even though I countered this barrage of arguments and recordings with illustrations of urban enjoyment ranging from Petula Clark's "Downtown" and Scott McKenzie's "San Francisco" and Frank Sinatra's "Chicago," I continued to encounter a movement by half of my class, which denied my initial "streets paved with gold" stereotype of urban life. Finally, a fourth group of students even suggested that migration from a rural setting to the city might occur for totally nonselfish, nonmaterialistic reasons. This small contingent argued, using John Sebastian's "Welcome Back," Timmy Thomas' "Why Can't We Live Together," and Rare Earth's "Hey Big Brother," that idealistic social reforms could be initiated by persons coming into a particular city seeking to improve the quality of urban politics, education, and race relations. Sensing an unrealistic overemphasis on humanitarianism and a failure to acknowledge the more materialistic elements of working life in the city, another student noted that employment opportunities in the city were often repetitive, boring, and dehumanizing. He made his case with lyrics from B.T.O.'s "Takin' Care of Business," the Easybeats' "Friday on My Mind," the Vogues' "Five O'Clock World," and O'Jays' "For the Love of Money."

By the time this three-day classroom exchange on the nature of rural existence, social mobility, and urban life had run its course, my students perceived that people in the United States could be simultaneously attracted and repelled by the city. They saw both advantages and disadvantages to living, working, and seeking to change the nature of metropolitan areas. From this broadened mindset, I then assigned portions of three books to be read and reviewed by the entire class. These studies were: Sinclair Lewis' *Main Street*, Jacob Riis' *How the Other Half Lives*, and Ulf Hannerz' *Soulside: Inquiries into Ghetto Culture and Community*.

# NINE

# The Black Roots of Popular Music

"We sing more colored than the Africans," said John Lennon, boastfully acknowledging the debt of the Beatles to Negro music.

—Arnold Shaw[1]

. . . The Beatles' first album included numbers that were originally hits for Arthur Alexander, the Isley Brothers, the Cookies and the Shirelles. And their second album contained . . . three cover versions of early Motown smashes—Barrett Strong's "Money," the Miracles' "You Really Got a Hold on Me" and the Marvelettes' "Please, Mr. Postman."

—Ian Hoare[2]

. . . The Stones managed an alarmingly effective xerox of American blues. Their first American album, *The Rolling Stones* (London PS 375), is a magnificent example of how important blues had become in England. It contains "I'm a King Bee," familiar in the American R & B market to Slim Harpo; Chuck Berry's "Oh, Carol;" Motown's "Can I Get A Witness;" Willie Dixon's "I Just Want to Make Love to You;" and Rufus Thomas' "Walking the Dog. . . ."

—Mike Jahn[3]

. . . The irony goes deeper, for it was the Beatles and the Liverpool 'Beat Music Scene' which largely changed attitudes and gave rise to a whole generation of guitarists and white blues singers in both Europe and America and changed the popular music world. . . . Chuck Berry and Bo Diddley attuned them to a new music and the Tamla-Motown

111

sound, in particular the singing of Mary Wells, gave impetus to the
Beatles; others, like the Rolling Stones and the Animals, were impressed
by the records of Lightnin' Slim and Slim Harpo when their names were
unknown in the newspapers of Baton Rouge.

— Paul Oliver[4]


Cover recordings and song revivals in the popular music field offer new
and exciting resources for history instruction. Complex elements related to the issues of racial integration, social change, and political
protest are amply illustrated in the evolutionary popularity of particular songs. For example, the 1963 revival by Peter, Paul, and Mary of
Bob Dylan's folk protest tune "Blowin' in the Wind" not only height-
ened public interest in Dylan but also helped to launch a decade of
lyrical criticism about political hypocrisy and governmental ineptitude.
Similarly, strong and often conflicting commentaries about topics including the war in Southeast Asia, sex roles, educational practices, and
ecological activities have dominated the lyrics of popular songs over the
past fifteen years. Literary historian Russel B. Nye and other scholars
have argued convincingly that the popular arts in general and popular
music in particular offers students and teachers vital, legitimate evidence for modern man's search for meaning.[5] High school and college
history students can benefit by joining popular culture analysts in
pursuing answers to one seemingly simple question: Why have white
performers so frequently chosen to revive songs that have been previously released by black recording artists? The search for potential
answers to this query can provide novel and stimulating classroom
exercise. The responses outlined below only begin to suggest the variety of social change indicators that a history teacher can explore with a
group of highly stimulated young record researchers.


### FINANCIAL EXPLOITATION

The path to popular music success was extremely difficult for black
performers in the early 1950s. Unless they were willing to adopt a
white-oriented singing style such as that of Nat "King" Cole, black
musicians invariably found themselves isolated from the dominant
recording companies — Decca, Columbia, RCA Victor, and Capitol —

and thus separated from the majority of the record-buying public. Worse yet, when a black artist developed an original, potentially successful tune through a small, independent recording outfit—Savoy, King, Specialty, or Peacock—white artists, including Pat Boone, Gale Storm, and the Fontane Sisters, hurriedly supplied the record purchasing audience with an acceptable "cover" version of the same tune. Yet, as several scholars have noted, not *all* black artists were co-opted.[6] This cover phenomenon, however, occurred frequently enough to confirm the suspicions that prejudice, plagiarism, and financial exploitation were central factors in American recording industry practices between 1953 and 1956.[7]

Below are some examples of cover songs:

| | |
|---|---|
| "I'm in Love Again" | Fats Domino (Imperial Records—4/8/1956); cover song by Fontane Sisters (Dot Records—5/16/1956) |
| "(My Heart Goes) Ka-Ding-Dong" | G-Clefs (Pilgrim Records—7/8/1956); cover song by Diamonds (Mercury Records—8/9/1956) |
| "Long Tall Sally" | Little Richard (Specialty Records—3/28/1956); cover song by Pat Boone (Dot Records—4/4/1956) |
| "Rip It Up" | Little Richard (Specialty Records—6/27/1956); cover song by Bill Haley and the Comets (Decca Records—8/1/1956) |
| "See Saw" | Moonglows (Chess Records—8/22/1956); cover song by Don Cornell (Coral Records—10/31/1956) |
| "Silhouettes" | Rays (Cameo Records—10/5/1957); cover song by Diamonds (Mercury Records—11/2/1957) |
| "Why Do Fools Fall in Love" | Frankie Lymon and the Teenagers (Gee Records—2/1/1956); cover song by Gale Storm (Dot Records—2/22/1956) |

But the bulk of cover recordings and revivals of black songs by white artists were not intended to inflict terminal financial hardship on Afro-American artists. Rather, they served as indirect acknowledgments of musical quality and sales attractiveness of original black material by white artists who were supported by more sophisticated marketing approaches and public distribution resources. Several major white recording artists, including Gale Storm, Elvis Presley, Pat Boone, the Crew Cuts, and the Chordettes profited directly and often by producing songs originally released by blacks. For example, the Drifters' "Money Honey," Wynonie Harris' "Good Rockin' Tonight," Junior Parker's "Mystery Train," and Willie Mae Thornton's "Hound Dog" were easily adapted to the Presley repertoire. But beyond the Presley revival recordings are two points of greater significance. First, black music—although slightly altered rhythmically and occasionally lyrically castrated—began to reach beyond the segregated "rhythm and blues" charts into *Billboard*'s "Top 100" lists during the 1955–59 period. Second, more and more white performers in the 1960s began to revive classic r & b tunes. In fact, the singing careers of white performers such as Dion DiMucci and Johnny Rivers have been shaped significantly by their ability to adapt black material for contemporary audiences. During the early 1960s Dion recorded the Drifters' "Ruby Baby" (1956), Chuck Berry's "Johnny B. Goode" (1958), and Muddy Waters' blues classic "Hoochie Coochie Man" (1954); meanwhile, Rivers revived several Chuck Berry hits, including "Brown-Eyed Handsome Man" (1956) and "Memphis, Tennessee" (1959), along with Chris Kenner's "Land of a Thousand Dances" (1963), Ray Charles' "I Got a Woman" (1955) and Lloyd Price's "Stagger Lee" (1958). Songs that had initially attracted positive attention from a limited audience—such as records played exclusively on black-oriented radio stations—were transformed into nationwide hits. The following list of white remakes of records originated by black artists during the 1953–1956 period further demonstrates this point.

"At My Front Door"          El Dorados (Vee Jay Records – 1955);
                             cover song by Pat Boone (Dot
                             Records – 1955)

| | |
|---|---|
| "Crying in the Chapel" | Orioles (Jubilee Records – 1953); cover songs by June Valli (RCA Victor Records – 1953) and Rex Allen (Decca Records – 1953) |
| "Earth Angel" | Penguins (Dootone Records – 1954); cover song by Crew Cuts (Mercury Records – 1954) |
| "Goodnight Sweetheart, Goodnight" | Spaniels (Vee Jay Records – 1954); cover song by McGuire Sisters (Coral Records – 1954) |
| "I'll Be Home" | Flamingos (Checker Records – 1956); cover song by Pat Boone (Dot Records – 1956) |
| "Sh-Boom" | Chords (Cat Records – 1954); cover song by Crew Cuts (Mercury Records – 1954) |

## SOCIAL COMMENTARY

Although the most blatant examples of white-over-black cover re-cording activities ended after 1956, the practice of reviving or altering the lyrics of black songs in the hope of satisfying white audiences continued for several years. Historically, this lyric alteration approach reached its peak during the Eisenhower years. One reason why most radio stations refused to play (and hence the white listening public failed to purchase) some black songs released in the mid-1950s was that the lyrics frequently contained earthy, off-color comments and explicit sexual references.

In 1954 Hank Ballard and the Midnighters recorded on the Federal label several suggestive songs—including "Work with Me Annie" and "Annie Had a Baby"—about the exploits of a notorious and promiscuous young lady. The explicit nature of her relationships with male courtiers was too vivid for the public airwaves. However, the catchy rhythm of Ballard's "Annie" songs prompted a black female artist to produce a slightly altered song for Modern Records entitled, "The

Wallflower." This new version eliminated much of the direct sexual commentary in the "Annie" numbers, while also serving as a female answer to Ballard's male-oriented original number. The sales success of Etta James' "Wallflower" then encouraged Mercury Recording Company staff writers to edit out all of the song's remaining suggestive lyrics in order to produce a bouncy, wholesome song entitled, "Dance with Me, Henry." Thus white pop singer Georgia Gibbs produced a king-sized pop hit in 1955, while Hank Ballard's tunes and Etta James' song continued to appeal only to a relatively small "race record" audience.

Another illustration of lyric alteration occurred in the case of one of the most famous early rock and roll hits, "Shake, Rattle, and Roll." This song, as first performed by Joe Turner for Atlantic Records in 1954, describes in detail the sheerness of a woman's nightgown (". . . the sun comes shinin' through") and her enticing physical endowments (". . . I can't believe that whole mess is you") in the bedroom. With slight line changes, which included shifting the domestic setting of the singer's commentary into the kitchen, Bill Haley and the Comets succeeded in transforming Turner's moderately successful Atlantic recording into a smash hit for Decca.

Other kinds of lyric alterations have been utilized to call attention to historic and present-day social injustices. In 1972, for instance, Roberta Flack interrupted her bluesy version of "Somewhere" with the startling cry – "This ain't no *West Side Story!*" – to emphasize the reality of racial inequality in New York City. Curtis Mayfield, in his 1972 "live" performance album, added several lines of rambling social commentary about the alleged disc jockey and radio station management censorship that was exercised against the Impressions' hit song "We're A Winner." And Solomon Burke cleverly converted Creedence Clearwater Revival's tale of youthful travel aboard the Mississippi sternwheeler "Proud Mary" into an attack against slavery and the post–Civil War caste system of black servitude.

## Musical Creativity and Artistic Tribute

Another interesting trend in the record revival syndrome has been the practice of black performers to return to their musical roots by successfully reproducing hit tunes originally performed by other Afro-American artists. This stylistic vitality has produced some of the most significant popular music of the past decade. Aretha Franklin's 1967 success with the tune "Respect," originally authored by the talented but ill-fated soul singer Otis Redding, is typical of the black-over-black revival practice. The peculiar genius of "Lady Soul" also led her to revive at least two other previously released black hits—Don Covay's "See Saw" and Dionne Warwick's "I Say a Little Prayer." Before his death in 1967, Otis Redding also offered new renditions of hits originally released by other noted black artists, including James Brown's "Papa's Got a Brand New Bag" and Sam Cooke's "Shake," which he dynamically performed at the Monterey Pop Festival. The following list of recordings provides ample evidence of the internal vitality of the black music community.

The following is a list of original black tunes which were reintroduced by other black artists, who brought to them innovative rhythm patterns or new vocal styling:

| | |
|---|---|
| "C. C. Rider" | Chuck Willis (Atlantic Records—1957); LaVern Baker (Atlantic Records—1962) |
| "Everybody Needs Somebody to Love" | Solomon Burke (Atlantic Records—1964); Wilson Pickett (Atlantic Records—1967) |
| "For Your Precious Love" | Jerry Butler (Falcon Records—1958); Garnett Mimms and the Enchanters (United Artists Records—1963) |
| "How Sweet It Is (To Be Loved by You)" | Marvin Gaye (Tamla Records—1964); Junior Walker and the All-Stars (Soul Records—1966) |
| "I Got a Woman" | Ray Charles (Atlantic Records—1955); Jimmy McGriff (Sue Records—1963) |
| "I Heard It through the Grapevine" | Gladys Knight and the Pips (Soul Records—1967); Marvin Gaye (Tamla Records—1968) |
| "Never Can Say Goodbye" | Isaac Hayes (Enterprise Records—1971); Jackson Five (Motown Records—1971); Gloria Gaynor (MGM Records—1974) |

| | |
|---|---|
| "Stagger Lee" | Lloyd Price (ABC Records – 1958); Wilson Pickett (Atlantic Records – 1967) |
| "Tracks of My Tears" | Smokey Robinson and the Miracles (Tamla Records – 1967); Aretha Franklin (Atlantic Records – 1969) |

An even more interesting question to investigate concerning the relationship of black music to record revivals is: How have black recording artists responded to the "new music" from Great Britain and elsewhere since 1964? The answer is obvious. When most white journalists sang the praises of the Beatles, the Rolling Stones, and other groups from the far side of the Atlantic, black artists recognized them as kindred musical spirits who shared respect for songs of the rhythm and blues tradition.[8] While the Beatles sang the hits of Chuck Berry ("Roll Over Beethoven") and Larry Williams ("Slow Down") and the Stones lauded Slim Harpo ("I'm a King Bee") and Marvin Gaye ("Hitch Hike"), American blacks commenced their own restyling of a variety of British song hits. The Beatles provided ample material for Wilson Pickett ("Hey Jude") and Ike and Tina Turner ("Let It Be" and "Get Back"). The Rolling Stones' lyrics proved appropriate for Muddy Waters ("Let's Spend the Night Together") and Otis Redding ("Satisfaction").

The use of white material by black musicians was not limited to British songwriting talent, either. As the list below indicates, black performers successfully transformed the record revival practice from a tactic of racial parasitism into a strategy for professional harmony and mutual musical exchange.

Listed below are several titles of established white tunes reintroduced with innovative rhythm patterns or new vocal styling by black artists:

| | |
|---|---|
| "Abraham, Martin and John" | Dion (Laurie Records – 1968); Moms Mabley (Mercury Records – 1969) and Smokey Robinson and the Miracles (Tamla Records – 1969) |

| "Bridge Over Troubled Water" | Simon and Garfunkel (Columbia Records – 1970); Aretha Franklin (Atlantic Records – 1971) |
| --- | --- |
| "Eleanor Rigby" | Beatles (Capitol Records – 1966); Ray Charles (ABC Records – 1968) and Aretha Franklin (Atlantic Records – 1969) |
| "Hey Jude" | Beatles (Apple Records – 1968); Wilson Pickett (Atlantic Records – 1968) |
| "Love the One You're With" | Stephen Stills (Atlantic Records – 1970); Isley Brothers (T-Neck Records – 1971) |
| "Proud Mary" | Creedence Clearwater Revival (Fantasy Records – 1969); Ike and Tina Turner (Liberty Records – 1971) |
| "(I Can't Get No) Satisfaction" | Rolling Stones (London Records – 1965); Otis Redding (Volt Records – 1966) |
| "We Can Work It Out" | Beatles (Apple Records – 1966); Stevie Wonder (Tamla Records – 1971) |
| "Yesterday" | Beatles (Capitol Records – 1967); Ray Charles (ABC Records – 1967) |

## CONCLUSION

The use of cover recordings and revivals of previously successful songs has undeniably broadened the base of the rock revolution in the United States. Black artists, at first victimized, have now joined their fellow white performers in prosperity through the revival system. The emergence of the black rock and rollers of the mid-1950s—Little-Richard, Fats Domino, Chuck Berry, Larry Williams, and Bo Diddley—provided the prophetic basis for what was to come in the mid-1960s—from Britain, Detroit, Memphis, New York City, and Chicago. The homogenization of rock, made possible through covers and revivals, was accomplished to a great extent during the decade before the Beatles. And just as the Supreme Court struck down the "separate, but equal" theory of education, so too the American buying public cracked the old race record barrier in popular music after 1954.

Several prominent American historians, including Richard Resh, Thomas R. Frazier, Roderick Nash, Leonard Dinnerstein, and Kenneth T. Jackson have included popular culture essays in their history survey course anthologies.[9] Obviously, these historians feel it is mandatory to have students examine scholarly interpretations about the relationship between modern music and social movements. But it is still the responsibility of the individual classroom teachers to translate the written messages of these essays into instructional materials. By combining the ideas suggested above with the audio resources provided below, a history instructor can generate student involvement in the investigation of contemporary social and political issues through the use of popular music.

## SELECTED DISCOGRAPHY

No single record album or preconstructed audio teaching aid currently on the market provides the song-by-song comparisons listed above. The albums listed in this discography should be considered as primary source material for initiating a revival-based instructional approach.

### Individual Soloists and Groups

Berry, Chuck. *Chuck Berry's Golden Decade* (CH 1514). New York: Chess/ Janus Records, 1972.

Blackwell, Otis. *These Are My Songs!* (IC 1032). New York: Inner City Records, 1977.

Charles, Ray. *A 25th Anniversary in Show Business Salute to Ray Charles: His All-Time Great Performances* (ABCH 731). New York: ABC Records, 1971.

Cooke, Sam. *The Best of Sam Cooke* (LSP 2625). New York: RCA Records, 1965.

Crudup, Arthur. *Arthur "Big Boy" Crudup – The Father of Rock and Roll* (LPV 573). New York: RCA Records, 1971.

Dixon, Willie. *I Am the Blues* (CS 9987). New York: Columbia Records/ CBS, n.d.

Domino, Fats. *Fats Domino – The Legendary Masters Series* (UAS 9958). Los Angeles: United Artists Records, 1971.

Dominoes. *The Dominoes* (KING 5005X). Nashville: Gusto (King/Federal) Records, 1977.

Drifters, *The Drifters' Golden Hits* (SD 8153). New York: Atlantic Recording Corporation, 1968.

Franklin, Aretha. *Aretha's Greatest Hits* (SD 8295). New York: Atlantic Recording Corporation, 1971.

Harris, Don "Sugarcane," and Dewey Terry. *Don and Dewey* (SPS 2131). Hollywood, Calif.: Specialty Records, 1970.

Howlin' Wolf. *Chester Burnett aka Howlin' Wolf* (2CH 60016). New York: Chess/Janus Records, 1972.

Little Richard. *Little Richard's Grooviest 17 Original Hits* (SPS 2113). Hollywood, Calif.: Specialty Records, Inc., n.d.

Pickett, Wilson. *Wilson Pickett's Greatest Hits* (SD 2-501). New York: Atlantic Recording Corporation, 1973.

Redding, Otis. *The Best of Otis Redding* (SD 2-801). New York: ATCO Records, 1972.

Taj Mahal, *The Natch'l Blues* (CS 9698). New York: Columbia Records, n.d.

Turner, Ike and Tina. *Workin' Together* (LST 7650). Los Angeles: Liberty/ United Artists, n.d.

Muddy Waters. *Folk Singer* (CHESS LP 1483). Chicago: Chess Recording Corporation, n.d.

Wilson, Jackie. *Jackie Wilson's Greatest Hits* (BL 754140). New York: Brunswick Record Corporation, 1968.

Stevie Wonder. *Looking Back* (M 804 LP 3). Hollywood, Calif.: Motown Record Corporation, 1977.

*Anthologies Featuring Various Artists*

*The Blues* – 5 vols. (LPS 4026/27/34/42/51). Chicago: Cadet (Chess) Records, n.d. Features Muddy Waters, Howlin' Wolf, John Lee Hooker, Willie Mabon, Lowell Fulson, Sonny Boy Williamson, Little Walter, Elmore James, Jimmy Witherspoon, and Willie Dixon.

*The Classic Blues* – 2 vols. (BLS 6061/62). New York: ABC Records, 1973. Features Ray Charles, T-Bone Walker, Jimmy Weatherspoon, John Lee Hooker, Jimmy Reed, and Otis Spann.

*Echoes of a Rock Era* – 3 vols. (RE 111/12/13). New York: Roulette Records, 1971. Features Sonny Til and the Orioles, the Penguins, Maurice Williams and the Zodiacs, the Moonglows, Mary Wells, and the Shirelles.

*14 Golden Recordings from the Historical Vaults of Vee Jay Records* (ABCX 785). Los Angeles: ABC Records, 1973. Features the Dells, Gene Chandler, Gladys Knight and the Pips, Jerry Butler, Dee Clark, Jimmy Reed, and John Lee Hooker.

*Alan Freed's Memory Lane* (R 42041). New York: Roulette Records, n.d. Features Jesse Belvin, the Moonglows, Jerry Butler, the Rays, and Little Anthony and the Imperials.

*From the Vaults of Duke/Peacock* (ABCX 789). Los Angeles: ABC Records, 1973. Features Bobby Bland, Johnny Ace, Junior Parker, Roy Head, Ernie K-Doe, and Willie Mae Thornton.

*Heavy Heads* (CHESS LPS 1522). Chicago: Chess Records, n.d. Features Bo Diddley, Little Milton, Howlin' Wolf, Muddy Waters, John Lee Hooker, and Sonny Boy Williamson.

*The History of Rhythm and Blues, 1947–1967* – 8 vols. (SD 8161/62/63/64/ 94 and 8208/09). New York: Atlantic Recording Corporation, 1968–69. Features the Ravens, the Cardinals, the Orioles, Joe Turner, the Chords, Ivory Joe Hunter, the Coasters, the Drifters, Clyde McPhatter, Ben E. King, Barbara Lewis, Wilson Pickett, Otis Redding, and Aretha Franklin.

*Motown's Preferred Stock* – 3 vols. (M 6-881/82/83 S1). Hollywood, Calif.: Motown Record Corporation, 1977. Features Gladys Knight and the Pips, the Spinners, Marvin Gaye and Tammi Terrell, the Marvelettes, the Four Tops, Mary Wells, Michael Jackson, Martha Reeves and the Vandellas, the Temptations, Smokey Robinson and the Miracles, Jr. Walker and the All Stars, and Edwin Starr.

*Rock 'N' Soul: The History of Rock in the Pre-Beatle Decade of Rock* – 9 vols. (ABCX 1955/56/57/58/59/60/61/62/63. Los Angeles: ABC Records, 1973. Features Willie Mae Thornton, the Cadillacs, Frankie Lymon and the Teenagers, Shirley and Lee, the Dells, Lloyd Price, the Olympics, Little Caesar and the Romans, Gene Chandler, and the Impressions.

*The Roots of Rock 'n Roll* (SJL 2221). New York: Arista Records, 1977. Features Wild Bill Moore, Johnny Otis, Nappy Brown, Big Maybelle, the Ravens, and Clarence Palmer and the Jive Bombers.

*This Is How It All Began: The Roots Of Rock 'N' Roll as Recorded from 1945 to 1955 on Specialty Records* – 2 vols. (SPS 2117/18). Hollywood, Calif.: Specialty Records, 1969–70. Features Roy Milton, Don and Dewey, Lloyd Price, Larry Williams, Sam Cooke, and Little Richard.

*The Very Best of the Oldies* — 2 vols. (UA – LA 335/84 E). Los Angeles: United Artists Music and Record Group, 1975. Features the Clovers, Jesse Hill, Garnet Mimms and the Enchanters, Thurston Harris, the Showmen, Benny Spellman, the Rivingtons, and Marv Johnson.

*You Must Remember These* — 2 vols. (BELL 6078/79). New York: Bell Records, 1972. Features the Mello Kings, the Nutmegs, the Turbans, the Silhouettes, the Delfonics, Lee Dorsey, and James and Bobby Purify.

PART THREE

# Popular Music
# and the Librarian

TEN

# An Interview with
# Audio Center Director
# William L. Schurk

(After reading several fascinating newspaper reports about the record and tape collections housed in the Bowling Green State University Library,[1] I finally had the good fortune of meeting William L. Schurk—Bowling Green's colorful, hyperactive Audio Center director—on October 28, 1977, during a "Popular Culture and the Library" symposium conducted at the University of Kentucky.[2] This encounter prompted me to tape a series of interviews with him. Spending several days with an unconventional, creative, encyclopedic library administrator helps one to understand the kind of enthusiasm that sparked the building of the nation's largest popular music collection. The following interview is the result of six hours of discussion with Mr. Schurk concerning the operation of Bowling Green's Audio Center.)

COOPER: I'm gratified that you've agreed to share some of your experiences at the Audio Center with me. Can you begin by outlining the history of the Center's creation?

SCHURK: I'll be happy to share my perspectives on the Audio Center's growth. In July 1967 I joined the university's library staff. After devoting a year to assembling a collection of recording industry trade journals (*Billboard*, *Record World*, and *Cash Box*) and discographic tools (*Gramophone*, the *Schwann Long*

*Playing Record Guide, American Record Guide,* and *Audio Cardolog*) as record selection guides; to developing student service procedures and staffing assignments; and to meeting with on-campus academic department heads, directors of traditional audiovisual library programs from several states, and a variety of folklorists, newsmen, and radio broadcasters, the Audio Center finally opened in 1968.[3] As you probably know, the center controls all record resources on the Bowling Green campus except for those classical recordings housed in the College of Musical Arts and the language tapes being utilized in University Hall listening labs by the foreign language department. Among the materials included in our collection are blues, folk, swing, rock, bluegrass, gospel, jazz, and country recordings; television and motion picture soundtrack music; prose, poetry, and dramatic readings; selected kiddie records; plus tapes of early radio shows and interviews with celebrities. These items of audio information are available on either LP albums, 45 r.p.m., and 78 r.p.m. records; cylinder recordings; or reel-to-reel and cassette tapes. During the past ten years the university's audio holdings have grown in market value by nearly $500,000. During the same period our service statistics have skyrocketed from only occasional use of an album or two to 7,765 record and tape users during the 1976–77 academic year.[4]

COOPER: In my efforts to locate written descriptions about the functions of Bowling Green's Audio Center, I was surprised to find only one published report by you—and that was a transcription of the 1977 speech which you delivered at the University of Kentucky.[5] Why haven't you made greater efforts to issue reports about the Audio Center's unique activities through professional library journals?

SCHURK: Honestly, the day-to-day responsibilities of managing Audio Center Operations, of searching for new sources to obtain recorded materials, of cataloging recordings, and of attempting to coordinate interlibrary loans and audio resource exchanges leave me very little time for personal publication activities. Nevertheless, I have given a number of oral presentations similar to the one which you heard me deliver in Lexington last October. In July of 1974, for instance, I addressed the Music Library Association at their annual meeting in New York City. I represented the field of popular music on a panel which included scholars and bookmen from several specialized record libraries. Although no transcript of my talk was printed, a bibliography of popular music books and magazines which I had compiled for the presentation was published by the Country Music Foundation (C.M.F.) as part of the small booklet. Bill Ivey, executive director of C.M.F., who was also on the panel representing the country music record collecting field, edited this pamphlet.[6] I gave a similar talk in Columbus, Ohio, in 1971 during the midwest regional meeting of the Music Library Association. It was very well received.

A few years ago Dr. Ray Browne, director of the Center for the Study of Popular Culture, and I published a pamphlet describing the collecting activities of both the Popular Culture Library and the Audio Center.[7] That same pamphlet, unbeknownst to either of us, was later published as an article in an anthology dealing with special library collections.[8] It was printed verbatim—the entire pamphlet—without my knowledge or permission.

I have planned to write an Audio Center essay for some time now, but I just haven't gotten around to it. The Association for Recorded Sound Collections publishes a journal which would certainly be an appropriate forum for me to describe our center. I'd also like to write articles about the center's activities for the *Wilson Library Bulletin* and *Library Journal.* Of course, I intend to continue to encourage other writers to investigate, analyze, and acquaint scholars and the general public with our audio resources.

COOPER: Are there other academic libraries which have attempted to preserve, catalog, and circulate recorded music resources?

SCHURK: There are several record collections which are extremely significant in specialized musical fields. Three of the most famous academic library illustrations are the Rutgers University Institute for Jazz Studies, Tulane's New Orleans jazz collection, and UCLA's John Edwards Memorial Foundation collection of traditional American blues and folk music. Some nonacademic libraries also assemble large ranges of recorded material. The Rogers and Hammerstein Archives of the New York Public Library System might be an example of this type of collection. Of course, the Library of Congress also maintains a music library.[9] On the other hand, the Country Music Foundation's collection is strictly a privately funded endeavor. There are quite a few other specialized collections, but they're too numerous to mention. Bowling Green has one of the largest audio collections retained by an academic institution primarily because it covers such a wide spectrum of recorded materials.

COOPER: In several newspaper and magazine reports that I've read about your collection-building techniques, you are quoted as saying that you take *everything*. One article printed in the *Nation* stated that among your "hundreds of special wants" were an album by a rock-and-roll Madrigal-styled group called the Jamies; a copy of "It's Love, Love, Love" by Guy Lombardo; any recordings on Sun, Chess, or Vee-Jay labels; a Frank Crumit and Julia Sanderson 78 r.p.m. album set; and any 78 r.p.m. records featuring Ku Klux Klan songs.[10] I realize that you can trade or sell duplicate records, so I can understand some aspects of your eclecticism. But exactly how have you formally defined the acquisition policy for the Audio Center?

SCHURK: As I stated before, we do not collect either classical records or foreign language tapes—so the "We'll take everything!" position is obviously an overstatement. Nevertheless, our acquisition policy (see figure 10.1) is broad enough to encompass the goals of an audio research resource department. The word *everything* really means that I do not qualitatively define recordings as "good" or "bad" according to some musical or library acquisition standard. I would rather not put myself into the judgmental position of rejecting a piece of audio material solely on the grounds that it was of inferior quality musically, either technically or artistically, only to later discover that it was indeed a key part of the American recording history. Because of limited funds, however, I am extremely selective about the individual records I *buy*. I try to gear my purchases to the stated classroom or research projects needs of those faculty members and students who request particular items. Also, when I discover reissue packages, which are usually limited pressings, I will attempt to purchase these immediately because they tend to have a very short market life span. In selecting the materials for the Audio Center, I always try to anticipate the needs of our patrons.

FIGURE 10.1

AUDIO CENTER MATERIALS SELECTION POLICY, JUNE 28, 1977

The Audio Center is an archival and research center and service unit to the University, the surrounding community, and serious scholars throughout the nation and world. The areas of concern in the Center include all fields of endeavor surrounding the Audio recording medium and the material contained within.

Materials included in the collection are of both a primary and secondary source nature. They are intended for studies up to and including those for doctoral research.

Types of material included in the Audio Center are as follows:

A. Audio recordings
   1. Phonograph records (all sizes, speeds, and groove cuts, and of all ages, from their inception up to the present; both disc and cylinder)
   2. Tape recordings (open reels concurrent with the speed capabilities of the Center's playback equipment, and cassettes)
   3. Piano rolls (Center retains a large collection, but does not have a player piano in its collection as of yet)

4. Wire recordings (None are presently in the collection, however, this does not preclude the possibility of the Center acquiring a machine and wire in the future)

B. Audio recording and playback equipment
   1. The console includes a complement of equipment to handle most of the tape and record configurations used on a daily basis
   2. A secondary collection of working historical machines for record playback are included both for historical study and for reproducing nonstandard record configurations (i.e., cylinders and "hill and dale" discs manufactured by Edison and also Pathé Bros.)

C. Printed support materials
   1. Reference books (i.e., discographies, bibliographies, biographical directories, heavily illustrated monographs, books issued with accompanying recordings, and historical studies of recordings and related subjects
   2. Periodicals (i.e., trade, critical, and scholarly journals, newsstand magazines, fanzines, and collector-oriented publications)
   3. Sheet music and song folios
   4. Dealer, manufacturer, and auction catalogs
   5. Record promotional material (i.e., posters, flyers, handbills, and retail establishment paraphernalia)
   6. Biographical and record promotional materials issued for media publication
   7. Record company release notices

Subjects included on the recordings and in the printed materials are as follows:

A. Popular music (personality, country, rhythm & blues and soul, rock and roll, reggae, etc.)
B. Jazz, big band, and the blues
C. Folk music and folklore
D. Musical revues and motion-picture music
E. Gospel and sacred
F. Comedy, and humorous songs
G. Poetry, prose, drama, and related readings
H. Documentary and histories
I. Old-time radio programs and television music
J. Conferences, seminars, presentations, panel discussions, etc., relating to all academic areas
K. Classical (an archive is being maintained through gifts and inexpensive purchases. A working collection for current music students can be found in the College of Musical Arts Audio Lab.)

L. Juvenile stories and music
M. International music
N. Miscellaneous
The Audio Center does not maintain a collection of language instruction recordings.

> Let me elaborate on the Audio Center's service function for a moment. When the center was first being organized during 1967, I spoke personally with faculty representatives from various academic departments and described the types of services which we planned to offer; I also urged them to assist me in selecting recorded materials for inclusion in the Audio Center's collection. I'm not saying they weren't receptive—but most faculty members are still very much bound by the "book" tradition which libraries and graduate schools fostered over many years. Most instructors were initially unwilling to accept nonprint resources from other media to supplement their educational endeavors. Since 1970, of course, the doors have opened wider and I have found that more and more people, *especially* Bowling Green's faculty members, are extremely receptive to the idea that recordings can be valuable teaching tools as well as significant primary source materials for research into political and social themes.

COOPER: I have heard that once a popular recording drops from the Top 40 charts, it is very difficult to acquire. How are you able to secure single records and albums which were popular several years, or even several decades ago?

SCHURK: I shop—or more accurately "scavenge"—anywhere that I can to secure recordings for the Audio Center. Frankly, Top 40, Top 50, and Top 100 records are the easiest ones to get— even *after* they have gone off the chart. My main sources for records have been garage sales, Salvation Army and Goodwill stores, Volunteers of America shops, flea markets, antique stores, and junk shops. These unorthodox outlets are the best sources for either the purchase of single discs at a very special price or of an album at a reduced rate.

In terms of acquisitions, the Audio Center has also been the recipient of a number of large gifts from both private record collectors and other individuals who have accumulated recordings. One of the largest single donations was made by Bill Randle, a former disc jockey from Cleveland. We got thousands of records from him — 33s, 45s, 78s — containing valuable early jazz and rhythm-and-blues performances. Another radio personality, who was known to his younger listeners from the early fifties as "Kousin Kay," also made a large donation to the center. Walter Kay had been featured on a children's radio show that programmed songs and moralistic "kiddies' stories" based on the exploits of commercial figures such as Hopalong Cassidy, Roy Rogers, and Bugs Bunny. He had kept copies of these broadcast recordings in his own home in Brecksville, Ohio. While debating what to do with this collection, he had contacted a number of other libraries, but the directors had responded that they could envision no use for them. Of course, when they were offered to us, I gladly accepted his entire collection. One of my student assistants and I rode with my father in his station wagon to Brecksville and picked up nearly five thousand juvenile recordings, mostly 78s — a lot of them very rare items. It's much easier when a significant gift collection is brought to the campus, though. Mr. Alfred K. Pearson of Gardner, Massachusetts, recently donated his entire jazz record collection to us — a thousand discs. Most of these recordings have been cataloged in the center's collection. In fact, almost every record we got from Mr. Pearson was a rare 78 dating between 1925 and 1945.

Another significant gift was acquired through an arrangement which I made with Dr. David Stupple of the sociology department at Eastern Michigan University in Ypsilanti. I met him at the Second Annual Popular Culture Association Meeting held in Toledo in 1971. He remarked to me that he'd heard several fine comments about the center's collection of recordings. Then he asked if we would be interested in acquiring his rhythm-and-blues record collection. I said "yes" without any hesitation, and he invited me to his home in Ypsilanti. I carefully went through all of his records, listening to ten hours of music in the process. We finally called it a night at 1:00 A.M., packed up all his records, and brought them back to Bowling Green to become part of our collection. They included nearly one thousand 45s dating from around 1954 to 1959 and including many very rare, very important recordings on such labels as Chess, Checker, Vee Jay, Atlantic — the key recording companies for rhythm and blues since the early fifties. I think that Dr. Stupple had been president of the Bill Haley Fan Club at one time, so his collection also yielded all of Bill Haley's early 45s. All of the records included in the Stupple Collection were in "mint" condition.[11]

In addition to donated collections and the junk shop/flea market buying, I also engage in the purchase of recordings from mail order auction lists. These forms are circulated by various types of people, some honest and some not so honest. They may be issued as single sheets or booklets from individual dealers, or they may come as an adjunct unit of a collector's trade magazine such as *Record Exchanger*.

For example, I recently subscribed to a magazine called *Goldmine*, which was originally published in Detroit, Michigan. It's a newspaper that just lists dealers and private individuals who are interested in selling or auctioning off records — single 45s, some 78s, and a number of LPs. The problem with this approach is that the prices are *very high* — at least they tend to be much higher than junk shop charges of twenty-five, fifty, or even seventy-five cents for an album. Through auction lists you may wind up paying five, ten, or even fifteen dollars for the same seventy-five-cent second-hand store album. The advantage of auctions is that they tend to sell records which are in better condition than the normal junk store variety. Many times I have gone into a junk shop and found a disc in one place and its LP cover in another. Some fool has separated the two items and thereby ruined the record.

It's also very touchy when you deal with people by mail. You must hope that they are honest and will honor your bid (if you *are* the highest bidder) and not simply elect to deal with friends who may be aware of the level of each bid which comes in. One must also be wary of the manner in which auction records are graded—as "new," "mint," or "very good."[12] Some people don't even want to consider an album unless it's in pristine condition; that is, the cover can't be split, it must be in its original sleeve, and it should be sealed. Recently, a friend of mine bought a sealed record, brought it to the Audio Center to tempt me, and opened it only to discover that the *wrong* record was inside. A number of unscrupulous dealers have gained access to cellophane wrap machines which can seal a record as cleanly as a record dealer, and no one is the wiser until the cover is exposed. Many times a buyer is miles away from where he purchased the album before he discovers the switch. Most times one is left with no recourse.

COOPER: Do you ever attempt to secure unauthorized or "bootleg" recordings for your collection?[13]

SCHURK: Remember that the term *bootleg* covers a variety of audio sins. These items are not simply taped copies of regularly released recordings. Mostly they are illegally released duplications of previously unreleased material, some made during concert performances and others stolen directly from recording company vaults. One general definition of a "bootleg" might be a record which is manufactured without the artist's knowledge or permission. Over the past decade we have acquired a number of bootleg recordings for the Audio Center.

Of course, the bootleg gambit is nearly as old as the recording business itself. Live opera performances of the early 1900s were recorded behind the scenes on cylinder recorders. There also were the six-inch Little Wonder records. We have quite a large collection of these. The most famous one I know of is a 1914 recording entitled "Back to the

Carolina You Love," by Al Jolson (Little Wonder #20), worth somewhere between twenty to twenty-six dollars, depending on the condition. When the *Great White Wonder* album, featuring out-takes from Bob Dylan's recording sessions, hit the market in the early 1970s, it became the hallmark of modern-day rock and roll bootlegging. Of course, being the social historian that I am, I thought that this important item should be added to our audio collection. Not that I ever intend to "rip off" anyone, certainly not Bob Dylan or Columbia Records, but I felt that the album was the prime example of what was being done in respect to illegal record marketing. After that first two-record bootleg set proved to be a financial success, hundreds of illegal recordings were released.

The quality of most concert-recorded bootleg discs is poor. Obviously, the need for taping secrecy, the type of low-visibility equipment employed (usually small, hand-held recorders), and the amateur skills of the operator contribute to this low-grade production. In addition, when the bootleg disc is printed, the vinyl quality is sometimes so poor that after a few plays the grooves fail to track smoothly. Finally, the bootleg packaging process is often strictly hit-or-miss with jumbled listings of songs and artists — and no information about the date or the location of the recorded event. There are occasional instances, however, when a bootleg disc — particularly one containing songs that have been lifted directly from unreleased studio-recorded master discs — is of the highest technical quality. I have even heard a few concert-recorded bootlegs that sounded clearer than the original record company studio-produced releases.

COOPER: How does the Audio Center staff catalog a record album once it arrives at the library?

SCHURK: Our records are shelved according to company label and number. This kind of information permits us to locate recordings easily. We have a number of student assistants who help us in shelving both cataloged and uncataloged recordings. We have manufacturers catalogs and other tools of the record trade including the *Record World, Cash Box, Billboard* and various collectors journals which feature special discographies, biographical notations, and reference sources which enable us to place recordings in a chronological sequence. The Record Research books published by Joel Whitburn list all Top 100 songs from the *Billboard* charts since 1940. Songs are listed alphabetically and by recording artists in Whitburn's books, along with the date the record first appeared on the *Billboard* chart, how many weeks it remained on the chart, the highest chart position reached, and also the record company name and number.[14]

COOPER: Bowling Green State University has become a national focal point for popular-culture study, research, and publication. In at least two instances I would suspect that you have designated assignments in regard to university-produced scholarly publications. In specific terms, what is your relationship with Dr. Ray B. Browne, director of the Center for the Study of Popular Culture at Bowling Green, and editor of the *Journal of Popular Culture*?

SCHURK: Dr. Browne is in charge of the Popular Culture Department and oversees all publishing ventures of the Bowling Green Popular Press. He's a fascinating man. He earned his Ph.D. at UCLA in American folklore. His dissertation research was conducted on foot in his native Alabama where he carried a tape recorder through the back hills gathering the state's oral history in folk songs and tales. Since I am employed by the university library, I do not report to Dr. Browne. We are close friends and colleagues, though, and I serve voluntarily as an advisory editor for the *Journal of Popular Culture* (JPC). In terms of publication activities, I have written numerous record reviews for the *JPC*.

Dr. R. Serge Denisoff is a professor of sociology at Bowling Green who is an expert on protest music of the mid-twentieth century. In 1971 he launched a journal entitled *Popular Music and Society* (PMS) as an offshoot of *JPC,* which specializes in the scholarly analysis of contemporary music. On request I contribute record reviews to this fine journal, too.

COOPER: There must be a great diversity in the levels of audio research which you are called upon to assist. I would suspect that the resource requests of undergraduate students are much easier to meet than those of Bowling Green professors and scholars from universities. Is that true?

SCHURK: Frankly, there is no correlation between the academic standing of the person requesting Audio Center assistance and the complexity of his or her record request. The reasons for this are numerous. Experienced researchers tend to initiate tightly structured, logically ordered audio resource requests which can easily be located in our stacks or through standard record references. Conversely, a freshman student may make requests that are so vague that an audio librarian becomes frustrated while attempting to provide specific answers to questions which defy resolution. "Do you have any songs about war?" is one of the most dreaded overkill questions at the center. Perhaps the most difficult requests I've encountered in the past ten years have come from nonacademic Audio Center patrons—a person seeking a recording of the Turkish National Anthem, a woman trying to create an audio background for her daughter's tap-dance routine, and an elderly couple looking for a tune they danced to when they were young (even though they can only remember one word—"Dream"—from the title).

Within the past two years, I can recall filling several unique requests for Bowling Green instructors and their students: (a) a program of ice skating music for a physical education teacher, (b) a variety of album covers from the 1950–75 period for an art professor who wanted his students to review the techniques of commercial album art, (c) soundtracks from selected radio and television news programs and documentaries for two history instructors, (d) a series of children's records for four elementary education student teachers, and (e) a taped recording of "Sparky's Magic Piano"—which was originally performed on a Sonovox, an electronic music device—for a music major.

COOPER: Do you permit Bowling Green students and other researchers to borrow albums or tapes from the Audio Center for designated periods of time?

SCHURK: Nothing circulates from our collection—but this is not unusual in research libraries which assemble original resource materials. We gladly tape specifically requested items which are to be used for either scholarly purposes or in classroom presentations. The new copyright laws have given us not only the right but also the responsibility to ask patrons to be concise in their duplication requests. Without this element of selectivity, our academic credibility would dissolve and we might become a subsidiary bootleg outlet.

COOPER: I have read several reports which estimate the value of the Audio Center's collection of recordings at between $250,000 and $500,000. Yet I note that your annual budget allocations to purchase new materials have never exceeded $4,000 during any one of the past ten years.[15] How have you been able to enrich your holdings so dramatically on such a meagre annual allowance?

SCHURK: As I mentioned earlier, I purchase most recordings for the Audio Center from sources which tend to sell singles and albums at very low prices. At the rate records are going today, a twelve-inch LP which sold for $3.98 ten years ago would now cost $7.98. From this perspective you can see why our collection is worth so much money. Just try to buy 65,000 LPs at an average list price of $6 each. You have $400,000 right there. And that's *just* list price. Considering the fact that at least half of our 65,000 albums are worth much more, that brings the value of the Audio Center collection close to a million dollars. And I haven't even included the 65,000 45 r.p.m. records, 30,000 78 r.p.m. discs, or the 700 cylinder recordings in that estimate.

COOPER: In a recent issue of the *Wilson Library Bulletin,* Gordon Stevenson decried the loss of valuable oral history resources—78 r.p.m. records created by black singers during the twenties, thirties, and forties—due to the failure of librarians to collect, catalog, and preserve these items.[16] The work you have been doing at Bowling Green since 1967 would seem to allay his fears. I assume that many humanistic scholars[17] and philanthropic organizations are anxious to assist you in your record collecting and cataloging activities. Have you been able to secure financial assistance from agencies such as the National Endowment for the Humanities or the Rockefeller Foundation to assist you in preserving contemporary recordings?

SCHURK: I'm not sure that your characterization of either the scholars or philanthropic organizations being "anxious" to help the Audio Center is entirely accurate. Nevertheless, I have received some grant money to assist in acquiring hardware—not records—for the Audio Center. In 1975 I was given a small faculty development grant by the university to purchase a portable cassette tape recorder for instructional experimentation. I also used HEW Title VI monies in 1977 to purchase several large pieces of recording equipment, including two Sony open-reel tape decks, four small cassette players, and eleven sets of headphones. I also used these grant funds to acquire a Soundcraftsman graphic sound-equalizer, which I use to enhance the sound of some of our radio tapes and older 78 r.p.m. recordings.

Representatives from the National Endowment for the Humanities were invited to visit the Audio Center a few years ago so that we could develop an appropriate grant request for that body. Unfortunately, these people weren't interested in fostering popular-culture studies at that time. The only other substantial grant that I can recall receiving was a $25,000 "seed money" allotment in the late 1960s from HEW Title II to build the book and recording collections in both the Audio Center and the Popular Culture Library. Although scholars such as Gordon Stevenson, Wayne A. Wiegand, R. Serge Denisoff, Russel B. Nye, and Ray B. Browne continue to argue for greater attention to preserving audio resources, I'm afraid that there isn't a groundswell within library organizations, governmental agencies, or private humanistic organizations to fund such activities.

COOPER: Have you encountered any efforts by overly enthusiastic private collectors to secure rare recordings from your collection by either purchase or theft?

SCHURK: Several years ago I was forced to change the locks to the Audio Center cataloging and record storage areas after we discovered that several recently acquired discs—including a Capitol recording of "Waitin' in Your Welfare Line," an RCA print entitled "Rindercella," and a Rojac-label tune called "Christmas in Vietnam"—had been stolen. I don't want to blame a serious collector for this activity, though. Since that incident we've had no security problem. No one is allowed to enter the stack area without my permission. My staff is paranoid about strangers in the collection area.

COOPER: You've accomplished so much during the past decade that I want to conclude our discussion with two speculative questions. How do you project the development of Bowling Green's Audio Center by the year 2000? And what impact do you envision the increased availability of popular music and other recorded resources will have on teaching and scholarly research over the next quarter of a century?

SCHURK: I hope that I'm still around—and directing the Audio Center—in twenty-three years. Most of my visions about collection building, sound delivery systems, cataloging and circulation practices for audio resources, and national recognition for Bowling Green as a scholarly resource are far from being fulfilled. Specifically, I want to rewire the entire Audio Center for stereo sound. I'd also like to improve the control console so that we could handle all types of audio recordings. This would mean some expansion from our present open-reel decks (ten and one-half inch maximum), cassette players, and standard or transcription turntables. Although some people may speculate that records and tapes might be obsolete by the turn of the century, I don't subscribe to that theory. Anyway, how could a social historian interpret America in the 1960s and 1970s without listening to 45s, albums, and cassette tapes?

By 2000 A.D. I pray that I'll have a sufficient staff to process all of the recordings that have been acquired since 1967. Now you've really got me dreaming. I'd like to think that several "angels" would provide restricted grants to the Audio Center to purchase private record collections which will become available during the next two decades. Other funding, from the university budget or federal grants, should be devoted to equipment acquisition and staff improvement.

Traditionally, writers who have conducted research in nonclassical music realms have dealt primarily with jazz and blues. By the year 2000 I trust that scholarly studies and discographic resources will be plentiful in all forms of contemporary music—rock and roll, country, gospel, rhythm and blues, and so on. Similarly, I expect additional development in the field of scholarly journals dealing with various audio subjects ranging from country discographies to radio programs. I also see greater international exchanges of ideas and resources. Not many Americans realize how thoroughly the music of the black man has been researched in Great Britain already. And can you imagine what will happen when the Germans begin to systematically organize record lists? Seriously, I know that you have already worked with essays from *Buch und Bibliographie*. That kind of discographic work is just the beginning. More song indexes are needed, too. I'm afraid that there are few library training programs that are currently paying much attention to specialized sound collections. Most media service librarians are more skilled in video than audio today.

COOPER: Thanks for sharing your ideas with me. I'm sure that you'll greet 2000 A.D. as director of the Audio Center. My dream would be that your Bowling Green collection would be the center of a nationwide network of audio resources for academic research. Good luck in your library work.

# ELEVEN

# An Annotated Bibliography of Popular Music Discographies

As more and more scholars, teachers, and librarians become involved in the serious investigation of popular music, there will be an increasing need for systematically organized information about recorded resources. The emergence of research facilities such as Bowling Green (Ohio) State University's Audio Center[1] illustrates the academic world's acknowledgment of the need to assemble library archives containing contemporary music materials.

In order to make effective analytical use of popular recordings, though, lists of available audio resources must be assembled. Just as bibliographies have served academicians in their searches for traditional print materials, the discography is a valuable research tool designed to assist scholars who are seeking oral information contained on 33⅓, 45, and 78 r.p.m. records.[2] Although the use of classical music discographies is a common practice among musicologists, the rock discography is just beginning to emerge as a scholarly tool. The geographical extent of recent discography study in popular music encompasses not only the United States and Canada, but also Great Britain and Germany.[3] Within the next decade it is likely that systematic discographies covering most areas of contemporary music will be available for scholars and librarians.

The following pages offer an introduction to a variety of rock discographies and record lists currently in print. Although the citation styles are inconsistent and the specific information provided about the recordings by each editor varies greatly, these discographies constitute the best information resources currently available.

Juul Anthonissen et al., comps. "Black Music Discography." *Billboard* (June 9, 1979): B.M. 30, 39–40.

This unannotated discography contains 325 entries, the vast majority of which are 33⅓ r.p.m. recordings. The citations are organized alphabetically by artist and consist of the album title and recording company. Performers included in this compilation begin with Louis Armstrong, Count Basie, Chuck Berry, Bobby Bland, James Brown, and Ray Charles . . . and end with the Temptations, Joe Turner, Ike and Tina Turner, Muddy Waters, Jackie Wilson, Stevie Wonder, and Lester Young.

Robert D. Barr. "Youth and Music." In *Values and Youth: Teaching Social Studies in an Age of Crisis—No. 2*. Washington, D.C.: National Council for the Social Studies, 1971. Pp. 99–103.

Features 41 entries of 33⅓ r.p.m. records, arranged in the following categories: "All-Time Greats" (13 albums—by Bob Dylan, the Beatles, Simon and Garfunkel, and the Jefferson Airplane), "Protest Songs" (6 albums—by Joan Baez and Pete Seeger), "Acid Rock and Soul" (11 albums—by Joe Cocker, Sly and the Family Stone, Jimi Hendrix, Janis Joplin, James Brown, and Richie Havens), "The New Rock Sounds" (7 albums—by James Taylor; Crosby, Stills, Nash, and Young; Paul McCartney; Elton John; and Cat Stevens, and "Rock Operas, Broadway Plays, and Other Extravaganzas" (four albums—*Hair, Woodstock, Jesus Christ Superstar*, and *Tommy*). Each entry consists of the performing artist, album title and record number, recording company, and examples of individual songs performed on the disc.

Carl Belz. *The Story of Rock*, 2d ed. New York: Harper and Row, 1972. Pp. 244–73.

Under the title "Selected Discography: 1953–1971," this compilation consists of both 33⅓ r.p.m. and 45 r.p.m. records. The 300 single recordings are chronologically arranged in songs-per-year sections beginning with 1953 and ending with 1963. Each entry includes the record title, performing artist, author(s) and publisher of the words and music, and the recording company. The 103 albums listed are alphabetized according to performing artists — from the Band, Beach Boys, and Beatles to the Temptations, Vanilla Fudge, and Velvet Underground. Each entry is from the 1964–71 period and includes the performing artist, album title and record number, and recording company.

Harry Castleman and Walter J. Podrazik, comps. *All Together Now: The First Complete Beatles Discography, 1961–1975.* New York: Ballantine Books, 1975.

Classic discographic study of the most popular contemporary music group ever contains full citations and background information on every record (including bootleg material) released by the Beatles — as a quartet and as individual performers — during a fifteen-year period.

Vivian Clair. "Discography." In *Linda Ronstadt.* New York: Quick Fox, 1978. Pp. 71–72.

This 14-album discography is arranged chronologically from 1967–1977. Each Linda Ronstadt recording listed is identified by title, recording company, record number, month and year of release, and producer. In addition, the individual songs contained on each 33⅓ r.p.m. disc are provided. No annotations are provided.

Norm Cohen, with the assistance of Arnold Shaw and George Lewis, comps. "Black Music Re-Issues: A Discography." *Billboard* (June 9, 1979): B.M. 30, 36.

This excellent discography of re-issued 33⅓ r.p.m. recordings is divided into seven sections: "Ragtime and Early (Pre-1917) Jazz" (16 albums); "Pre-Blues Folk (commercially recorded)" (7 albums); "Jug Bands" (7 albums); "Early (acoustic, rural) Blues" (48 albums); "Religious Music Prior to World War II" (19 albums); "Jazz of the 1920s and 1930s" (23 albums); and "Blues (urban), 1940s–1950s; R&B" (58 albums). This latter areas of contemporary recordings includes black artists ranging from Professor Longhair, Blind Willie Metell, and John Lee Hooker . . . to Chuck Berry, Little Richard, and Diana Ross. No annotations are provided in this lengthy record list. Each citation contains the artist's name, album title, recording company, and record number.

R. Serge Denisoff. *Great Day Coming: Folk Music and the American Left.*
    Baltimore: Penguin, 1971. Pp. 190–92.

Alphabetically arranged discography emphasizes albums by folk artists such as Bob Dylan, Woody Guthrie, Phil Ochs, Tom Paxton, Pete Seeger, and the Weavers. The 65 entries are listed according to performing artist, album title and record number, and recording company.

Paul Gambaccini, comp. *Rock Critics' Choice: The Top 200 Albums.* New
    York: Quick Fox, 1978. Pp. 7–79.

This specialized discography features 200 albums selected by music critics, rock journalists, and record collectors. Each entry contains the artist, album title, recording company, record number, date of release, and list of single tunes on the 33⅓ r.p.m. disc. The annotations consist of personal observations by several critics about the immediate impact and historical influence of the particular album. The list begins with: (No. 1) The Beatles' *Sgt. Pepper's Lonely Hearts Club Band,* (No. 2) Bob Dylan's *Blonde on Blonde,* and (No. 3) Bob Dylan's *Highway 61 Revisited* . . . and ends with (No. 198) The Temptations' *Greatest Hits,* (No. 199) New York Dolls' *New York Dolls,* and (No. 200) Richie Havens' *Mixed Bag.*

Phyl Garland. *The Sound of Soul: The Story of Black Music.* New York:
    Pocket Books, 1969. Pp. 199–202.

Lists 90 albums. Although the majority of recordings cited are performed by black artists—including Herbie Mann, Lou Rawls, James Brown, Aretha Franklin, Nina Simone, Otis Redding, Diana Ross and the Supremes, B. B. King, Ray Charles, Chuck Berry, Mahalia Jackson, and Dinah Washington—a few albums by so-called "white soul" artists—including José Feliciano, Janis Joplin, the Righteous Brothers, Tom Jones, and Elvis Presley—are also included. Each entry contains the performing artist, album title and record number, and recording company.

Charlie Gillett. *The Sound of the City: The Rise of Rock and Roll.* New York: Outerbridge and Dienstfrey, 1970. Pp. 343–46.

This "play list" consists of 32 single records identified only by artist and title. They have been arranged in chronological order from 1954 – Hank Ballard and the Midnighters, Joe Turner, the Spaniels, Elvis Presley, and Guitar Slim – to 1970 – Sly and the Family Stone and Creedence Clearwater Revival. The second part of the discography features 30 relatively rare album anthologies featuring rock and roll and rhythm and blues tunes by Wynonie Harris, Little Willie John, Joe Turner, Lloyd Price, Carl Perkins, Percy Sledge, and James Brown. The 33⅓ r.p.m. records are randomly listed by performing artist, album title, and record number.

John Goldrosen, with Bill Griggs. "Discography." In *The Buddy Holly Story,* rev. ed. New York: Quick Fox, 1979. Pp. 244–50.

This fascinating discography of Buddy Holly songs qualitatively supersedes all earlier lists by Goldrosen, Laing, and The Peers (listed below). The detailed compilation is organized in four parts: (1) All of Holly's American releases – 45 r.p.m. singles on Decca, Brunswick, and Coral released between 1956–59; singles released after Holly's death; extended-play singles; and albums; (2) A list of all Holly recording dates and accompanying personnel; (3) Tribute records to Holly; and (4) Cover versions of Holly songs.

Peter Guralnick. *Feel Like Going Home: Portraits in Blues and Rock 'N' Roll.* New York: Outerbridge and Dienstfrey, 1971. Pp. 212–17.

Highly specialized discography containing 65 albums. Structured in a loose chronological fashion, the author includes references to recorded selections by Blind Lemon Jefferson, Lightnin' Hopkins, Robert Johnson, Elmore James, Big Joe Williams, Muddy Waters, Johnny Shines, Skip James, Robert Pete Williams, Howlin' Wolf, Jerry Lee Lewis,

Charlie Rich, Bo Diddley, and Chuck Berry. Each entry lists the performing artist, album title and record number, and recording company.

Peter Guralnick. "Selected Discography." In *Lost Highway: Journeys and
    Arrivals of American Musicians.* Boston: Godine, 1979. Pp.
    341–50.

The 115 entries in this annotated discography are organized according
to the chapters in Guralnick's text and by the personalities being ex-
plored in *Lost Highway.* Each citation contains the artist's name, album
title, recording company, and record number. The variety of country,
rhythm and blues, rockabilly, and blues performers listed in this compilation include Jimmie Rodgers (4), Ernest Tubb (3), Rufus Thomas (5),
Bobby Bland (9), Charlie Feathers (5), Elvis Presley (9), Charlie Rich
(6), Sleepy LaBeef (4), Waylon Jennings (6), Merle Haggard (13),
Howlin' Wolf (10), Otis Spann (7), and Big Joe Turner (3).

Mike Jahn. *Rock: From Elvis Presley to the Rolling Stones.* New York:
    Quadrangle 1973. Pp. 295–302.

Arranged in alphabetical order by the performing artist, this discography begins with Eric Anderson, the Animals, Joan Baez, John Baldry,
and the Band and ends with T. Rex, Loudon Wainwright III, the Who,
Hank Williams, and Frank Zappa. Among the 179 albums listed, each
entry features the performing artist, album title and record number,
and recording company.

James Karnback and David Dalton, comps. "Discography." In *Rolling
    Stones: An Unauthorized Biography in Words and Photographs,*
    revised edition. New York: Quick Fox, 1979. Pp. 123–27.

This unannotated discography of Rolling Stone records includes thirty-
eight (38) 45 r.p.m. discs released between 1968 and 1978 and thirty-
two (32) albums released during the same period. The singles list ranges
from "Not Fade Away"/"I Wanna Be Your Man" to "Beast of Burden"/
"When the Whip Comes Down" and contains two song titles, the
month and year of release, the composers of the songs, and the record
number in each citation. The album list ranges from *The Rolling Stones*
to *Some Girls* and includes the album title, the recording company,

record number, date of release, all songs on the album, the composers of the songs, and the album's producer in each entry.

Rochelle Larkin. *Soul Music!* New York: Lancer, 1970. Pp. 181–89.

Lenghthy discography features 336 albums performed by a variety of black artists such as Duke Ellington, James Brown, the Mighty Clouds of Joy, Aretha Franklin, Harry Belafonte, Charlie Parker, Ruth Brown, Ike and Tina Turner, Booker T. and the M.G.'s, Stevie Wonder, Dionne Warwick, Ella Fitzgerald, Sam Cooke, Wilson Pickett, Muddy Waters, John Coltrane, Ray Charles, and Leon Bibb. The entries, which contain only the performing artist, album title, and recording company, are arranged in fourteen unequal sections corresponding with the chapters in the text.

Paul Lichter. "Discography and Films." In *The Boy Who Dared to Rock: The Definitive Elvis.* Garden City, N.Y.: Dolphin, 1978. Pp. 199–298.

This remarkably detailed Elvis Presley discography contains all Sun and RCA 45 r.p.m. and 78 r.p.m. single recordings, all RCA 45 r.p.m. extended-play albums, and all RCA 33⅓ r.p.m. long-playing albums arranged in chronological order. Complete citations and photographs of all record jacket/album covers are also included. Various kinds of rare Elvis Presley promotional recordings are included, along with a section on bootleg discs and recent foreign releases.

Dave Marsh, with John Swenson, eds. *The Rolling Stone Record Guide.* New York: Random House, 1979. Pp. 3–596.

This extensive discographic guide offers nearly ten thousand citations of album-length recordings. The annotations are interesting and informative, but highly personalized. Each entry features the artist's name, the album title, the recording company, and record number. The text is divided into the following major categories with individual artists listed alphabetically: "Rock, Soul, Country, and Pop" (pp. 3–427) with artists ranging from Aalon, Abba, AC/DC, Ace, and Johnny Ace . . . to Warren Zevon, the Zombies, Zoom, Zvider Zee, and Zulema; "Blues" (pp. 431–49) featuring performers ranging from

Luther Allison, Big Bill Broonzy, Big Maceo, and Big Maybelle . . . to Bukka White, Sonny Boy Williamson, Jimmy Witherspoon, Howlin' Wolf, and Mighty Joe Young; "Jazz" (pp. 453–531) with artists ranging from John Abercrombie, Muhal Richard Abrams, and Cannonball Adderley . . . to Larry Young, Lester Young, and Joe Zawinul; "Gospel" (pp. 535–45) featuring performers ranging from professor Alex Bradford, Shirley Caesar, and the Reverend James Cleveland . . . to the Swan Silvertones, the Violinaires, and the Ward Singers; and "Anthologies, Soundtracks, and Original Casts" (pp. 549–96).

Christopher May. "A Basic List of Rock Records." *BRIO* 13 (Autumn 1976):34–38.

Contains 125 long-playing records. The list is organized in alphabetical order by performing artist—starting with the Band, Beach Boys, Beatles, Jeff Beck, and Chuck Berry and ending with Stevie Wonder, Link Wray, the Yardbirds, and Yes. Each 33⅓ r.p.m. entry includes the performing artist, album title, recording company, and year of initial release.

Jim O'Connor. "A Rock and Roll Discography." *School Library Journal* 22 (September 1975):21–24.

Contains 237 album entries structured in two unequal sections (according to the compiler's personal preferences) and arranged alphabetically according to performing artists. This dual list begins with Alice Cooper, the Allman Brothers Band, the Animals, and the Association and ends with Yes, Neil Young, the Youngbloods, and the Zombies. Individual listings contain the performing artist, album title and record number, and the recording company. The author also utilizes a twelve-letter coding system ("A" means "acid" or "psychedelic" rock, "B" means "blues," "CW" means "country and western," and so on) to identify the style/genre of each recommended 33⅓ r.p.m. record.

Michael Olds. "From Sargeant Pepper to Captain Fantastic: A Basic Rock Collection." *Hoosier School Libraries* 16 (December 1976):17–19.

Consists of 37 albums presented in alphabetical order from Alice

Cooper, Allman Brothers Band, and America to Bruce Springsteen, the Who, and Stevie Wonder. Each entry offers the performing artist, album title and record number, recording company, and a one-sentence comment by the compiler.

David Pichaske. "Suggested Recordings." In *A Generation in Motion: Popular Music and Culture in the Sixties.* New York: Schirmer, 1979. Pp. 229–31.

This discography, organized alphabetically by the performer's last name, contains 109 album entries. Each citation includes the artist, the album title, the record company, and the record number. No annotation is provided. The performers in this discography range from Joan Baez, the Band, the Beach Boys, the Beatles, and Chuck Berry . . . to Simon and Garfunkel, Sly and the Family Stone, the Weavers, the Who, and Neil Young.

Ulrich Raschke. "One Hundred Times Pop Music: Concrete Advice for the Construction of a Basic Collection." *Buch und Bibliographie* 27 (July/August 1975):661–82ff.

Features 100 albums performed by artists such as the Animals, Beatles, James Brown, Johnny Cash, Bob Dylan, Otis Redding, Steppenwolf, Johnny Winter, and Stevie Wonder. Arranged alphabetically by performing artist, each entry also contains the album title and record number, the recording company, the year of release, and a brief annotation including songs featured on the record and the arrangement/production techniques utilized in the studio.

Jerome L. Rodnitzky. *Minstrels of the Dawn: The Folk-Protest Singer as a Culture Hero.* Chicago: Nelson-Hall, 1976. Pp. 181–84.

This 100-album "selected discography" is arranged alphabetically by performing artists. Each entry consists of the singer's name, album title, recording company, and year of release. The folk-music emphasis of the discography is illustrated by the number of 33⅓ records contributed by Joan Baez (15), Bob Dylan (13), Woody Guthrie (5), Phil Ochs (7), and Pete Seeger (8).

William L. Schurk. "Recommended Popular Records for a Non-
Classical Record Library." In *Selected Recordings and Publications
in the Popular Music Field,* ed. William Ivey. Nashville: Country
Music Foundation Press, 1975. Pp. 1–9.

Contains sixty-eight entries arranged alphabetically by recording artists
and is structured in the following categories: "Rock and Roll" (31
albums, including Bob Dylan, Bill Haley, and Jerry Lee Lewis).
"Rhythm and Blues and Soul" (14 albums, including Chuck Berry, Fats
Domino, and Little Richard), "The Blues" (fourteen albums, including
Muddy Waters, Blind Lemon Jefferson, and Bukka White), and "Gospel" (9 albums, including the Mighty Clouds of Joy, the Original Five
Blind Boys, and the Sensational Nightingales). Performing artists, album title and record number, and recording company are listed in each
entry.

Arnold Shaw. *The Rockin' '50's: The Decade That Transformed the Pop
Music Scene.* New York: Hawthorn Books, 1974. Pp. 282–88.

Consists of 185 long-playing records divided into twenty-five unequal
sections as a supplement to the chapters in the text. The albums listed
vary greatly – ranging from *Kiss Me Kate* and *Call Me Madam* to *Chuck
Berry's Golden Decade* and Bill Haley's *Rock around the Clock.* Each entry
consists of the performing artist, an abbreviated album title and record
number, and the recording company.

Arnold Shaw. *The World of Soul.* New York: Paperback Library, 1971.
Pp. 361–68.

Consists solely of black artists and contains 220 albums arranged in
twenty unequal sections which correspond with the organizational
structure of the text. Included among the 33⅓ r.p.m. records listed are
albums by Bessie Smith, Sarah Vaughan, the Platters, Jimmy Reed, the
Isley Brothers, Nina Simone, James Brown, Jimi Hendrix, Otis Redding, Aretha Franklin, and Ray Charles. Each entry features the performing artist, album title and record number, and the recording company.

Dean Tudor and Nancy Tudor. *Black Music.* Littleton, Colo.: Libraries
Unlimited, 1979. Pp. 31–188.

This book, along with the Tudor's companion volume entitled *Contemporary Popular Music,* constitute the two most comprehensive, systematic, authoritative discographic resources on rock music available. Although the individual citations in these books contain only the artist's name, album title, and record number, more than 1,300 discs are reviewed in these texts. The majority of entries are fully annotated with exceptionally detailed historical commentaries. The 33⅓ r.p.m. records are arranged in the following categories: "Blues"—featuring 434 albums by artists like Blind Lemon Jefferson, Sonny Boy Williamson, Big Bill Broonzy, B. B. King, Muddy Waters, Joe Turner, and Jimmy Witherspoon; "Rhythm 'N' Blues"—with 74 albums by artists including the Clovers, the Coasters, the Drifters, Ray Charles, Little Richard, Chuck Berry, LaVern Baker, and Ruth Brown; "Gospel"—featuring 66 albums by artists including James Cleveland, the Dixie Hummingbirds, Edwin Hawkins Singers, Mahalia Jackson, the Soul Stirrers, the Staple Singers, and the Swan Silvertones; "Soul"—with 80 albums by artists including Curtis Mayfield, the Supremes, the Temptations, James Brown, Wilson Pickett, Otis Redding, Smokey Robinson and the Miracles, Stevie Wonder, Marvin Gaye, Aretha Franklin, Gladys Knight and the Pips, Esther Phillips, and Ike and Tina Turner; and "Reggae"—featuring 8 albums.

Dean Tudor and Nancy Tudor. *Contemporary Popular Music.* Littleton, Colo.: Libraries Unlimited, 1979. Pp. 35–232.

The 33⅓ r.p.m. records in this lengthy discography (see stylistic details explained in the previous entry) are presented in the following categories: "Mainstream Popular Music"—featuring 177 albums by artists including Tony Bennett, Bing Crosby, Frank Sinatra, Neil Diamond, Sarah Vaughan, Petula Clark, Patti Page, Barbara Streisand, the Fifth Dimension, and Tony Orlando and Dawn; "Instrumental Ensembles"—with 23 albums; "Novelty and Humor"—with 12 albums; "Big Bands"—with 112 albums; "Stage and Film"—featuring 170 albums; "Rockabilly"—with 18 albums by artists including Bill Haley and the Comets, Buddy Holly, Jerry Lee Lewis, Elvis Presley, Carl Perkins, and Gene Vincent; "Rock 'N' Roll"—featuring 51 albums by performers including Roy Orbison, Dion and the Belmonts, Rick Nelson, and the Shirelles; "Modern Rock 'N' Roll"—with 25 albums by artists including the Beach Boys, the Beatles, Creedence Clearwater

Revival, the Four Seasons, Guess Who, Johnny Rivers, the Righteous Brothers, and Carly Simon; "Rock"—featuring 47 albums by performers including Elton John, the Rolling Stones, the Who, Chicago, Leon Russell, and the Zombies; "Blues rock"—with 23 albums by artists including Paul Butterfield, the Yardbirds, the Animals, Led Zeppelin, Janis Joplin, and Eric Clapton; "Acid Rock"—with 14 albums by performers including the Doors, Grateful Dead, and Jefferson Airplane; "Country/Folk rock"—featuring 21 albums by artists including the Band, the Byrds, Crosby, Stills, Nash, and Young, the Eagles, and Neil Young; "Heavy Metal (hard rock)"—with 22 albums by performers including Cream, Jimi Hendrix, Deep Purple, and Steppenwolf; and "Notable Experimentation"—featuring 28 notable discs such as the Beatles' *Sgt. Pepper's Lonely Hearts Club Band*, Jethro Tull's *Aqualung*, and the Rolling Stones' *Their Satanic Majesties Request*.

Jacques Vassal. *Electric Children: Roots and Branches of Modern Folkrock*. New York: Taplinger, 1976. Pp. 252–57.

Consists of nearly 300 albums arranged alphabetically by performing artists. The entries consist only of singers and album titles. Among the artists included in this folk-oriented record list are Joan Baez, Judy Collins, Donovan, Bob Dylan, Phil Ochs, Tom Paxton, Buffy Sainte-Marie, and Pete Seeger.

Graham Vulliamy and Ed Lee. *Pop Music in School*. Cambridge: Cambridge University Press, 1976. Pp. 195–204.

Extensive discography, with 232 album entries chronologically divided into the following sections: "Folk Anthologies" (10 records), "Popular Music prior to Rock 'N' Roll" (9 records), "Blues" (8 records, including B. B. King and John Lee Hooker), "Country and Western" (2 records, featuring Jimmie Rodgers and Hank Williams), "Rhythm and Blues" (9 records, including Fats Domino and Louis Jordan and his Tympany Five), "The Fusion Into Rock 'N' Roll" (5 records, featuring Elvis Presley, Jerry Lee Lewis, and Joe Turner), "Rock 'N' Roll" (18 records, including Bill Haley and the Comets, Chuck Berry, Little Richard, Buddy Holly, and Elvis Presley), "1959/1960 Payola" (1 record), "Britain—The Early 1960's and the Clubs" (4 records—including the

Animals and the Yardbirds), "Britain—The Beatles, Stones, and Five Other Groups" (9 records), "America—The Mid-1960's" (6 records, including the Beach Boys, the Byrds, and Bob Dylan), "Changes, 1966/1967" (9 records, including Cream, the Mothers of Invention, the Beatles, and Bob Dylan), "The Late 1960's—Britain" (17 records, including Jimi Hendrix, Led Zeppelin, Jethro Tull, and Pink Floyd), "The Late 1960's—America" (17 records, including the Band, Steve Miller Band, and Buffalo Springfield), "Black Music in the 1960's and 1970's" (20 records, including the Supremes, Otis Redding, Aretha Franklin, James Brown, and Stevie Wonder), "The 1970's (78 records, including Bob Dylan, John Lennon, Paul McCartney and Wings, Carole King, Rod Stewart, Elton John, the Eagles, and the Who), and "The Breaking of Barriers" (10 records, including Chick Corea, Miles Davis, and John McLaughlin and the Mahavishnu Orchestra). Each entry contains the performing artist, album title and record number, the recording company, and the year of release.

ADDITIONAL DISCOGRAPHIES AND LISTS OF POPULAR RECORDS

*The All-Time Million Seller Records.* Woodland Hills, Calif.: Phono-Graph Publications, 1969.

Chris Beachley, with assistance from Mike Redmond and Marv Goldberg. "The 'New' Drifters—A Total Reorganization, 1959–1971: Part 2 of the Drifters Story." *It Will Stand* 1 (1979): 4–7.

Peter E. Berry. "*. . . And The Hits Just Keep on Comin'.*" (Syracuse, N.Y.: Syracuse University Press, 1977. Pp. 169–276.

Alan Betrock, comp. *Girl Groups: An Annotated Discography, 1960–65.* New York: A Betrock, n.d.

John Blair, comp. *The Illustrated Discography of Surf Music, 1959–1965.* Riverside, Calif.: J. Bee Productions, 1978.

John Broven. "The Best Selling New Orleans Singles, 1946–72" and "Album Discography." In *Rhythm and Blues in New Orleans.* Gretna, La. Pelican, 1978. Pp. 228–42.

Harry Castleman and Walter J. Podrazik. *The Beatles Again?* Ann Arbor, Mich.: Pierian Press, 1977.

Ken Clee, comp. *A Discography Collection of Artists and Labels,* 2d ed. Philadelphia, Pa.: Stak-O-Wax Publications, 1979.

B. Lee Cooper. "An Opening Day Collection of Popular Recordings: Searching for Discographic Standards." In *20th Century Popular Culture in*

*Museums and Libraries*, ed. Fred E. H. Schroeder. Bowling Green, Ohio: Bowling Green University Popular Press, 1980.

B. Lee Cooper. "Popular Music Resources—Audio Collection Guidelines." *The Library-College Experimenter* 4 (May 1978): 11–22.

Jim Davis and Chris Beachley. "The Early Drifters, 1953–1959, and the Bill Pinkney Story." *It Will Stand* 1 (1979):4–7.

R. Serge Denisoff, comp. "American Protest Songs of War and Peace: A Selected Bibliography and Discography." Santa Barbara, Calif.: American Bibliographical Center—Clio Press, 1973.

Ted Dicks, ed. "Discography." In *A Decade of The Who: An Authorized History in Music, Paintings, Words, and Photographs*. London: Fabulous Music, 1977. Pp. 238–39.

L. R. Docks, comp. *The American Premium Record Guide, 1915–1965: Identification and Values of 78's, 45's, and LP's*. Florence, Ala.: Books Americana, 1980.

Joe Edwards, comp. *Top 10's and Trivia of Rock and Roll and Rhythm and Blues, 1950–1973*. St. Louis, Miss.: Blueberry Hill, 1974. (Supplements for 1974, 1975, etc. are also available.)

Colin Escott and Martin Hawkins. *Catalyst: The Sun Records Story*. London: Aquarius, 1975. Pp. 117–52.

Colin Escott and Martin Hawkins, comps. *The Complete Sun Label Session Files*, revised edition. Bexhill-On-Sea, East Sussex: Swift Record Distributors, 1978.

Anthony Fawcett. "John Lennon Discography." In *John Lennon—One Day at a Time: A Personal Biography of the Seventies*. New York: Grove Press, 1976. Pp. 188–90.

Robert D. Ferlingere, comp. *A Discography of Rhythm and Blues and Rock 'N' Roll Vocal Groups, 1945 to 1965*. Hayward, Calif.: California Trade School, 1976.

*The 45 RPM Handbook of Oldies: A Complete Guide To All The Available Hit Singles of the Past*. Los Angeles, Calif.: Record Rack, 1976.

Pete Fowler and Annie Fowler. "Chart Toppers: U. K. Singles, 1955–73." In *Rock Almanac*, ed. Stephen Nugent and Charlie Gillett. Garden City, N.Y.: Anchor Press/Doubleday, 1976. Pp. 354–66.

Phyl Garland. "Basic Library of Rhythm-and-Blues." *Stereo Review* 42 (May 1979):72–77.

Steve Gelfand, comp. "Vinyl Confusion: A Beach Boys Album Discography." *Goldmine* 33 (February 1979):10.

Charlie Gillett, Simon Frith, and Dave Marsh. "Hot One Hundred: Singles and Albums." In *Rock Almanac,* ed. Stephen Nugent and Charlie Gillett. Garden City, N.Y.: Anchor Press/Doubleday, 1976. Pp. 1–15.

Bruce Golden. "Discography." In *The Beach Boys: Southern California Pastoral.* San Bernardino, Calif.: Borgo Press, 1976. Pp. 40–52.

Stewart Goldstein and Alan Jacobson, comps. *Oldies but Goodies: The Rock 'N' Roll Years.* New York: Mason/Charter, 1977.

Jay Goldsworthy, ed. *Casey Kasem's American Top 40 Yearbook.* New York: Grosset and Dunlap, 1979.

Fernando Gonzalez, comp. *Disco-File: The Discographical Catalog of American Rock and Roll and Rhythm and Blues Vocal Harmony Groups, 1902 to 1976,* 2d ed. Flushing, N.Y.: F. L. Gonzalez, 1977.

Barbara Farris Graves and Donald J. McBain. "Discography." In *Lyric Voices: Approaches to the Poetry of Contemporary Song.* New York: Wiley 1972. Pp. 195–204.

Michael Haralambos. "Discography." In *Right On: From Blues to Soul in Black America.* New York: Drake, 1975. Pp. 179–81.

Randal C. Hill, comp. *The Official Price Guide to Collectible Rock Records.* Orlando, Fla.: House of Collectibles, 1979.

Thomas N. Jewell. "Rock: The Best Recordings of 1979." *Library Journal* 107 (February 15, 1980):473–80.

Ernst Jorgensen, Erik Rasmussen, and Johnny Mikkelsen. *Elvis Presley – Recording Sessions.* Baneringen, Denmark: JEE Publications, 1977. Pp. 3–103.

Don R. Kirsch, comp. *Rock 'N' Roll Obscurities – Volume One.* Tacoma, Wash.: D. R. Kirsch, 1977.

Dave Laing. "Discography." In *Buddy Holly.* New York: Macmillan 1971. Pp. 141–44.

Jon Landau. *It's Too Late to Stop Now: A Rock and Roll Journal.* San Francisco, Calif.: Straight Arrow Books, 1972. Pp. 224–27.

Alan "Bo" Leibowitz. *The Record Collector's Handbook.* New York: Everest House, 1979.

Nick Logan and Bob Woffinden, eds. *The New Musical Express Book of Rock – 2,* rev. ed. London: William H. Allen, 1977.

Greil Marcus. *Mystery Train: Images of America in Rock 'N' Roll Music.* New York: E. P. Dutton, 1975. Pp. 209–64.

Jean-Charles Marion. "Essential Recordings: Part 1 – A Beginner's Basic Library." *Record Exchanger* 4 (1975):25,30.

Jean-Charles Marion. "Essential Recordings: Part 2 – A Collector's Basic Library. *Record Exchanger* 4 (1976):13,19.

Mitchell McGeary, comp. *The Beatles Discography*, rev. ed. Lacey, Wash.: Ticket To Ryde, 1976. Pp. 1–33.

John "Ned" Mendelsohn. "Discography." In *The Who*. San Francisco, Calif.: Straight Arrow Books, 1975. Pp. 82–85.

Daniel J. Miles, Betty T. Miles, and Martin J. Miles, comps. *The Miles Chart Display—Volume I: 1955–1970*. Boulder, Colo.: Convex Industries, 1973.

Daniel J. Miles, Betty T. Miles, and Martin J. Miles, comps. *The Miles Chart Display of Popular Music—Volume II: 1971–1975*. New York: Arno Press, 1977.

Bill Millar. "Discography." In *The Drifters: The Rise and Fall of the Black Vocal Group*. New York: Collier, 1971. Pp. 169–79.

Charles Miron, comp. *Rock Gold: All the Hit Charts from 1955 to 1976*. New York: Drake, 1977.

*The Motown Era*. New York: Grosset and Dunlap, 1971. Pp. 5–16.

Joseph Murrells, comp. *The Book of Golden Discs: The Records That Sold A Million*, rev. ed. London: Barrie and Jenkins, 1978.

Ed Naha, comp. *Lillian Roxon's Rock Encyclopedia*, rev. ed. New York: Grosset and Dunlap, 1978.

Ralph M. Newman and Alan Kaltman. "Lonely Teardrops: The Story of A Forgotten Man." *Time Barrier Express* 3 (1979):29–32.

A. X. Nicholas, comp. *The Poetry of Soul*. New York: Bantam, 1971. Pp. 93–98.

A. X. Nicholas, comp. *Woke Up This Mornin': Poetry of the Blues*. New York: Bantam, 1973. Pp. 119–22.

Stephen Nugent and Charlie Gillett, comps. *Rock Almanac: Top Twenty American and British Singles and Albums of the '50s, '60s, and '70s*. Garden City, N.Y.: Anchor Press/Doubleday, 1976.

Jerry Osborne, comp. "Elvis 1977–78 Checklist." *Record Digest* 2 (January 1, 1979):44–64.

Jerry Osborne, comp. *55 Years of Recorded Country/Western Music*. Phoenix: O'Sullivan, Woodside, 1976.

Jerry Osborne and Bruce Hamilton, comps. *A Guide to Record Collecting*. Phoenix: O'Sullivan, Woodside, 1979.

Jerry Osborne, comp. *Popular and Rock Records, 1948–1978*, 2d ed. Phoenix: O'Sullivan, Woodside, 1978.

Jerry Osborne, comp. *Record Albums, 1948–1978*, 2d ed. Phoenix: O'Sullivan, Woodside, 1978.

Robert Palmer. "A Chronological Listing of Records Produced by Leiber and

Stoller." In *Baby, That Was Rock 'N' Roll: The Legendary Leiber and Stoller.* New York: Harcourt Brace Jovanovich, 1978. Pp. 128–31.

Robert Palmer. "Recordings of Works by Leiber and Stoller." In *Baby That Was Rock 'N' Roll: The Legendary Leiber and Stoller.* New York: Harcourt Brace Jovanovich, 1978. Pp. 120–27.

Elizabeth Peer and Ralph Peer II. "Discography." In *Buddy Holly . . . A Biography in Words, Photographs, and Music.* New York: Peer International Corporation, 1972. Pp. 135–44.

David R. Pichaske, ed. "A Select List of Recordings." In *Beowulf to Beatles: Approaches to Poetry.* New York: Free Press, 1972. Pp. 391–97.

John Pidgeon. "Discography." In *Eric Clapton: A Biography.* Frogmore, St. Albans: Panther Books, 1976. Pp. 139–44.

Michael R. Pitts and Louis H. Harrison, comps. *Hollywood on Record: The Film Stars' Discography.* Metuchen, N.J.: Scarecrow Press, 1978.

Dan Price. "Bibliography of Bob Dylan: Articles and Books, By and About; Albums and Singles Published; and Unreleased Recordings." *Popular Music and Society* 3 (1974):227–41.

Steve Propes. *Golden Goodies: A Guide to 50's and 60's Popular Rock & Roll Record Collecting.* Radnor, Pa.: Chilton, 1975.

Steve Propes. *Golden Oldies: A Guide to 60's Record Collecting.* Radnor, Pa.: Chilton, 1974.

Steve Propes. *Those Oldies but Goodies: A Guide to 50's Record Collecting.* New York: Collier, 1973.

Jim Quirin and Barry Cohen, comps. *Chartmasters' Rock 100: An Authoritative Ranking of the 100 Most Popular Songs for Each Year, 1956 Through 1975*, 2d ed. Covington, La.: Chartmasters, 1976.

Richard Robinson et al. "Creem's List of Top Rock Albums, 1955–75." In *Rock Revolution.* New York: Popular Library, 1976. Pp. 209–14.

Richard Robinson. *Pop, Rock, and Soul.* New York: Pyramid, 1972. Pp. 181–82.

Richard Robinson and Andy Swerling. *The Rock Scene.* New York: Pyramid, 1971. Pp. 162–66.

Mike Rowe. *Chicago Breakdown.* New York: Drake, 1975. Pp. 217–18.

Ellen Sander, "Pop in Perspective: A Profile," *Saturday Review* (October 26, 1968):80–93.

Ellen Sander and Tom Clark. "A Rock Taxonomy." In *Trips: Rock Life in the Sixties.* New York: Scribner's, 1973. Pp. 162–258.

Frank Scott et al., comps. *Vintage Rock and Roll Catalog – 1979.* El Cerrito, Calif.: Down Home Music, 1979.

Arnold Shaw. *Honkers and Shouters: The Golden Years of Rhythm and Blues.* New York: Collier, 1978. Pp. 529–41.

Arnold Shaw. *Rock Revolution.* New York: Crowell-Collier, 1969. Pp. 242–50.

John L. Smith, comp. *Johnny Cash Discography and Recording History, 1955–1968.* Los Angeles: John Edwards Memorial Foundation, 1969.

Clive Solomon, comp. *Record Hits: The British Top 50 Charts, 1954–1976.* London, Eng.: Omnibus Press, 1977.

Irwin Stambler and Grelun Landon, comps. "Discography." In *Encyclopedia of Folk, Country and Western Music.* New York: St. Martin's Press, 1969. Pp. 377–90.

Irwin Stambler, comp. *Encyclopedia of Pop, Rock, and Soul.* New York: St. Martin's Press, 1974. Pp. 569–99.

Friedrich Summan and Manfred Jagnow. "A Basic Collection of Rock 'N' Roll Records and Tape Cassettes." *Buch und Bibliographie* 27 (July-August 1975):682–84.

"Sun Record Company Discography." *Mean Mountain Music* 4 (1979):15–21.

Steve Turner. "Discography." In *Conversations with Eric Clapton.* London: Sphere Books, 1976. Pp. 112–16.

John Voight. "Rock Music: The Sacred Squeal of Now." *Wilson Library Bulletin* 46 (October 1971):130–31.

Pete Welding. "The Best of Blues and Roots: A Guide to Blues, Gospel, R&B, and Ragtime on Records." In *Downbeat Music '68* Chicago: down beat magazine, 1968. Pp. 56–59, 86–93.

Joel Whitburn, comp. *Pop Annual, 1955–1977.* Menomonee Falls, Wis.: Record Research, 1978.

Joel Whitburn, comp. *Top Country & Western Records, 1949–1971.* Menomonee Falls, Wis.: Record Research, 1972. (Supplements for 1972–73, 1974, etc. are also available.)

Joel Whitburn, comp. *Top Easy Listening Records, 1961–1974.* Menomonee Falls, Wis.: Record Research, 1975. (Supplements for 1975, 1976, etc. are also available.)

Joel Whitburn, comp. *Top LP Records, 1945–1972.* Menomonee Falls, Wis.: Record Research, 1973. (Supplements for 1973, 1974, etc. are also available.)

Joel Whitburn, comp. *Top Pop Records, 1940–1955.* Menomonee Falls, Wis.: Record Research, 1973.

Joel Whitburn, comp. *Top Pop Records, 1955–1972.* Menomonee Falls, Wis.: Record Research, 1973. (Supplements for 1973, 1974, etc. are also available.)

Joel Whitburn, comp. *Top Rhythm and Blues Records, 1949–1971.* Menomonee Falls, Wis.: Record Research, 1972. (Supplements for 1972–73, 1974, etc. are also available.)

Rick Whitesell. "The Brightest Comet of Them All—Bill Haley." *Record Exchanger* 4 (1976):4–9.

Paul Williams. "Discography." In *Outlaw Blues: A Book of Rock Music.* New York: Pocket Books, 1969. Pp. 189–91.

Richard Williams. "Phil Spector Discography." In *Out of His Head: The Sound of Phil Spector.* London: Abacus, 1972. Pp. 140–51.

# TWELVE

# An Opening-Day Collection of Popular Music Albums for Libraries

It is obvious that if academic librarians begin to take popular culture as seriously as [teaching and writing] scholars, there are likely to be a number of complex problems of a practical nature which will have to be considered. Because we have been taught to exercise qualitative judgments in building collections, we will need to find new guidelines and strategies to provide alternatives to our traditional selections criteria.
— Gordon Stevenson

Despite the growing number of articles published in scholarly journals, the many presentations delivered at professional meetings, and the numerous courses that have been implemented and taught on campuses throughout the United States, it is notable that informed discussions about the acquisition, classification, and distribution of contemporary music resources have not surfaced in many library journals.[1] In addition, only one brief essay has been published since 1970 that attempts to define the role of a reference librarian in assembling media and print resources and in providing technical assistance to a faculty member teaching a course on popular music.[2] Worse yet, the larger question of collection construction has been almost totally neglected.[3] Most librarians would readily acknowledge that responding to a specific album request from a single professor is an easy task compared to the complex challenge of assembling an entire library of contemporary recordings appropriate for general use by both students and instructors. Clearly, the library profession needs to establish a set of guidelines for creating a general collection of popular music sources.

Traditional training in library science does not include the critical review and evaluation of popular recordings. The following pages offer discographic assistance to librarians who are searching for constructive suggestions about building basic, representative holdings in the area of popular music.

Librarians should be forewarned that several special interest groups would like to influence library acquisition practices in respect to popular records. For several years sales directors of commercial recording companies such as RCA, Columbia, and Capitol have observed the growing interest of academicians in nonprint instructional resources. They have also noted with great interest the bulk purchasing potential of library budgets. This has led to the institution of a variety of special sales arrangements. To cite just one example, Columbia Records offers a one-year library subscription service that permits a librarian to select 70 records from an annual list of 250 choices. The fee for this record purchasing plan is $250 annually. The Columbia advertising letter notes that this service

> . . . offers you the *very latest* CBS, Columbia, Epic and associated label releases, at the same time that they are delivered to regular retail record shops—but you pay only 45% of the suggested list prices: a 55% discount!
>
> Leonard Bernstein and the New York Philharmonic; Barbra Streisand; Glenn Gould; E. Power Biggs; Neil Diamond; Eugene Ormandy and the Philadelphia Orchestra; Bob Dylan; Willie Nelson; Walter Carlos; the Isley Brothers; Chicago; Lazar Berman; Paul Simon; Johnny Cash; Rudolf Serkin; Miles Davis. . . . These are just a few of the artists whose releases will be sent *directly from the CBS/Columbia pressing plant to your library, postpaid.*[4]

The issue is not the cost efficiency of the Columbia plan, but how Columbia determines *which* recordings should be available in a general collection. Although the brochure describing the Columbia Subscription Service states that the company will provide "a permanent classic 'basic repertory' list" to enable librarians "to build or replenish your classical foundation," no such list of contemporary music "classics" is mentioned. This leaves the librarian with the impression that recordings by Bob Dylan, Willie Nelson, the Isley Brothers, and Chicago are of equal worth (or, from a negative standpoint, nonworth).

The librarian concerned with record selection might begin with the question, "What is popular music?" The answers to this query vary so dramatically that some librarians might wonder whether any reasonable (or rational) discographic guidelines for a core collection of contemporary recordings are possible. Among recent definitions of "popular music," the following selections are typical:

> . . . From a theoretical standpoint rock and roll music is a regular, continuous four-beat rhythm in a twelve-beat or thirty-two beat blues song pattern. The accompaniment usually includes electronically-amplified guitars. Typical performances contain extreme voice range and a standard change of tone.[5]

> Pop music, normally called "rock music" today, cannot be defined by musical scores. Cataloging of its notes and music has been done in retrospect. Playing and listening enjoyment, rhythm, loud beat and variation, immediacy, casual and improvised composition, experimentation and stereotypes, dissonance and displacement, irony and earnest but naive seriousness, sentimentality and bad taste, pathos and brutality, thought, coldness, reflection, vibration, pulsation, tenderness, intelligence, abstraction, intoxication, sorrow, forgetfullness, stimulation, trembling, dreams, and life: that is pop music.[6]

> For a time rock 'n' roll had become a life style, but in the early '70's it tended to recede more to the old-time status of pop music as primarily an entertainment form. . . . Almost any type of number—hard rock, soft rock, rock revival, country and western, soul, ballad—had a chance at hit status, and the "Top 40 Charts" in both albums and singles indicated that no one type of music had a monopoly on public attention.[7]

> Popular music is the sum total of those taste units, social groups and musical genres which coalesce along certain taste and preference similarities in a given space and time. These taste publics and genres are affected

by a number of factors, predominately age, accessibility, race, class, and education. . . . People select what they like from what they hear. The reasons for this selection are influenced by many factors some of which have little to do with the esthetic quality of a song or instrumental piece.[8]

Carl Belz has suggested the ultimate commentary on this definitional dilemma by noting that "any listener who wants rock defined *specifically* is probably unable to recognize it."[9]

The "opening day collection" of 33⅓ r.p.m. recordings suggested in the following pages should adequately serve sociology, English, history, psychology, and political science teachers who wish to involve their students in a critical examination of lyrical commentaries about contemporary American society. While it would be easier to provide complete record lists from major music corporations—Columbia, RCA, Capitol, or MCA—and to claim that academic libraries should acquire *all* of the recordings released by these companies, such an assertion would be financially disastrous in an age of shrinking library budgets. The careful selection of appropriate popular music resources by academic librarians is mandatory. But who should initiate such judgments? Ideally, the foremost popular music scholars and teachers experienced in the use of musical resources should offer suggestions to assist acquisitions librarians. On the one hand, though, librarians have not demonstrated much interest in collecting the social commentaries contained in contemporary lyrics; on the other hand, most popular music scholars have condemned academic bookmen as bibliographic elitists who treasure only the latest printed literary criticism on Steinbeck and Hemingway while ignoring the audio observations of Phil Ochs, Bob Dylan, Les McCann, Joni Mitchell, Janis Ian, Stevie Wonder, and others. Such unproductive relations must cease. Instead, they should be replaced by tough-minded, critical exchanges over *which* records by *which* artists ought to be housed in the library for student and faculty use.

The following recommendation of an "opening-day collection" of popular music resources attempts both to fill a gap in library literature and to foster discussion and debate among librarians and their academic patrons. Obviously, a discographer inevitably falls prey to subjectivity in assembling a brief list of recordings designed to illustrate the most relevant musical trends and social commentary over the past quarter-century. The criteria and organizational structure used to assemble this listing are outlined below:

1. Although the 45 r.p.m. record remains the chief quantitative source of identifying "hit" music (even though it is clearly *not* the financial basis for celebrity status when compared to concert performance receipts and album sales income), this discography consists entirely of 33⅓ r.p.m. recordings. Stated simply, albums offer academic librarians greater cost efficiency on a song-per-dollar-invested basis.

2. The record anthology, featuring either popular tunes by various artists or the "greatest hits" of a group or an individual performer, constitutes this discography's structural backbone.

3. With few exceptions, the recordings listed in this discography are currently available at most retail music stores or can be easily purchased by librarians through wholesale record distribution outlets. Exotic foreign rock import discs, bootleg records, and rare, out-of-print 1950s rhythm and blues albums have been omitted purposely from this discography.

4. The organizational pattern of this discography avoids two traditional arrangements. First, the "alphabetical listing by artist" format was rejected because of the desire to emphasize album-length anthologies. Second, the traditional division of songs or albums into genre categories such as "jazz," "rock," "rhythm and blues," "pop," "folk," "country," "soul," and "bluegrass" was avoided because so many popular artists, such as Bob Dylan, Elvis Presley, Carole King, and Paul Simon, frequently cross these narrow stylistic barriers. The specific discographic structure utilized in the following pages is outlined below:

I. Anthology Albums — Songs by various artists
   A. Chronological song order
   B. Random song order
   C. Recordings of "live" performances
   D. Special collections
II. Greatest Hits Albums — Individual or group performances
   A. Chronological song order
   B. Random song order

      C.  Recordings of "live" performances
      D.  Special collections
III.  Standard Albums
      A.  Individual artists
      B.  Group performances
IV.  Other Types of Albums
      A.  Motion picture soundtracks
      B.  Novelty and comedy recordings
      C.  Bootleg releases
      D.  Imported recordings
      E.  Special collections and documentary recordings

### AN OPENING DAY COLLECTION OF POPULAR MUSIC RECORDINGS

I.  Anthology Albums — Songs by Various Artists
      A.  Chronological song order
          *Dick Clark/20 Years of Rock and Roll* (BDS 5133-2). New York: Buddah Records, 1973. Features Carl Perkins, the Kingsmen, Van Morrison, Curtis Mayfield, and others.
          *History of Rhythm and Blues, 1947–1967* — 8 vols. (SD 8161-4/8193-4/8208-9). New York: Atlantic Recording Corporation, 1968 (vols. I–VI) and 1969 (vols. VII–VIII). Features the Ravens, the Cardinals, Leadbelly, the Orioles, Joe Turner, the Chords, Ivory Joe Hunter, the Coasters, the Drifters, Clyde McPhatter, Ben E. King, Barbara Lewis, Wilson Pickett, Aretha Franklin, Otis Redding, and others.
          *Rock 'N' Soul: The History of Rock in the Pre-Beatle Decade of Rock* — 9 Vols. (ABCX 1955–64). Los Angeles: ABC Records, 1973. Features Willie Mae Thornton, the Cadillacs, Frankie Lymon and the Teenagers, Shirley and Lee, the Dells, Lloyd Price, the Olympics, Little Caesar and the Romans, Gene Chandler, the Impressions, and others.
          *The Roots of Rock 'N Roll* (SJL 2221). New York: Arista Rec-

ords, 1977. Features Wild Bill Moore, Johnny Otis, Nappy Brown, Big Maybelle, the Ravens, Clarence Palmer and the Jive Bombers, and others.

*This Is How It All Began: The Roots of Rock 'N' Roll as Recorded from 1945 to 1955 on Specialty Records* – 2 vols. (SPS 2117/2118). Hollywood, Calif.: Specialty Records, 1969/1970. Features Roy Milton, Don and Dewey, Larry Williams, Lloyd Price, Little Richard, and others.

B.  Random song order

*And the Rock Lives On* . . . 3 Vols. (SVL 1020/21/22). Sunnyvale, Calif.: Sunnyvale Records, 1978. Features Robert and Johnny, the Capris, Billy Bland, the Fiestas, the Royaltones, Lee Allen, Billy Myles, the Turbans, and others.

*At the Hop* (AA 1111/12). Los Angeles: ABC Records, 1978. Features Danny and the Juniors, Three Dog Night, Del Shannon, the Impressions, Lloyd Price, Sonny James, the Royal Teens, Pat Boone, George Hamilton IV, and others.

*The Blues* – 5 vols. (LPS 4026/27/34/42/51). Chicago: Cadet (Chess) Records, n.d. Features Little Walter, Chuck Berry, Howlin' Wolf, Muddy Waters, Willie Mabon, and others.

*The Blues Are Black* (P 13211). New York: Columbia Records/CBS, Inc., 1976. Features Mississippi John Hurt, Blind Lemon Jefferson, Leadbelly, Bessie Smith, Robert Johnson, Billie Holiday, Elmore James, and others.

*Cadence Classics* – 3 vols. (BR 4000/4001/4002). Los Angeles: Barnaby Records, 1975. Features the Everly Brothers, Link Wray, the Chordettes, Eddie Hodges, Bill Hayes, Johnny Tillotson, and Lenny Welch.

*Classic Blues* – 2 Vols. (BLC 6062/6062). New York: ABC Records, 1973. Features Ray Charles, T-Bone Walker, Jimmy Witherspoon, John Lee Hooker, Jimmy Reed, and Otis Spann.

*Cruisin' the Fifties and Sixties: A History of Rock and Roll Radio* — 13 vols. (INCM 2000-2012). Sunnyvale, Calif.: Increase Records, 1970 (vol. 1956–62), 1972 (vol. 1955 and 1963), and 1973 (vol. 1964–67). Features Janis Ian, Sandy Posey, Barry McGuire, Chuck Berry, Shep and the Limelites, Little Anthony and the Imperials, Big Jay McNeeley, Wilbert Harrison, Bobby Day, the Tuneweavers, Bo Diddley, the Charms, and others.

*Discotech #1* (M6 824 S1). Hollywood, Calif.: Motown Record Corporation, 1975. Features Stevie Wonder, Martha Reeves and the Vandellas, Temptations, Junior Walker and the Allstars, Marvin Gaye, and others.

*Echoes of a Rock Era* — 3 vols. (RE 111/112/113). New York: Roulette Records, 1971. Features Sonny Til and the Orioles, the Penguins, the Moonglows, Maurice Williams and the Zodiacs, Mary Wells, the Shirelles, and others.

*The 50's Greatest Hits* (G 30592). New York: Columbia Records/CBS, Inc., 1972. Features Johnny Mathis, Doris Day, Johnny Ray, the Four Lads, and others.

*14 Golden Recordings from the Historic Vaults of Duke/Peacock Records* — 2 Vols. (ABCX 784/789). New York: ABC Records, 1973. Features Johnny Ace, Bobby Bland, Roy Head, Ernie K-Doe, Junior Parker, Willie Mae Thornton, and others.

*14 Golden Recordings from the Historical Vaults of Vee Jay Records* (ABCX 785). Los Angeles, Calif.: ABC Records, 1973. Features Dee Clark, Gladys Knight and the Pips, John Lee Hooker, and others.

*Alan Freed's "Golden Pics"* (LP 313). New York: End Records, n.d. Features Little Richard, the Nutmegs, Chuck Berry, the Willows, Little Walter, and others.

*Alan Freed's Memory Lane* (R 42041). New York: Roulette Records, n.d. Features the Moonglows, Jesse Belvin, Little Anthony and the Imperials, Jerry Butler, and others.

*Golden Goodies* — 19 vols. (R 25207/09-19/38-42/47-48). New York: Roulette Records, n.d. Features the Spaniels, Joey Dee, Buddy Knox, Frankie Lymon, the Tune Weavers, the Dubs, Dave "Baby" Cortez, Johnny and the Hurricanes, the G-Clefs, Larry Williams, Jack Scott, the Rays, and others.

*Great Bluesmen* — Recorded Live at the Newport Folk Festivals in Newport, Rhode Island, 1959–1965 (VSD 77/78). New York: Vanguard Recording Society, 1976. Features Son House, Skip James, Sonny Terry, Brownie McGhee, Mississippi, Fred McDowell, and others.

*Greatest Folksingers of the 'Sixties* (VSD 17/18). New York: Vanguard Recording Society, n.d. Features Ian and Sylvia, Buffy Sainte-Marie, Joan Baez, Odetta, Phil Ochs, John Hammond, Bob Dylan, Judy Collins, Theodore Bikel, Tom Paxton, Pete Seeger, and others.

*Heavy Hands* (CS 1048). New York: Columbia Records/CBS, n.d. Features Taj Mahal, Freddie King, Johnny Winter, and others.

*Heavy Heads* (LPS 1522). Chicago: Chess Records, n.d. Features Bo Diddley, Little Milton, Muddy Waters, and others.

*History of British Rock* — 2 Vols. (SASH 3704-2/3705-2/3712-2) Los Angeles: Sire Records, (ABC Records, Inc.), 1974, 1975.

*Jim Pewter's 10th Anniversary Salute to Rock 'N Roll* (FR 1006). Los Angeles: Festival Records, 1976. Features Dale Hawkins, Chuck Berry, Mickey and Sylvia, the Big Bopper, Bobby Herb, the Diamonds, and others.

*Juggernauts of the Early 70's* (DSX 50146). Los Angeles: ABC Records, 1973. Features Jim Croce, Three Dog Night, Smith, Mama Class, and others.

*Jukebox Jive* (NU 9020). Minnetonka, Minn.: K-tel International, 1975. Features Ronnie Hawkins, Paul Anka, Del Shannon, Buddy Knox, Chris Montez, the Clovers, and Sue Thompson.

*King-Federal Rockabillys* (King 5016X). Nashville: Gusto Records, 1978. Features Mac Curtis, Charlie Feathers, Ronnie Moleen, Joe Penny, Bob and Lucille, Bill Beach, and Hank Mizell.

*Don Kirshner Presents "Rock Power"* (P 12417). New York: CBS Records, 1974. Features the Doobie Brothers, Bachman-Turner Overdrive, Dr. John, Alice Cooper, and others.

*Mindbender* (TU 2440). Minnetonka, Minn.: K-tel International, 1976. Features Neil Sedaka, Kiss, LaBelle, Elton John, C. W. McCall, and others.

*Motown's Preferred Stock* — 3 Vols. (m 6-881/882/883 S1). Hollywood, Calif.: Motown Record Corporation, 1977. Features the Four Tops, Mary Wells, Michael Jackson, Martha Reeves and the Vandellas, Gladys Knight and the Pips, the Spinners, Marvin Gaye and Tammi Terrell, the Marvellettes, the Temptations, Smokey Robinson and the Miracles, Edwin Starr, and Jr. Walker and the All Stars.

*Nuggets: Orginial Artyfacts from the First Psychedelic Era, 1965–1968* (Sash 3716-2). Los Angeles: Sire Records, 1976. Features the Mojo Men, the Castaways, the Amboy Dukes, the Knickerbockers, the Standells, and others.

*Old King Gold* — 10 vols. (KS 16001-10). Nashville: Gusto Records, 1975. Features Hank Ballard and the Midnighters, Platters, Otis Williams and the Charms, Bill Doggett, Billy Ward and the Dominos, Little Willie John, Freddy King, Wynonie Harris, Earl Bostic, and others.

*Original Early Top 40 Hits* (PAS 1013). New York: Paramount Records, 1974. Features Pat Boone, Gale Storm, Tab Hunter, Sanford Clark, and others.

*Original Golden Hits of the Great Blues Singers* — 3 vols. (MHG 25002-3/11). Chicago: Mercury Records, n.d. Features Lightnin' Hopkins, Little Junior Parker, Lowell Fulsom, Howlin' Wolf, Bobby Bland, Willie Mabon, Muddy Waters, and others.

*Original Golden Hits of the Great Groups* — 3 vols. (MGH 25000/07/10). Chicago: Mercury Records, n.d.

*Original Golden Instrumental Hits* (MGH 25001). Chicago:

Mercury Records, n.d. Features Phil Upchurch, Lee
Allen, Mar-Keys, Ace Cannon, Booker T. and the
MG's, Champs, Les Cooper, and others.

*Original Golden Rhythm and Blues Hits* (MGH 25006). Chicago: Mercury Records, n.d. Features Jimmy McCrack-
lin, Don Gardner and Dee Dee Ford, Clarence Henry,
Little Walter, and others.

*Original Golden Teen Hits* — 3 vols. (MGH 25004-5/09). Chicago: Mercury Records, n.d. Features Thomas Wayne,
the Shirelles, Sammy Turner, Gary U.S. Bonds, Rufus
Thomas, Jan Bradley, Johnny Preston, and others.

*Original Golden Town and Country Hits* (MGH 25008). Chicago: Mercury Records, n.d. Features Jerry Wallace,
Patti Page, Patsy Cline, Rusty Draper, Leroy van Dyke,
and others.

Price, Lloyd, Sam Cooke, Larry Williams, and Little Richard.
*"Our Significant Hits."* (SP 2112). Hollywood, Calif.:
Specialty Records, n.d.

*Rock and Roll Show* (GT 0002). Nashville: Gusto Records,
1978. Features Bill Doggett, Sammy Turner, the Moonglows, Chuck Berry, Billy Wards and the Dominos,
Jerry Lee Lewis, and others.

*Rock Begins* — 2 vols. (SD 33-314/315). New York: ATCO
Records, 1970. Features Bobby Darin, Ray Charles, the
Coasters, La Vern Baker, Chuck Willis, and others.

*Rock Invasion, 1956–1969* (LC 50012). New York: London
Records, 1978. Features Rod Stewart, Joe Cocker, Lon-
nie Donegan, Unit Four + 2, Zombies, Nashville Teens,
and others.

*Rock On — The Musical Encyclopedia of Rock N' Roll: The Solid
Gold Years* (PG 33390). New York: Columbia Records/
CBS, 1975. Features Jimmy Dean, Johnny Horton,
Don Cherry, Guy Mitchell, Marty Robbins, Frankie
Laine, Johnny Mathis, Bobby Vinton, and others.

*A Salute to Rock 'N' Roll: 20 Original Hits* (FR 1006A). Sher-
man Oaks, Calif.: Festival Records, 1976. Features Jan
Bradley, Mickey and Sylvia, Dale Hawkins, Johnnie and
Joe, and others.

*Solid Gold Old Town* (SD 9032). New York: Cotillion Records, 1971. Features the Royaltones, the Fiestas, the Harptones, Billy Bland, and others.

*Soul Train Hall of Fame* (AVIII 8004). New York: Adam VIII, 1973. Features Sam and Dave, the Isley Brothers, Otis Redding, the Edwin Hawkins Singers, James Brown, Clarence Carter, and others.

*Soul Train Hits That Made It Happen* (AVIII 8005). New York: Adam VIII, 1973. Features Joe Tex, the Cornelius Brothers and Sister Rose, Al Green, Curtis Mayfield, the O'Jays, the Four Tops, and others.

*Sounds Spectacular* (TU 2400). Minnetonka, Minn.: K-tel International, 1975. Features the Ohio Players, the Edgar Winter Group, Gloria Gaynor, Frankie Valli, B. W. Stevenson, and others.

*Phil Spector's Greatest Hits* (2 SP - 9104). Los Angeles: Warner Brothers Records, 1977. Features the Ronettes, the Crystals, the Righteous Brothers, Sonny Charles and the Checkmates Ltd., Ike and Tina Turner, and others.

*Super Bad* (NU 427). N.E. Minneapolis: Minn. K-tel International 1973. Features the Staple Singers, Timmy Thomas, the Chi-Lites, the Main Ingredient, and others.

*Super Groups of the 50's* (SPC 3271). Long Island City, N.Y.: Pickwick International (Mercury Records), n.d. Features the Diamonds, Platters, Crew Cuts, and Gaylords.

*The Super Hits* — 5 Vols. (SD 501/8188/8203/8224/8274). New York: Atlantic Recording Corporation, 1967 (vol. I), 1968 (vols. II and III), and 1970 (vols. IV and V). Features Crosby, Stills, Nash and Young, Led Zeppellin, Cream, Vanilla Fudge, Wilson Pickett, the Buffalo Springfield, the Bee Gees, Aretha Franklin, Barbara Lewis, the Young Rascals, Eddie Floyd, and others.

*Superhits of the Superstars* (TU 2451). Minnetonka, Minn.: K-tel International, 1975. Features Sugarloaf, Phoebe Snow, Hot Chocolate, Gwen McCrae, and others.

*Surfin' Roots* (FR 1010). Sherman Oaks, Calif.: Festival Records, 1977. Features the Beach Boys, the Surfaris, the Chantays, Dick Dale and the Del-Tones, and others.

*20 Original Winners of 1964* (R 25293). New York: Roulette
   Records, n.d. Features Marvin Gaye, the Reflections,
   Jimmy Hughes, and others.
*26 Hit Rock Classics* (P 212065). New York: Columbia
   Records/CBS, 1974. Features Johnny Nash, Curtis
   Mayfield, the O'Jays, the Isley Brothers, Lenny Welch,
   the Chambers Brothers, Aretha Franklin, and others.
*The Unforgettable Hits of the '40's and '50's* (R 214291). Univer-
   sal City, Calif.: MCA Records, n.d. Features the An-
   drews Sisters, Bing Crosby, the Mills Brothers, Ray
   Bolger, and others.
*The Very Best of the Oldies* — 2 vols. (UA-LA 335E). Los An-
   geles: United Artists Music and Record Group, 1975.
*You Must Remember These* — 2 vols. (Bell 6078/6079). New
   York: Bell Records, 1972. Features the Mello Kings, the
   Nutmegs, the Turbans, the Silhouettes, the Delfonics,
   the Box Tops, Lee Dorsey, and James and Bobby Purify.
*Your Hit Parade* (P 12750). New York: HRB Music Company
   (Columbia Records, Inc.), 1975.
C. Recordings of "live" performances
   *The Blues . . . "A Real Summit Meeting"* (BDS 5144-2). New
      York: Buddah Records, 1973. Features Willie Mae
      Thornton, Eddie Vinson, Arthur Crudup, Muddy Wa-
      ters, and others.
   *New Orleans Jazz and Heritage Festival — 1976* (SLD 9424). Los
      Angeles: Island Records, 1976. Features Professor
      Longhair, Lee Dorsey, Ernie K-Doe, Robert Parker,
      Irma Thomas, Allen Toussaint, Earl King, and Lightnin'
      Hopkins.
   *Newport in New York '72: The Soul Sessions — Vol. 6* (CST
      9028). New York: Buddah Records, Inc., 1972. Fea-
      tures Billy Eckstine, Curtis Mayfield, B. B. King, Herbie
      Mann, Les McCann, and Roberta Flack.
   *Stars of the Appollo Theatre* (KG 30788). New York: Columbia
      Records/CBS, 1973. Features Bessie Smith, Big May-
      belle, Cab Calloway, Sarah Vaughan, Billie Holiday,
      and Ella Fitzgerald.
D. Special collections

> *Alan Freed's Rock 'N' Roll Dance Party* — 4 vols. (Wins 1010-13). New York: Wins Records, n.d.
>
> Clapton, Eric, Jeff Beck, and Jimmy Page. *Guitar Boogie* (LPS 46242). New York: RCA Records, 1971.
>
> *Dance! Dance! Dance!* (CD 2023). New York: Telehouse, Inc., n.d. Features Little Eva, Joey Dee and the Starliters, the Orlons, Wilson Pickett, Hank Ballard and the Midnighters, the Olympics, and others.
>
> Freed, Alan. *Rock 'N' Roll Radio — Starring Alan Freed "The King of Rock 'N' Roll"* (MR 1087). Sandy Hook, Conn.: Radiola Company, 1978.
>
> *The Guitar Album* (Polydor Super 2659-027). London: Polydor, Ltd., 1972. Features Jimi Hendrix, Duane Allman, Freddie King, Eric Clapton, Albert King, Peter Townshend, B. B. King, Shuggie Otis, John McLaughlin, Link Wray, and others.
>
> *Pop Origins* (LP 1544). Chicago: Chess Records, n.d. Features Howlin' Wolf, Dale Hawkins, Bo Diddley, Muddy Waters, and others.
>
> *Risky Blues* (KS 1133). Nashville: Gusto Records, Inc., 1976. Features Bull "Moose" Jackson, Checkers, Hank Ballard and the Midnighters, and others.
>
> *A Tribute to Burt Bacharach: Composer, Arranger, Conductor* (SPS 5100) New York: Scepter Records, 1972. Features Dionne Warwick, Jackie DeShannon, Chuck Jackson, Jerry Butler, and others.

II. Greatest Hits Albums — Individual or Group Performances

   A. Chronological song order

> Beatles, *The Beatles/1962–1966* (SKBO 3403). New York: Apple Records, 1973.
>
> Beatles, *The Beatles/1967–1970* (SKBO 3404). New York: Apple Records, 1973.
>
> Charles, Ray. *The Ray Charles Story — Volume One* (SD 8063). New York: Atlantic Recording Corporation, 1962.
>
> Charles, Ray. *The Ray Charles Story — Volume Two* (SD 8064). New York: Atlantic Recording Corporation, 1962.
>
> Clapton, Eric. *History of Eric Clapton* (SD2-803). New York: ATCO (Atlantic Records), 1972.

Presley, Elvis. *Elvis – The Sun Session*. New York: RCA Records, 1976.

*The Sun Story, Volumes 1–6: The Story of the Legendary Sun Label of Memphis, Tennessee* (9930-901/2/3/4/5/6). Sunnyvale, Calif.: Sunnyvale Records, 1977. (Individual albums by Johnny Cash, Jerry Lee Lewis, Charlie Rich, Carl Perkins, Roy Orbison, and Carl Mann.)

B. Random song order

Bachman-Turner Overdrive, *Best of B.T.O.* (SRM-1-11-1). Chicago: Phonogram, (Mercury Records), 1976.

Baez, Joan. *The First 10 Years* (VSD 6560/61). New York: Vanguard Recording Society, n.d.

Baker, La Vern. *La Vern Baker: Her Greatest Recordings* (SD 33-372). New York: ATCO Records, 1971.

Band. *Anthology* (SKBO 11856). Hollywood, Calif.: Capital Records, 1978.

Hank Ballard and the Midnighters. *Hank Ballard and the Midnighters* (King 5003X). Nashville: Gusto Records, 1977.

Beach Boys. *Endless Summer* (SVBB 11307). Hollywood, Calif.: Capitol Records, 1974.

*The Beatles, Rock 'N' Roll Music* (SKBO 11537). Hollywood, Calif.: Capitol Records, 1976.

Bee Gees. *Bee Gees Gold* (RS 1-3006). New York: RSO Records, 1976.

Berry, Chuck. *Chuck Berry's Golden Decade* (CH 1514). New York: Chess/Janus Records, 1972.

Berry, Chuck. *Chuck Berry's Golden Decade – Volume 2* (CH 60023). New York: Chess/Janus Records, 1972.

Bo Diddley. *Bo Diddley's 16 All-Time Greatest Hits* (CK 2989). New York: Chess Records, 1973.

Brown, James. *Solid Gold: 30 Golden Hits in 21 Golden Years* (2679044). New York: Polydor, 1978.

Captain and Tennille. *The Captain and Tennille's Greatest Hits* (SP 4667). Beverly Hills, Calif.: A & M Records, 1977.

Carpenters. *The Singles, 1969–1973* (SP 3601). Beverly Hills, Calif.: A & M Records, 1973.

Cash, Johnny. *Johnny Cash's Greatest Hits – Volume One* (CS 9478). New York: Columbia Records/CBS, n.d.

Cash, Johnny. *The Johnny Cash Collection: His Greatest Hits – Volume II* (KC 30887). New York: Columbia Records/CBS, n.d.

Charles, Ray. *Greatest Hits* (ABCS 415). New York: ABC Records, 1971.

Chicago. *Chicago IX: Chicago's Greatest Hits* (PC 33900). New York: Columbia Records/CBS, 1975.

Clapton, Eric. *Clapton* (PD 5526). New York: Polydor, 1973.

Clovers. *The Clovers: Their Greatest Hits* (SD 33-374). New York: ATCO Records, 1971.

Coasters. *The Coasters – Their Greatest Recordings: The Early Years* (SD 33-371). New York: ATCO Records, 1971.

Cochran, Eddie. *Eddie Cochran: Legendary Masters Series* (UAS 9959). Los Angeles: United Artists Records, 1971.

Collins, Judy. *Colors of the Day: The Best of Judy Collins* (Elektra 75030). New York: Elektra Records, 1972.

Cooke, Sam. *The Best of Sam Cooke* (LSP 2625). New York: RCA Records, 1965.

Creedence Clearwater Revival. *Creedence Gold* (9418). Berkeley, Calif.: Fantasy Records, 1972.

Creedence Clearwater Revival. *More Creedence Gold* (9430). Berkeley, Calif.: Fantasy Records, 1973.

Croce, Jim. *Bad, Bad LeRoy Brown: Jim Croce's Greatest Character Songs* (JZ 35571). New York: Lifesong Records, 1978.

Croce, Jim. *Photographs and Memories: His Greatest Hits* (JZ 35010). New York: Lifesong Records, 1974.

Deep Purple. *When We Rock We Rock – And When We Roll, We Roll* (PRK 3223). Burbank, Calif.: Warner Brothers Records, 1978.

Denver, John. *John Denver's Greatest Hits* (CPL 1-0374). New York: RCA Records, 1973.

Denver, John. *John Denver's Greatest Hits – Volume 2* (CPL 1-2194). New York: RCA Records, 1977.

Diamond, Neil. *His 12 Greatest Hits* (MCA 2106). Universal City, Calif.: MCA Records, 1974.

Dion and the Belmonts. *The Dion Years, 1958–1963* (2103-707). Sunnyvale, Calif.: GRT Corporation, 1975.

Fats Domino. *Fats Domino: Legendary Masters Series* (USA 9958). Los Angeles: United Artists Records, 1971.

Donovan. *Donovan's Greatest Hits* (PE 26439). New York: Epic Records/CBS, n.d.

Doobie Brothers. *Best of the Doobies* (BSK 3112). Burbank, Calif.: Warner Brothers Records, 1976.

Doors. *13* (EKS 7407a). New York: Elektra Records, 1970.

Drifters. *The Drifters Golden Hits* (SD 8153). New York: Atlantic Recording Corporation, 1968.

Drifters. *The Drifters – Their Greatest Recordings: The Early Years* (SD 33–375). New York: ATCO Records, 1971.

Dylan, Bob. *Bob Dylan's Greatest Hits* (PC 9463). New York: Columbia Records/CBS, n.d.

Dylan, Bob. *Bob Dylan's Greatest, Vol. II* (PG 31120). New York: Columbia Records/CBS, 1971.

Eagles. *Their Greatest Hits, 1971–1975* (Asylum 7E-1052). Los Angeles: Elektra/Asylum/Nonesuch Records, 1976.

Eddy, Duane. *The Vintage Years* (SASH 3707-2). Los Angeles: Sire Records, 1975.

Everly Brothers. *The Golden Hits of the Everly Brothers* (WS 1471). New York: Warner Brothers Records, 1962.

Fifth Dimension. *Greatest Hits* (SCS 33900). Los Angeles: Liberty/U.A., Soul City Records, n.d.

Five Keys. *The Five Keys* (King 5013X). Nashville: Gusto Records, 1978.

Five Royales. *The Five Royales* (King 5014X). Nashville: Gusto Records, 1978.

Flamingos. *Flamingos: Chess Rock 'N' Rhythm Series* (ACRR 702). Englewood, N.J.: Chess Records, 1976.

Four Seasons. *The Four Seasons Story* (PS 7000). New York: Private Stock Records, 1975.

Franklin, Aretha. *Aretha's Greatest Hits* (SD 8295). New York: Atlantic Recording Corporation, 1971.

Franklin, Aretha. *Aretha Franklin's Greatest Hits, 1960–1965.* New York: Columbia Records/CBS, n.d.

Gaye, Marvin. *Marvin Gaye Anthology* (M9 791 A3). Hollywood, Calif.: Motown Record Corporation, 1974.

Grand Funk. *Grand Funk Hits* (ST 11579). Hollywood, Calif.: Capitol Records, 1976.

Guess Who. *The Greatest of the Guess Who* (AFL 1-2253). New York: RCA Records, 1977.

Bill Haley and His Comets. *Golden Hits* (MCA 2-4010). Universal City, Calif.: MCA Records, 1972.

Harris, Don "Sugarcane," and Dewey Terry. *Don and Dewey* (SP 2131). Hollywood, Calif.: Specialty Records, 1970.

Hawkins, Dale. *Dale Hawkins: Chess Rock 'N' Rhythm Series* (ACRR 703). Englewood, N.J.: Chess Records, 1970.

Hendrix, Jimi. *The Essential Jimi Hendrix* (2RS 2245). Burbank, Calif.: Warner Brothers Records, 1978.

Buddy Holly and the Crickets. *Buddy Holly Lives: 20 Golden Greats* (MCA 3040). Universal City, Calif.: MCA Records, 1978.

Howlin' Wolf. *Chester Burnett Aka Howlin' Wolf* (2 CH–60016). New York: Chess/Janus Records, 1972.

Impressions. *The Impressions, Featuring Jerry Butler and Curtis Mayfield: The Vintage Years* (Sash 3717-2). Los Angeles: Sire Records, 1976.

Jay and the Americans. *The Very Best of Jay and the Americans* (UA-LA 357). Los Angeles: United Artists Records, Inc., 1975.

Jefferson Airplane. *Flight Log, 1966–1976* (CYL 2-1255). New York: Grunt (RCA) Records, 1977.

John, Elton. *Elton John's Greatest Hits – Volume II* (MCA 3027). Universal City, Calif.: MCA Records, 1977.

John, Elton. *Greatest Hits* (MCA 2128). Universal City, Calif.: MCA Records, 1974.

Joplin, Janis. *Janis Joplin's Greatest Hits* (PC 32168). New York: Columbia Records/CBS, 1973.

King, Carole. *Her Greatest Hits: Songs of Long Ago* (JE 34967). New York: Ode Records/CBS, 1978.

Kristofferson, Kris. *Songs of Kristofferson* (PZ 34687). New York: Monument Records (Columbia Records/CBS), 1977.

Lennon, John. *Shaved Fish* (SW 3421). New York: Apple Records, 1975.

Lewis, Jerry Lee. *Jerry Lee Lewis: Original Golden Hits – Volume 1* (Sun 102). Nashville: Sun International Corporation, n.d.

Little Richard, *Little Richard's Grooviest 17 Original Hits* (SPS 2113). Hollywood, Calif.: Specialty Records, n.d.

Lovin' Spoonful. *The Very Best of the Lovin' Spoonful* (KSBS 2013). New York: Buddah Records, n.d.

Clyde McPhatter and the Dominoes. *The Dominoes, Featuring Clyde McPhatter* (King 5006X). Nashville: Gusto Records, 1977.

Mamas and the Papas. *Farewell to the First Golden Era* (DS 50025). New York: ABC Records, n.d.

Manilow, Barry. *Greatest Hits* (A 2L 8601). New York: Arista Records, 1978.

Mathis, Johnny. *All-time Greatest Hits* (PG 31345). New York: Columbia Records/CBS, 1972.

Mayfield, Curtis. *Curtis Mayfield: His Early Years With the Impressions* (ABCX 780-2) Los Angeles, California: ABC Records, 1973.

The Moonglows, *Moonglows: Chess Rock 'N' Rhythm Series* (UAS 9960) Los Angeles, California: United Artists Records, 1971.

Nelson, Ricky. *Ricky Nelson: Legendary Masters Series* (UAS 9960). Los Angeles: United Artists Records, 1971.

Nilsson, Harry. *Greatest Hits* (AFL 1-2798). New York: RCA Records, 1978.

Ochs, Phil. *Chords of Fame* (A & M SP 4599). Beverly Hills, Calif.: A & M Records, 1977.

Orbison, Roy. *The All-time Greatest Hits of Roy Orbison* (MP 8600). Nashville: Monument Record Corporation, 1972.

Otis, Johnny. *The Original Johnny Otis Show* (SJL 2230). New York: Savoy (Arista) Records, 1978.

Peter, Paul and Mary. *10 (Ten) Years Together: The Best of Peter, Paul and Mary* (WB 2552). Burbank, Calif.: Warner Brothers, 1970.

Pickett, Wilson. *Wilson Pickett's Greatest Hits* (SD 2-501). New York: Atlantic Recording Corporation, 1973.

Platters. *Encore of Golden Hits* (SR 60243). New York: Mercury Record Corporation, n.d.

Presley, Elvis. *Elvis* (DPL 2-0056). New York: RCA Records, 1972.

Ravens. *"The Greatest Group of Them All": Roots of Rock and Roll, Volume 3* (SJL 2227). New York: Savoy (Arista) Records, 1978.

Rawls, Lou. *The Best from Lou Rawls* (SKBB-S11585). New York: Capitol Records, 1976.

Redding, Otis. *The Best of Otis Redding* (SD 2-801). New York: ATCO Records, 1972.

Reddy, Helen. *Helen Reddy's Greatest Hits* (ST 511467). New York: Capitol Records, 1975.

Reed, Jimmy. *The Greatest Hits of Jimmy Reed – Volume I* (KST 553). Los Angeles: Kent Records, n.d.

Reed, Jimmy. *Jimmy Reed's Greatest Hits – Volume 2* (KST 562). Los Angeles: Kent Records, n.d.

Paul Revere and the Raiders Featuring Mark Lindsay, *All-Time Greatest Hits* (CG 31464). New York: Columbia Records/CBS, 1972.

Righteous Brothers. *The History of The Righteous Brothers* (SE 4885). Hollywood, Calif.: MGM Records, 1972.

Rivers, Johnny. *Superpack* (UXS 93). Los Angeles: United Artists Records, 1972.

Robbins, Marty. *Marty Robbins' All-time Greatest Hits* (CG 31361). New York: Columbia Records/BCS, 1972.

Smokey Robinson and the Miracles. *Smokey Robinson and the Miracles' Anthology* (793 R 3). Hollywood, Calif.: Motown Record Corporation, 1973.

Rogers, Kenny. *Ten Years of Gold* (VA-LA 835 H). Los Angeles: United Artists Records, 1977.

Rolling Stones. *Hot Rocks 1964–1971* (London 2PS 606-7). New York: ABKCO Records (London), 1972.

Rolling Stones. *Made in the Shade* (COC 79102). New York: Rolling Stone Records, 1975.

Ronstadt, Linda. *Greatest Hits* (Asylum 7E-1092). Los Angeles: Elektra/Asylum/Nonesuch Records, 1976.

Ronstadt, Linda. *A Retrospective* (SKBB 511629). New York: Capitol Records, 1977.

Diana Ross and the Supremes. *Diana Ross and the Supremes Anthology* (M7-794Ac). Hollywood, Calif.: Motown Record Corporation, 1974.

Russell, Leon. *Best of Leon* (SRL 52004). Los Angeles: Shelter Recording Company, 1976.

Sedaka, Neil. *Neil Sedaka's Greatest Hits* (PIG 5297). Universal City, Calif.: Rocket Record Company, 1977.

Seeger, Pete. *Pete Seeger's Greatest Hits* (CS 9416). New York: Columbia Records/CBS, n.d.

Shirelles. *The Very Best of the Shirelles* (UA-LA 340E). Los Angeles: United Artists Records, 1975.

Simon, Carly. *The Best of Carly Simon* (7E 1048). Los Angeles: Elektra/Asylum/Nonesuch Records, 1975.

Simon, Paul. *Greatest Hits, Etc.* (JC 35032). New York: Columbia Records/CBS, 1977.

Spinners. *The Best of the Spinners* (SD 19179). New York: Atlantic Recording Corporation, 1978.

Steppenwolf. *Steppenwolf Gold: Their Greatest Hits* (DSX 50099). New York: ABC Records, n.d.

Cat Stevens. *Greatest Hits* (SP 4519). Beverly Hills, Calif.: A & M Records, 1975.

Streisand, Barbra. *Barbra Streisand's Greatest Hits – Volume 2* (FC 35679). New York: Columbia Records/CBS, 1978.

Taylor, James. *Greatest Hits* (BS 2979). Burbank, Calif.: Warner Brothers Records, 1976.

Temptations. *The Temptations – Anthology: A Tenth Anniver-*

*sary Special* (M 782 A3). Hollywood, Calif.: Motown Record Corporation, 1973.

Three Dog Night. *Golden Biscuits* (DSX 50098). New York: ABC Records, n.d.

Three Dog Night. *Joy To The World – Three Dog Night: Their Greatest Hits* (DSD 50178). New York: ABC Records, 1974.

Turner, Joe. *Joe Turner: His Greatest Recordings* (SD 33-376). New York: ATCO Records, 1971.

Turtles. *The Turtles' Greatest Hits* (WW 115). Los Angeles: White Wale Records, n.d.

Billy Ward and the Dominoes. *The Dominoes* (King 5008X). Nashville: Gusto Records, 1977.

Warwick, Dionne. *Dionne Warwick's Golden Hits – Part One* (SPS 565). New York: Scepter Records, n.d.

Who. *Meaty Beaty Big and Bouncy* (DL 79184). Universal City, Calif.: MCA Records, 1971.

Williams, Hank. *24 of Hank Williams' Greatest Hits* (SE 4755-2). Hollywood, Calif.: MGM Record Corporation, n.d.

Otis Williams and the Charms. *Otis Williams and His Charms* (King 5015X). Nashville: Gusto Records, 1978.

Willis, Chuck. *Chuck Willis: His Greatest Recordings* (SD 33-372). New York: ATCO Records, 1971.

Wilson, Jackie. *Jackie Wilson's Greatest Hits* (BL 754140). New York: Brunswick Record Corporation, 1968.

Wings. *Wings Greatest* (500 11905). New York: Capitol Records, 1978.

Stevie Wonder. *Looking Back* (M 804 LP 3). Hollywood, Calif.: Motown Record Corporation, 1977.

Z Z Top. *The Best of Z Z Top* (PS 706). New York: London Records, 1977.

C. Recordings of "live" performances

Baez, Joan. *From Every Stage* (SP 3704). New York: A & M Records, 1976.

Beatles. *The Beatles at the Hollywood Bowl* (SMAS 11638). Hollywood, Calif.: Capitol Records, 1977.

Beatles. *The Beatles Live! At the Star-Club in Hamburg, Ger-*

*many—1962* (LS 2-7001). London, Eng.: Lingasong, 1977.

Belafonte, Harry. *Belafonte at Carnegie Hall: The Complete Concert* (LSO 6006). New York: RCA Victor, n.d.

Campbell, Glen. *Glen Campbell Live at the Royal Festival Hall* (SWBC 11707). Hollywood, Calif.: Capitol Records, 1977.

Cash, Johnny. *Johnny Cash at Folson Prison* (CS 9639). New York: Columbia Records/CBS, n.d.

Cash, Johnny. *Johnny Cash at San Quentin* (KC 9827). New York: Columbia Records/CBS, n.d.

Chapin, Harry. *Greatest Stories—Live* (E7-2009). Los Angeles: Elektra/Asylum/Nonesuch Records, 1976.

Charles, Ray. *Ray Charles Live* (SD 2-503). New York: Atlantic Recording Corporation, 1973.

Cocker, Joe. *Mad Dogs and Englishmen* (SP 6002). Hollywood, Calif.: A & M Records, 1970.

Diamond, Neil. *Hot August Night: Recorded in Concert at the Greek Theatre in Los Angeles* (MCA 2-8000). Universal City, Calif.: MCA Records, 1972.

Diamond, Neil. *Love at the Greek* (KC 2-34404). New York: Columbia Records/CBS, 1977.

Bob Dylan and the Band. *Before the Flood* (Asylum AB 201). New York: Elektra/Asylum/Nonesuch Records, 1974.

Frampton, Peter. *Frampton Comes Alive!* (SP3703). Beverly Hills, Calif.: A & M Records, 1976.

Franklin, Aretha. *Aretha—Live at Fillmore West* (SD 7205). New York: Atlantic Recording Corporation, 1971.

Jones, Tom. *Live in Las Vegas—At the Flamingo* (PAS 71031). New York: Parrot Records, n.d.

Kershaw, Doug. *Alive and Pickin'—Recorded Live in Atlanta* (BS 2851). Burbank, Calif.: Warner Brothers Records, 1975.

King, Albert. *Live Wire/Blues Power* (STS 2003). Memphis: Stax Records, n.d.

King, B. B. *Live in Cook County Jail* (ABCS 723). Los Angeles: ABC/Dunhill Records, 1971.

King, B. B., and Bobby Bland. *Together for the First Time . . . Live* (DSY 50190/2). Los Angeles: ABC Records, 1974.

Lewis, Jerry Lee. *The Greatest Live Show on Earth* (SRS 67056). Chicago: Smash (Mercury) Records, n.d.

Little Richard. *Little Richard's Greatest Hits* (OKS 14121). New York: Okeh Records, 1967.

McCann, Les, and Eddie Harris. *Swiss Movement* (SD 1537). New York: Atlantic Recording Corporation, 1969.

Manilow, Barry. *Barry Manilow Live* (Arista 8500). New York: Arista Records, 1977.

Mayfield, Curtis. *Curtis/Live!* (CRS 8008). New York: Buddah Records (Curtom). n.d.

Nelson, Willie. *Willie and Family Live* (KC 2-35642). New York: Columbia Records/CBS, 1978.

Peter, Paul and Mary. *In Concert* (2 WS 1555). Burbank, Calif.: Warner Brothers Records, n.d.

Presley, Elvis. *Elvis: Aloha from Hawaii via Satellite* (CPD 2-2642). New York: RCA Records, 1972.

Presley, Elvis. *Elvis in Concert* (APL 2-2587) New York: RCA Records, 1977.

Otis Redding and the Jimi Hendrix Experience. *Otis Redding/ The Jimi Hendrix Experience* (MS 2029). New York: Reprise Records, 1970.

Simon, Paul. *Live Rhymin': Paul Simon in Concert* (PC 32855). New York: Columbia Records/CBS, 1974.

Wings. *Wings over America* (SWCO 11593). New York: MPL Communications (Capitol Records), 1976.

D. Special collections

Blackwell, Otis. *These Are My Songs!* (I.C. 1032). New York: Inner City Records, 1977.

Blackwell, Otis, Eddie Cooley, Lincoln Chase, Winfield Scott, Ollie Jones, and Billy Dawn Smith, *We Wrote 'Em and We Sing 'Em* (MGM E 3912). Hollywood, Calif.: MGM Record Corporation, n.d.

Charles, Ray. *A 25th Anniversary Show Business Salute to Ray Charles: His All-Time Great Performances* (ABCH – 731). New York: ABC Records, 1971.

Crudup. Arthur "Big Boy." *Arthur "Big Boy" Crudup – The Father of Rock and Roll* (LPV 573). New York: RCA Records, 1971.

Dixon, Willie. *I Am the Blues* (CS 9987). New York: Columbia Records/CBS, n.d.

Franklin, Aretha. *The Gospel Soul of Aretha Franklin* (CH 10009). New York: Chess/Janus Records, 1972.

Lewis, Jerry Lee. *The Session* (SRM 2-803). Chicago: Phonogram, (Mercury), 1973.

III. Standard Albums

A. Individual artists

Gordon, Robert. *Rock Billy Boogie* (AFL 1-3294). New York: RCA Records, 1979.

Ian, Janis. *Between the Lines* (PC 33394). New York: Columbia Records/CBS, 1975.

Joel, Billy. *The Stranger* (JC 34987). New York: Columbia Records. CBS, 1977.

John Elton. *Captain Fantastic and the Brown Dirt Cowboy* (MCA 2142). Universal City, Calif.: MCA Records, 1975.

King, B. B. *Indianola Mississippi Seeds* (ABCS 713). Los Angeles: ABC/Dunhill Records, 1970.

King, Carole. *Tapestry* (SP 77009). Hollywood, Calif.: A & M Records, 1971.

Lennon, John. *Rock 'N' Roll* (SK 3419). New York: Apple Records, 1975.

Manilow, Barry. *Tryin' to Get the Feeling* (Arista 4060). New York: Arista Records, 1975.

Michaels, Lee. *Barrel* (SP 4249). Hollywood, Calif.: A & M Records, n.d.

Rivers, Johnny. *Blue Suede Shoes* (UA-LA 075F). Los Angeles: United Artists Records, 1972.

Ronstadt, Linda. *Living in the USA* (6E 155). Los Angeles: Elektra/Asylum Records, 1978.

Sedaka, Neil. *Sedaka's Back* (MCA 463). Universal City, Calif.: MCA Records, (Rocket Record Company), 1974.

Simon, Paul. *Still Crazy after All These Years* (PC 33540). New York: Columbia Records/CBS, 1975.

Summer, Donna. *Bad Girls* (NBLP 2-7150). Los Angeles, Calif.: Casablanca Records, 1979.

Taj Mahal. *The Natch'l Blues* (CS 9698). New York: Columbia Records, n.d.

Stevie Wonder. *Songs in the Key of Life* (T13-340C2). Hollywood, Calif.: Motown Record Corporation, 1976.

B. Group performances

Beatles. *Sgt. Pepper's Lonely Hearts Club Band* (SMAS 2653). Hollywood, Calif.: Capitol Records (EMI), 1967.

Crosby, Stills, Nash and Young (with Dallas Taylor and Greg Reeves). *Deja Vu* (SD 7200). New York: Atlantic Recording Corp., 1970.

Derek and the Dominos (Eric Clapton). *Layla* (ATCO SD 2-704). New York: ATCO Records, 1970.

Eagles. *Hotel California* (Asylum 6E-103). Los Angeles, Calif.: Elektra/Asylum/Nonesuch Records, 1976.

Fleetwood Mac. *Rumors* (BSK 3010). Burbank, Calif.: Warner Brothers Records, 1977.

Buddy Holly and the Crickets, *The Buddy Holly Story* (SRL 57279). New York: Coral Records, n.d.

Jefferson Airplane. *Volunteers* (LSP 4238). New York: RCA Records, 1969.

Loggins and Messina. *"So Fine"* (PC 33810). New York: Columbia Records, 1977.

Steve Miller Band. *Book of Dreams* (SO 11630). Los Angeles: Capitol Records, 1977.

Persuasions. *The Chirpin' Persuasions* (7E 1099). Los Angeles: Elektra/Asylum Records, 1977.

Rolling Stones. *Some Girls* (COC 39108). New York: Rolling Stones Records, 1978.

Bob Seger and the Silver Bullet Band. *Stranger in Town* (SW 11698). Hollywood, Calif.: Capitol Records, 1978.

Simon and Garfunkel. *Bridge over Troubled Water* (KCS 9914). New York: Columbia Records/CBS, n.d.

Simon and Garfunkel. *Sounds of Silence* (CS 9269) New York: Columbia Records, 1965.

Ike and Tina Turner. *Workin' Together* (LST 7650). Los Angeles: Liberty/U.A., n.d.

Who. *Tommy* (MCA 2-10005). Universal City, Calif.: MCA Records, 1973.

Jackie Wilson and Count Basie, *Manufacturers of Soul* (BL 754134). New York: Brunswick Record Corporation, 1968.

IV. Other types of albums

  A. Motion picture soundtracks

    *American Graffiti* (MCA 2-8001). Universal City, Calif.: MCA Records, 1973. Features the Crests, Heartbeats, Frankie Lymon and the Teenagers, Buddy Knox, Clovers, and others.

    *American Hot Wax* (SP 6500). Beverly Hills, Calif.: A & M Records, Inc., 1978. Features the Spaniels, Little Richard, Moonglows, Buddy Holly, Drifters, Jackie Wilson, and others.

    *Animal House* (MCA 3046). Universal City, Calif.: MCA Records, 1978. Features Sam Cooke, Chris Montez, Paul and Paula, Bobby Lewis, and others.

    Band. *The Last Waltz* (3 WS 3146). Burbank, Calif.: Warner Brothers Records, 1978. Features Bob Dylan, Neil Diamond, Joni Mitchell, Ringo Starr, Neil Young, Eric Clapton, and others.

    Beatles. *Yellow Submarine* (SW 153). Hollywood, Calif.: Capitol Records, 1968.

    Busey, Gary. *The Buddy Holly Story* (SE 35412). New York: Epic Records, 1978.

    *Bye Bye Birdie* (LSO 1081). New York: RCA Records, 1963.

    *Car Wash* (MCA 2-600). Universal City, Calif.: MCA Records, 1976.

    *Cooley High* (M7 840 R2). Hollywood, Calif.: Motown Record Corporation, 1975. Features Diana Ross and the Supremes, Stevie Wonder, the Four Tops, Martha Reeves and the Vandellas, the Marvellettes, the Temptations, Mary Wells, and others.

*F.M.* (MCA 2-12000). Universal City, Calif.: MCA Records, 1978. Features Boston, Jimmy Buffett, the Doobie Brothers, the Eagles, Foreigner, Billy Joel, Steve Miller, Queen, Linda Ronstadt, Boz Scaggs, Bob Seeger, James Taylor, Joe Walsh, Steely Dan, and others.

*Godspell: A Musical Based upon the Gospel According to St. Matthew* (Bell 1102). Scarborough 703, Ontario, Canada: Quality Records (Bell Records), 1971.

*The Graduate* (OS 3180). New York: Columbia Records/CBS, n.d. Features Simon and Garfunkel.

*Grease* (RS 2-4002). Los Angeles: RSO Records, 1978. Features Sha-Na-Na, Frankie Valli, John Travolta, Olivia Newton-John, Frankie Avalon, and others.

*Hair: The American Tribal Love-Rock Musical* (LSO 1150). New York: RCA Records, 1973.

Hamlisch, Marvin. *The Sting* (MCA 2040). Universal City, Calif.: MCA Records, 1973.

*Jesus Christ Superstar* (MCA 2-11000). Universal City, Calif.: MCA Records, 1973.

*Let the Good Times Roll* (Bell 9002). New York: Bell Records, 1973. Features Chubby Checker, Bill Haley and the Comets, Danny and the Juniors, Fats Domino, the Shirelles, the Coasters, Bo Diddley, the Five Satins, and Little Richard.

*Looking for Mr. Goodbar* (JS 35029). New York: Columbia Records/CBS, 1977. Features Donna Summer, the Commodores, Thelma Houston, Diana Ross, the O'Jays, Boz Scaggs, Bill Withers, and others.

Mayfield, Curtis. *Superfly* (CRS 8014-ST). New York: Curtom (Buddah) Records, 1972.

*Rocky* (UA-LA 693 G). Los Angeles: United Artists Records, 1976.

Ross, Diana. *Lady Sings the Blues* (M 756 D). Detroit: Motown Record Corporation, 1972.

*Saturday Night Fever* (RS 2-4001). Los Angeles: RSO Records, 1977. Features the Bee Gees, Yvonne Elliman, Walter Murphy, Tavares, K. C. and the Sunshine Band, and the Trammps.

*Sgt. Pepper's Lonely Hearts Club Band* (RS 2-4100). New York: RSO Records, 1978. Features Peter Frampton; the Bee Gees; Aerosmith; Alice Cooper; Billy Preston; Earth, Wind and Fire; and others.

*"Thank God It's Friday"*. Los Angeles: Casablanca Records, 1978. Features Donna Summer, Diana Ross, the Commodores, Santa Esmeralda, Thelma Houston, Cameo, and others.

*Tommy* (PD 2-9502). New York: Polydor, 1975. Features Elton John, Eric Clapton, Tina Turner, the Who, and others.

*Wattstax: The Living Word* (STS 2-3018). Memphis: Stax Records, 1973. Features Kim Weston, Johnny Taylor, Isaac Hayes, and others.

*Wattstax 2: The Living Word* (STS 2-3018). Memphis: Stax Records, 1973. Features Kim Weston, Johnny Taylor, Isaac Hayes, and others.

Williams, John. *Close Encounters of the Third Kind* (AL 9500). New York: Arista Records, 1977.

*Woodstock* (SD 3-500). New York: Cotillion Records, 1970. Features Jimi Hendrix, Jefferson Airplane, Richie Havens, Arlo Guthrie, Country Joe McDonald and the Fish, Joan Baez, and others.

B. Comedy albums

Buchanan and Goodman. *The Original Flying Saucers* (NCS 9000). New York: IX Chains, n.d.

*25 Years of Recorded Comedy* (3 BX 3131). Burbank, Calif.: Warner Brothers Records, 1977. Features Lenny Bruce, Shelley Berman, Richard Pryor, Lily Tomlin, Gabriel Kaplan, Stan Freberg, Cheech and Chong, David Frye, and others.

C. Bootleg albums

(Librarians seeking to fulfill a patron's request for a bootleg album should contact William L. Schurk, director of the Audio Center at the Bowling Green State University Library in Bowling Green, Ohio. The exorbitant prices of bootleg discs and the lack of quality control in these recordings should discourage all but the most specialized collectors from attempting to add bootleg items to standard audio holdings.)

D.  Imported recordings

It may seem peculiar that Japan, England, Holland, and Germany are producing some of the best reissue recordings of American rock music. The albums listed in this section are currently available in most large record stores at prices competitive with American records.

*The American Dream: The Cameo-Parkway Story, 1957–1962* (Dream U¾). London: London Records, n.d. Features Chubby Checker, Dee Dee Sharp, the Orlons, the Dovells, Jo Ann Campell, Charlie Gracie, the Rays, and others.

*Charly's Angels* (CR 30143). London: Charly (Pye) Records, n.d. Features the Shangri La's, the Jelly Beans, the Ad Libs, the Butterflies, Evie Sands, and the Dixie Cups.

Domino Fats, *The Fats Domino Story – 6 Volumes* (UAS 30067/68/69/99/100/118). London: United Artists Records, 1977.

*"Don't You Step on My Blue Suede Shoes"* (CR 30119). London: Charly (Pye) Records, n.d. Features Charlie Rich, Johnny Cash, Carl Mann, Roy Orbison, Warren Smith, Jerry Lee Lewis, and others.

*Flashbacks: 20 Rock and Roll Favourites – Volume 1* (SNTF 780). London: Sonet Productions, 1978. Features Don and Dewey, Lloyd Price, Little Richard, Sam Cooke, and others.

Holly, Buddy. *Legend* (CDMSP 802). Middlesex, Eng.: MCA Coral, n.d.

Presley, Elvis. *Elvis: The '56 Sessions – Volume 1* (PL 42101). London: RCA LTD., 1978.

*The Red Bird Era: The Hit Factory – Volume 1* (CR 30108). London: Charly (Pye) Records, n.d. Features the Dixie Cups, the Shangri La's, the Ad Libs, the Jelly Beans, the Tradewinds, Sid Barnes, Sam Hawkins, and the Robbins.

*The Red Bird Era: The New York Sound and the New Orleans Connection — Volume 2* (CR 30109). London: Charly (Pye) Records, n.d. Features Alvin Robinson, the Dixie Cups, the Ad Libs, Evie Sands, the Robbins, "Shadow" Morton, Jeff and Ellie, and the Butterflies.

*Sun — The Roots of Rock: The History of the Legendary Sun Record Company of Memphis, Tennessee — 13 Volumes* (CR 30101-06/14-17/26-28). London: Charly Records, n.d.

*Walking the Back Streets and Crying: The Stax Blues Masters* (STM 7004). Middlesex, Eng.: Stax (EMI Records), 1978. Features Little Milton, Little Sonny, Albert King, Johnnie Taylor, Freddie Robinson, and Isreal "Popper Stopper" Tolbert.

E.  Special collections and documentary recordings

*The Beatles' Story: A Narrative and Musical Biography of Beatlemania* (STBO 2222). Hollywood, Calif.: Capitol Records, n.d.

*Elvis Presley: Interviews and Memories of the Sun Years* (Sun 1001). Memphis: Sun International Corporation, 1977.

*50 Years of Film: Original Motion Picture Soundtrack Recordings of the Great Scenes and Stars from the Warner Brothers Classics, 1923 to 1973.* Burbank, Calif.: Warner Brothers Records, 1973.

Holly, Buddy. *Buddy Holly "Live": The Only Unreleased "Live" Recordings of Buddy Holly and His Crickets — Volume 1* (C 001000). N.p.: Cricket Records, n.d.

Holly, Buddy. *Buddy Holly "In Person" — Volume 2* (C 002000). N.p.: Cricket Records, n.d.

*The Motown Story* (MS 5-726). Detroit: Motown Record Corporation, 1970.

Presley, Elvis. *Elvis — The King Speaks: February 1961 in Memphis, Tennessee* (GNW 4006). Seattle: Great Northwest Music Company, 1977.

Presley, Elvis. *Elvis: A Legendary Performer — Volume 1* (CPL 1-0341). New York: RCA Records, 1973

Presley, Elvis. *Elvis: A Legendary Performer – Volume 2* (CPL 1-1349). New York: RCA Records, 1976.

Presley, Elvis. *Elvis: A Legendary Performer – Volume 3* (CPL 1-3082). New York: RCA Records, 1978.

Presley, Elvis. *"The Elvis Tapes"* (GNW 4005). Seattle: Great Northwest Music Company, 1977.

*Twenty-Five Years of Recorded Sound from the Vaults of M-G-M Records.* New York: DRG Archive, 1979.

# THIRTEEN

# Record Reviews
# as Teaching Resources

AMERICAN GRAFFITI

*41 Original Hits from the Soundtrack of "American Graffiti"*
(MCA 2-8001). Universal City, Calif.: MCA Records, Inc., 1973.

Can a historian create an authentic image of American society between 1955 and 1962 through the use of popular records? If the forty-one songs provided on the *American Graffiti* album are all that he has to work with, then the answer is an emphatic "No!" This conclusion, however, does not preclude the possibility of developing an audio sequence that *does* depict an accurate historical picture; it merely condemns a single effort that is lacking in thematic continuity, social and political content, and chronological reliability.

*American Graffiti* presents a random selection of songs from the early age of rock which provide the lyrical background for a motion picture directed by George Lucas. The music is employed as an audio bridge to the year 1962—where carhops, going steady, petting, burger stands, disc jockeys, sock hops, hoods, and drag races were the dominant fads among teenagers. Under the mystical guidance of platterman Wolfman Jack, the youngsters in the film cruise along a seemingly endless river of sound as they pursue their urban-based Huck Finn fantasies. For a thirty-year-old, the "oldies but goodies" presented on the album should create a strong sense of nostalgia; for the contemporary teenager, the sounds might provide a unique passage into the pre-Beatles era; but for the social historian, the melodies and lyrics resemble the ruins of Pompeii, demanding a monumental effort in reorganization and interpretation in order to come close to reconstructing reality.

The two-record *American Graffiti* album creates myths and shuns reality. The year 1962 was the nadir, not the pinnacle, of the "golden age of rock." Elvis Presley had chosen the military and the movies over the rock and roll circuit, Chuck Berry was in jail and Jerry Lee Lewis was in "social exile," Little Richard had abandoned rock for religion, and Buddy Holly, Ritchie Valens, the Big Bopper, and Eddie Cochran were dead. Although glamour boys of the Bobby Vinton/Bobby Vee mold had attempted to replace the missing rockers, it wasn't until 1964 that the Beatles and the Rolling Stones launched a rebirth of rock in the United States. It is ironic, and historically unbelievable, that the *American Graffiti* album omits the works of the master rockers – "Heartbreak Hotel" (1956), "Whole Lotta Shakin' Goin' On" (1957), and "Good Golly Miss Molly" (1958). Director Lucas should have read Charlie Gillett's Columbia University master's thesis *The Sound of The City: The Rise of Rock and Roll.*

The real nightmare for the historian in *American Graffiti* is its lack of chronological order and its unidentifiable thematic pattern. The songs of side one/record one, for instance, are arranged in the following disorder: 1955, 1958, 1961, 1956, 1957, 1959, 1957, and 1959. These songs deal with a series of seemingly unrelated topics ranging from dancing ("Rock around the Clock,'" "At the Hop" and "The Stroll"), to birthdays ("Sixteen Candles"), to lost love ("Runaway" and "Fanny Mae"), to arrogance ("That'll Be the Day"), and to love ("She's So Fine" and "See You in September"). A more sophisticated approach to combining pop lyrics with identifiable social and political themes can be found in two lyric anthologies: Stephanie Spinner's *Rock Is Beautiful* (1970) and Bruce L. Chipman's *Hardening Rock: An Organic Anthology of the Adolescence of Rock 'N' Roll* (1972).

No artistic work is completely without merit or historical value. Although *American Graffiti* falls far short of becoming the audio historian's answer to Frederick Lewis Allen's brilliant text *Only Yesterday*, it does provide an accurate sense of the low level of electronic equipment employed by Fifties groups. It also demonstrates, if only negatively, the lack of lyrical sophistication and the dearth of social commentary provided by pre-Vietnam, pre-Dylan, pre-Watts, and pre-Kent State songwriters. Finally, the stylistic distinctions of the present music industry—the "Motown sound" et al.—are not nearly as vivid in the classic discs. There are several other albums depicting the evolution of the rock era, such as the *History of Rhythm and Blues, 1947–1967* (eight vols.) by the Atlantic Recording Corporation, *Echoes of a Rock Era* (three vols.) by Roulette Records, Inc., and *Cruisin' 1955–63* (nine vols.) by Increase Records, which accomplish all of these low-level objectives in a more successful fashion than *American Graffiti*.

If you are seeking entertainment for the faculty lounge or background music for a reunion of the class of 1960, then you may wish to purchase *American Graffiti*. But if you are committed to pursuing the reflective examination of American society through the study of lyrics from popular songs, then an investment in an album by Bob Dylan, Marvin Gaye, Curtis Mayfield, Simon and Garfunkel, Phil Ochs, or the Beatles would be far more appropriate.

## CHUCK BERRY'S GOLDEN DECADE

*Chuck Berry's Golden Decade.* (CH 1514). New York: Chess/Janus Records, 1972.

*Chuck Berry's Golden Decade, Volume 2.* (CH 60023) New York: Chess/Janus Records, 1972.

*The London Chuck Berry Sessions.* (CH 60020) New York: Chess/ Janus Records, 1972.

The magazine commentaries of H. L. Mencken and Walter Lippmann have been crucial to social historians in analyzing the nature of American life during the 1920s. Although the opinions of these men were couched in brief articles, the perceptiveness of their observations is of far greater value than thousands of pages drafted by less cogent thinkers. This same principle of condensed verbiage may be applied to examining musical lyrics for historical purposes. Just as there were many journalists in the 1920s and only a few of the Mencken-Lippmann standard, so today there are many popular singers and songwriters but only a small number with the descriptive and analytical talents of Bob Dylan, Paul Simon, Joe South, Joni Mitchell, or Paul McCartney. One of these contemporary lyrical giants is Charles Edward Berry.

Chuck Berry emerged as a popular recording star for Chess Records of Chicago in 1955. His first release – "Maybellene" – ranked as high as 42 on the *Billboard* Top 100 chart. Despite the racist label attached to the rhythm and blues songs of black artists in the mid-1950s, Chuck Berry produced hit after hit. "Roll Over Beethoven" rose to 29; "School Day" peaked at 5 after twenty-six weeks on the *Billboard* list; "Rock and Roll Music" and "Johnny B. Goode" both climbed to position 8 in 1957 and 1958, respectively; and "Sweet Little Sixteen" closed at 2 during a sixteen-week period of popularity. The Chuck Berry hit phenomenon stretches from 1955 to the present. During the 1960s his recording productivity slowed considerably, but eight of his 45 r.p.m. releases reached *Billboard*'s Top 100. And in early 1970, on the strength of laudatory comments by the Beatles and the Rolling Stones and during a surge of rock and roll nostalgia, Chuck Berry regained his hit-making power with a revised version of his classic "Reelin' and Rockin' " and a new novelty song entitled "My Ding-A-Ling."

The release of three Chuck Berry albums in 1972 provides a fine opportunity for cultural historians to examine the scope and quality of his lyrical social commentary. The two *Golden Decade* collections and the *London Session* performance provide excellent classroom materials for reflective examination of the images and issues presented by a youth-oriented black performer. His consistent popularity among young people, the fact that he has always been a total performer (singer, writer, dancer, and musician), and the dramatic effect of his songs on the entire field of popular music make him a seminal figure in contemporary audio production. The themes of his songs are manifestly personal. They evince a minstrel's approach to life. Chuck Berry's song-poems are pointed observations about the life-styles of young people in urban-industrial America. He notes the lack of relevance in the public school experience ("School Day," "Too Much Monkey Business," and "Anthony Boy"); he depicts the universal reliance of the young on popular music as a medium of emotional communication and celebration ("Rock and Roll Music," "Round and Round," and "Go, Go, Go");

he capsules the invigorating but confusing process of social maturation ("Almost Grown," "Sweet Little Sixteen," and "Sweet Little Rock and Roller"); he constructs a series of twentieth-century Horatio Algers ("Johnny B. Goode," "Bye Bye Johnny," and "You Never Can Tell"); he eulogizes the role of the automobile in the youth culture ("Maybellene," "Carol," "Come On," "No Particular Place to Go," and "No Money Down"); he condemns the fickleness of the female heart ("Nadine" and "Little Queenie"); and he describes the image of America to teenagers everywhere ("Back in the U.S.A.").

The thematic consistency of Chuck Berry's lyrics constitutes only one aspect of his uniqueness. He is also a creative force in language usage (a quality that Mencken surely would have applauded). In addition to employing standard slang terminology such as "machine" for automobile and "cruisin' " for driving in his tunes, Chuck Berry initiates fascinating verbal images which come to symbolize the characters or scenes that he describes. For instance, Johnny B. Goode doesn't just sit beside a railroad track and play his guitar; the rhythm of the trains becomes the rhythm of his strumming. The fellow who trades his beat-up Ford for a new Cadillac shuns ordinary gasoline, preferring to fill his new car with aviation fuel instead. Students at a dance do not merely listen to their favorite rock-and-roll songs;.the music becomes a physical experience for them. Finally, the young women of Chuck Berry's lyrical world inevitably face the transition period called "The Grown-Up Blues" when they must begin to wear sophisticated clothes, cosmetics, and high heeled shoes.

For the social historian, the literary analyst, or the cultural sociologist, these three Chuck Berry albums are potential gold mines for study. The sources of youthful pleasure are lyrically cataloged (dating, driving, dames, dancing, and deejays), along with the causes for teenage unrest and alienation (unemployment, public school irrelevance, parental distrust, lack of physical mobility, and the insecurity of love). Beneath these themes one notes the tremendous influence of money and materialistic goals. The image of California as the "Promised Land" and the notion that the "big car" symbolizes success and happiness are also significant. Almost all of the factors that have been identified as sources of human frustration by such respected scholars as David Riesman, C.

Wright Mills, Theodore Roszak, and Edgar Z. Friedenberg are illustrated poetically in the lyrics of Chuck Berry. Although this undoubtedly wasn't the reason for releasing these three albums, it is certainly ample justification for utilizing these discs in high school or college classrooms.

## RAY CHARLES' GREATEST HITS

Ray Charles, *Greatest Hits* (ABCS-
415). New York: ABC-Paramount
Records, 1971.

He's the "Genius of Soul," a "classic rocker," the "Blues Giant," and a "Jazz King." Each of these laudatory titles has been used to describe gifted singer-pianist-composer-arranger Ray Charles. The breadth of his musical talent is staggering. One critic recently noted that the lyrical material presented by "Uncle Ray" is always of secondary importance. From ballads to blues and beyond, the source of his magic stems from the personalized quality of the man's sound. "Through the myriad of musical styles runs the unique, dominating voice of Ray Charles — sometimes tender, sometimes guttural, sometimes pleading, sometimes demanding. Ray's vocal style changes the music; the music never changes him."

This *Greatest Hits* album may seem to be an unlikely selection for a record review today. It was originally released in 1962 as a mono disc; nine years later ABC Records reissued the same songs in a stereo package. Historically, this leaves quite a void. The album ignores Ray Charles' "country and western" involvement during the pre-Beatles period; it fails to reckon with his major motion picture scores — *Cincinnati Kid* and *In the Heat of the Night*; and it omits several of his more recent hits such as "Busted," "Crying Time," "Let's Go Get Stoned," "Yesterday." Nevertheless, this twelve-song record offers the most concise audio statement of the versatility of the magnificent "Mr. C." For the full treat(ment), listen to the thirty-six tunes featured on *A 25th Anniversary in Show Business Salute to Ray Charles: His All-Time Great Performances* (ABCH-712/2 records).

Ray Charles handles the common blues theme of wicked, cheating female trickery with style and grace. His response to the liberationist image of the misunderstood Ms. is obvious. Man's greatest problem has never been his inhumanity to his fellow man; the biblical Eve has always been in cahoots with some shady snake, seeking to cause the honest Adams of the earth garden pain, misery, sorrow, jealousy—the genuine stuff of the blues.

Personal feelings dominate most of this album. The songs illustrate an introspective viewpoint as the singer expresses doubts about his girl friend's fidelity, about the nature of his freedom, and about his inability to endure the pain of lost love. Only one tune from the disc—"Sticks and Stones"—proclaims the power of the individual to ignore social criticism. Elsewhere, Ray Charles seems to bemoan his fate in tones of singular despair and insecurity. Love is at the same time the cause and the cure of pain, as the wounded lover seeks comfort from the woman who causes his grief.

The organ-playing magic of Ray Charles dominates "One Mint Julep," the final piece of the album. The rolling chords and the soft-spoken request to the invisible barkeeper for a soda are unmistakable signs of the gentle genius at work. Other cuts of merit on the album include "Georgia on My Mind," "Hit the Road Jack," "Ruby," and "Unchain My Heart." This record is truly an audio feast.

Unfortunately, the history of the "Age of Rock" will probably be written by a few men with little imagination and less talent. Biography and history often happen that way. But if the footnote-mongers will pause long enough to reflect upon the giants of the age, they will have to apply capital letters to a few names—BOB DYLAN, CHUCK BERRY, RAY CHARLES.

## LET THE GOOD TIMES ROLL

*Let the Good Times Roll* (Bell 9002).
New York: Bell Records, 1973.

This album is an unbalanced mixture of historical commentary, promotional trivia, and musical nostalgia. For the history teacher seeking to enrich a popular culture unit through a nontraditional instructional resource, however, the selections on this recording might be ideal. The two-record package, created by promoter Richard Nader from the soundtrack of the Columbia motion picture *Let the Good Times Roll* is presented in systematic patterns of documentary radio comments, disc jockey introductions, and contemporary performances of nostalgia tunes from the late 1950s. The music on this album was originally taped during the Fourth Annual Rock and Roll Festival, which was held in 1972 at the Felt Forum of Madison Square Garden. The featured artists and songs include: Chubby Checker ("Pony Time," "Let's Twist Again," and "The Twist"), Bill Haley and the Comets ("Rock around the Clock" and "Shake, Rattle, and Roll"), Danny and the Juniors ("At the Hop"), Fats Domino ("My Blue Heaven" and "Blueberry Hill"), the Shirelles ("Everybody Loves a Lover" and "Soldier Boy"), the Coasters ("Poison Ivy" and "Charlie Brown"), Bo Diddley ("I'm a Man" and "Hey Bo Diddley"), the Five Satins ("Save the Last Dance for Me," "Sincerely," "Earth Angel," "[I'll Remember] In the Still of the Night," and "I'll Be Seeing You"), and Little Richard ("Lucille," "Good Golly Miss Molly," and "Rip It Up").

The value of this oral history resource is two-fold. First, the songs presented clearly depict the low degree of literary merit and the scarcity of political commentary that typified the music of the Eisenhower years. With the exception of Bo Diddley and Little Richard, the artists on this album utilize material developed either by commercial writers (Jerry Leiber and Mike Stoller) or by other little-known rhythm and blues performers (Don Covay, Harvey Fuqua, and Hank Ballard); the age of singing-composing superstars – Stevie Wonder, Bob Dylan, Neil Diamond, Carole King, John Lennon, Paul McCartney, and Joni Mitchell – was clearly a decade away. Second, the radio clips and off-stage commentaries that precede each musical rendition are priceless. For example, the fear of an American cultural collapse voiced by the commissioner of public safety of Jersey City, New Jersey, in response to a request to conduct a rock concert in his town is indicative of the white, middle-class response to the growing popularity of "race records." But even more significant are the impromptu observations about early '50s social life by several black rock giants, illustrating the overriding pressure of the American caste system. Bo Diddley recalls the harsh segregation system that required "colored singers" to go to the back door of a restaurant to get served "a damned cheese sandwich"; Little Richard reflects on Pat Boone's "white sound" plagiarism of many of his original hits; and the Coasters discuss the failure of most students of pop music to understand or acknowledge the key musical contributions of early rhythm and blues groups such as the Orioles, the Five Royales, the Dominoes, and the Midnighters.

The shortcomings of *Let the Good Times Roll* are numerous. Some are forgivable; some are not. Since no producer can be faulted for failing to bring the dead back to life, it is simply sad to note the absence of Frankie Lymon, Clyde McPhatter, Buddy Holly, Eddie Cochran, Sam Cooke, and Gene Vincent from the album. Other omissions, however, are unexplainable; why Elvis Presley, Chuck Berry, Carl Perkins, the Platters, and Jerry Lee Lewis are omitted is a mystery. Similarly, the use of '60s singer Chubby Checker in place of the other original '50s greats is a critical historical error. Numerous technical problems also mar this disc. These conditions can be variously attributed to crowd noises, the inconsistency of the support bands, and ineffective microphone placement. A final problem with the album is related to song selection. The editing seems arbitrary and uneven, to the point of providing too much of the Five Satins (8:52) and too little of Danny and the Juniors (2:35).

This nostalgia disc, which was an unsuccessful attempt to duplicate the commercial success of *American Graffiti* (MCA 2-8001), offers no objective standards by which to select "classic" tunes or from which to rate the "real" stars of the early "Age of Rock." Perhaps this is an unfair criticism, though, since nostalgia defies quantification. This album would have been more valuable to a historian if the "good times" had been rolled from original radio tapes from the 1950s, as on the thirteen-volume *Cruisin'* series produced by Increase Records, which features real deejays playing original sounds with authentic commercial breaks.

*Let the Good Times Roll* also fails to approach some of the most difficult questions of popular music history: What happened to the "magic" of '50s rock and roll during the early '60s? Why have Fats Domino and Chuck Berry been lionized, while other early rock stars such as Hank Ballard and Bo Diddley continue to be ignored? What fundamental elements of musical innovation and commercialism have enabled the rock era to thrive for more than two decades? Who were the prime movers behind the rhythm and blues revolution which brought black artists from the shadows to the spotlight in American popular music?

The innovative history instructor should not hesitate to *Let the Good Times Roll* in his or her classroom. However, even a light dose of this musical nostalgia album should be carefully tempered with warnings about the numerous limitations of this audio learning resource.

## STILL CRAZY AFTER ALL THESE YEARS

Paul Simon, *Still Crazy after All These Years* (PC 33540). New York City: Columbia Records/CBS. Inc., 1975.

Early in 1976 rock critic Steve Simels described the songs on Paul Simon's *Still Crazy after All These Years* as ". . . so vile that they have cast a retroactive pall on some of his earlier work." This is a heavy indictment. But Simels' criticism didn't end there. Reflecting on Simon's past hits, the *Stereo Review* pundit labeled "The Sounds of Silence" sophomoric, referred to "Bridge over Troubled Water" as pure corn, and condemned most of the songwriter's other tunes as vintage kitsch. Is this negative assessment of Paul Simon common among other record reviewers, rock performers, and fans of popular music? Of course not. But Simels' feelings should call attention to one undisputable fact. The highly acclaimed *Still Crazy* album deserves special attention.

In a 1970 *Psychology Today* interview Warren G. Bennis, full-time sociologist and sometime college president, remarked, "Perhaps only a Homer or Herodotus, or a first-rate folk-rock composer, could capture the tumult and tragedy of the last five years and measure their impact upon our lives." Among the first-rate folk-rock composers of today, Paul Simon is preeminent. Bob Dylan is clearly the past master; Paul McCartney flies high but also dips low with his new Wings; Stevie Wonder offers fascinating glimpses into the consciousness of black America; and Janis Ian continually mystifies our senses. Still, it is the

impish Simon who poetically captures the sense of his time and trans-
lates it into memorable, personal vignettes.

Unfortunately, the image of American society presented in *Still
Crazy after All These Years* is something less than favorable. Paul Simon
has created an album of black humor and dark thoughts. The nostalgic
element of the title song is marred by the singer's haunting fear that he'll
"Do some damage one fine day." In "My Little Town," Simon describes
adolescence as a dreary period of "Dreaming of glory. / Twitching like
a finger on the trigger of a gun." The themes of lost love, fading trust,
and noncommitment in personal relationships dominate offerings such
as "I Do It for Your Love" and "Fifty Ways to Leave Your Lover." And
finally, a moribund alienation and a sense of fatalism emerge in lyrical
statements such as, "I've had a long streak of that bad luck / But I'm
praying it's gone at last." This sentiment, articulated in upbeat terms in
"Gone At Last," is followed by the down tempo generalization that ". . .
most folks' lives, they stumble / Lord they fall / through no fault of
their own most folks never catch their stars."

The impact of Simon's apocalyptic words is somewhat masked by
the beautiful orchestration of the album. The joyous sounds to be
found on this album seem an unlikely vehicle for a poet's warnings of
impending personal disaster. Yet the folk-rock genre frequently blends
messages of unrest with rhythms of joy and abandon. It is difficult to
believe the majestic humanism exhibited by the writer of "Bridge over
Troubled Water" has been replaced by such depths of disenchantment.
Of course, before he crossed the "Bridge" Paul Simon had already
walked the dark side of the emotional street with "I Am a Rock,"
"Richard Cory," "A Most Peculiar Man," and "The Sounds of Silence."

What solution does Paul Simon offer to this situation? Sadly, none —
unless one believes that his invocation about "Have a Good Time" is an
existential way out. This album is particularly disturbing because it is
the product of one of popular music's most respected minds. It is not
social protest or propaganda; it is not sensationalism; it is not even,
entirely morbid in the sense of combining heavy, crushing melodies
with apocalyptic words. But it is significant. And to look closely at the
album cover, one can see the faded image of urban America behind the
figure of a Jacob Riis-type character standing on a fire escape. It is
enough to make Paul Simon grin.

ELVIS—THE SUN SESSIONS

Elvis Presley, *Elvis — The Sun Sessions*
(AOM 1 - 1675). Distributed by RCA
Records, Inc., of New York, New
York. Released 1976.

For more than two decades the voice of Elvis Presley dominated the American popular music scene. In a realm of entertainment where popularity ebbs and flows as frequently as the New England tides, Elvis remained a durable constant. Perhaps it was because of his uncanny ability to attract fans from all age brackets; perhaps it was due to his skills in performing songs from every musical genre—pop, gospel, country, rock, and rhythm and blues. Whatever the reason, the singer who launched the "Rock Revolution" in 1955 continued to straddle the movement. Elvis was undeniably "The King."

But why have historians and history teachers chosen to ignore such a potent cultural force? Elvis and the popular music phenomenon have commanded the attention of millions of Americans for twenty years, yet both are virtually unrepresented in the pages of historical scholarship.

Responding to the counsel of respected authors ranging from Thomas Carlyle to John A. Garraty, history teachers have frequently attempted to spark student enthusiasm for studying historical trends by utilizing biographies. Obviously, pivotal figures and their roles in watershed events can provide the basis for exciting investigations of the past. The images of great men—Washington, Jefferson, Lincoln, Edison, Rockefeller, and others—are the personal links to the impersonal facts, dates, and trends in history. The reader might reflect for a moment on his or her own experience in studying America in the 1950s. Undoubtedly, your textbook systematically assessed the rise and fall of Joseph McCarthy, the ascendency of Dwight D. Eisenhower, and the personalities involved in the Suez Crisis, the Hungarian Revolt, and the launching of Sputnik. These events were admittedly "crucial," to borrow Eric Goldman's term. Yet one must acknowledge that they touched the lives of only a limited portion of the American public during that decade. It is time for historians to begin to broaden their studies to include fields such as popular music, a cultural experience which has united millions of Americans, from the generation of Korea and Alger Hiss to the generation of Vietnam and Watergate. Instructors must develop a historical perspective on the cultural milieu in which popular music thrives. And if biography is indeed a valuable teaching tool — as a means to the end of historical study — then *Elvis — The Sun Sessions* offers an excellent resource for launching an examination into this neglected area.

This album is a genuine classic. It provides numerous clues (though little conclusive evidence) for explaining the Presley mystique. Initially, it suggests that there was more to the rise of rock than the vocal talents of a lone truckdriver from Tupelo, Mississippi. The sixteen songs which appear on *Elvis — The Sun Sessions* were originally taped in the Memphis Recording Service's downtown studio between July 1954 and July 1955. Under the direction of Sam C. Phillips of Sun Records, young Elvis Presley was joined by house musicians Scotty Moore, Bill Black, and D. J. Fontana to create a series of demo recordings. The tunes selected for the Sun Sessions included an unusual combination of white country and western standards ("Blue Moon of Kentucky," "I Forgot to Remember to Forget," and "I Don't Care if the Sun Don't Shine") and black rhythm and blues numbers ("That's All Right (Mama)," "Baby, Let's Play House," and "Mystery Train"). Elvis' embryonic rockabilly style, as translated through Phillips' recording techniques, still sounds dramatically distinctive; it was to become a national phenomenon within two years. This album offers students the opportunity to listen to the vocal tip of a soon-to-be-discovered musical iceberg.

The key to utilizing this album as a teaching tool rests in a history teacher's ability to foster classroom speculation concerning Elvis' sensational rise to fame. Among the questions that might be considered are: (1) How did the change of personal managers from Sam Phillips to Colonel Tom Parker affect Elvis' professional activities? (2) How did the switch from the tiny Sun Record Company to the more prestigious RCA Victor label affect the production and marketing of the Presley sound? (3) How did Elvis' ability to meld black and white tunes into his performing repertoire enhance his popularity? (4) Why was Elvis able to outshine and ultimately outlast all of the other rock singers of the late

1950s including such notables as Little Richard, Fats Domino, Larry Williams, Chuck Berry, Carl Perkins, Bill Haley, Roy Orbison, and Jerry Lee Lewis? (5) How did the technological innovations in the communications media and the sociological changes within the youth culture of the late '50s and early '60s contribute to the rise of Elvis? (6) Why have traditional definitions of musical quality failed as barometers for dictating the success or failure of rock stars since Elvis? (7) Why did Elvis, who did not write his own music or lyrics, achieve even more public recognition as a recording artist than such talented singer-composers as Carole King, Joni Mitchell, Bob Dylan, or Paul Simon? (8) What comparisons and contrasts exist between the rise of Elvis in the '50s and the emergence of the Beatles in the '60s? (9) Why was Elvis able to survive a tour of military duty, the payola scandals, the emergence of soul music from Motown, Atlantic, and Stax, the Beatles and Rolling Stones, the era of protest songs, and competition from diverse talents such as Chicago, Jimi Hendrix, and Elton John and still remain the single dominant figure of rock music?

Obviously, a history teacher will need to provide his class with supplementary materials on Elvis and the history of American popular culture if students are to be expected to critically and creatively pursue these complex questions. Articles including the recent one by Ashely R. Griffith and Kerrin L. Griffith ("Elvis Presley," *Stereo Review* (July 1976):76–80) are mandatory; scholarly studies such as Jerry Hopkins' biography *Elvis* (Warner Paperback Library, 1971, are significant; histories of the Sun Record Company by Colin Escott and Martin Hawkins, (*Catalyst*, Aquarius Books, 1975), and Paul Vernon (*The Sun Legend*, Steve Lane, 1969) are interesting though often difficult to acquire; and the oral history of twenty years of record-making success which is readily available from RCA Records can provide insights into Elvis' vocal background and social commentary.

If more could be asked of this album, it might be that introductory comments about each song be provided by Elvis himself or by some of his Sun Record contemporaries. It is also ironic that rock journalist Roy Carr, in his record jacket comments, elects to praise "the Sun Sound" instead of the dynamic Elvis as the real musical foundation of the rock era. He notes, "Though everyone from the Beatles right on

# Notes

## Introduction

1. The following essays of mine have resulted from this intensive research period: "Bob Dylan, Isaac Asimov and Social Problems: Non-Traditional Materials for Reflective Teaching," *International Journal of Instructional Media* 4 (1976–77:105–115; "Futurescope," *Audiovisual Instruction* 21 (January 1976):31–45; and "Beyond Flash Gordon and 'Star Wars': Science Fiction and History Instruction," *Social Education* 42 (May 1978):392–97. Ironically, I even co-authored one science fiction story: B. Lee Cooper and Larry S. Haverkos, "An Error in Punctuation," in *Stellar#3: Science Fiction Stories*, ed. Judy-Lynn del Rey (New York: Ballantine, 1977), pp. 108–15.

2. Stephen Traiman, "Print Music Has Brilliant Future with Top Songbooks: Education, Religious Markets Blossom," *Billboard* (March 12, 1977): 42ff.

3. Carl I. Belz, *The Story of Rock*, 2d ed. (New York: Harper and Row, 1972); R. Serge Denisoff, *Sing a Song of Social Significance* (Bowling Green, Ohio: Bowling Green University Popular Press, 1972); Charles Keil, *Urban Blues* (Chicago: University of Chicago Press, 1966); Greil Marcus, *Mystery Train: Images of America in Rock 'N' Roll Music* (New York: E. P. Dutton, 1975); and Arnold Shaw, *The Rockin' 50's: The Decade That Transformed the Pop Music Scene* (New York: Hawthorn Books, 1974).

4. Steve Chapple and Reebee Garofalo, *Rock 'N' Roll Is Here to Pay: The History and Politics of the Music Industry* (Chicago: Nelson-Hall,

1977); Charlie Gillett, *Making Tracks: Atlantic Records and the Growth of a Multi-Billion-Dollar Industry* (New York: E. P. Dutton, 1974); Charles Gillett, *The Sound of the City: The Rise of Rock and Roll* (New York: Outerbridge and Dienstfrey, 1970); Jonathan Ramin, "Parallels in the Social Reactions to Jazz and Rock," *Journal of Jazz Studies* 2 (December 1974):95–125; Richard A. Peterson and David G. Berger, "Cycles in Symbol Production: The Case of Popular Music," *American Sociological Review* 40 (April 1975): 158–72; Peterson and Berger, "Entrepreneurship in Organizations: Evidence from the Popular Music Industry," *Administrative Science Quarterly* 16 (March 1971):97–106; Peterson and Berger, "Three Eras in the Manufacture of Popular Music Lyrics," in *The Sounds of Social Change: Studies in Popular Culture*, ed. R. Serge Denisoff and Richard A. Peterson (Chicago: Rand McNally, 1972), 282–302; and Jon H. Rieger, "The Coming Crisis in the Youth Music Market," *Popular Music and Society* 4 (1975), 19–35.

## Chapter 1

1. R. Serge Denisoff, *Solid Gold: The Popular Record Industry* (New Brunswick, N.J.: Transaction Books, 1975), pp. 92–282.

2. C. A. Schicke, *Revolution in Sound: A Biography of the Recording Industry* (Boston: Little, Brown, 1974), pp. 114–70 and 209–38; Ivan Berger, "One Hundred Years of Recording," *Stereo Review* 39 (July 1977):62–65.

3. David R. Pichaske, ed., *Beowulf to Beatles: Approaches to Poetry* (New York: Free Press, 1972), pp. 3–50; Harold F. Mosher, Jr., "The Lyrics of American Popular Music: A New Poetry," *Popular Music and Society*, 1 (Spring 1972):167–76.

4. Gary Allen, "More Subversion than Meets the Ear," in *The Sounds of Social Change: Studies in Popular Culture*, ed. R. Serge Denisoff and Richard A. Peterson (Chicago: Rand McNally, 1972), pp. 151–66. Also see the September 14, 1970, speech by Spiro T. Agnew entitled, "Talking Brainwashing Blues," which is reprinted in the same anthology, pp. 307–10.

## Chapter 2

1. B. Lee Cooper, "The Traditional and Beyond: Resources for Teaching Women's Studies," *Audiovisual Instruction* 22 (December 1977):14.

2. Anne Firor Scott, "Women in American Life," in *The Reinterpretation of American History and Culture*, eds. William H. Cartwright and Richard L. Watson, Jr. (Washington, D.C.: National Council for the Social Studies, 1973), p. 151.

3. James Baldwin, *Notes of a Native Son* (New York: Bantam, 1964), p. 138.

**Chapter 3**

1. Not infrequently the terms *devil* and *communism* have been employed interchangeably by these critics. See Gary Allen, "That Music: There's More to It Than Meets the Ear," in *The Age of Rock-2*, ed. Jonathan Eisen (New York: Vintage Books, 1970), pp.193–213, and David A. Noebel's books and pamphlets published by the Christian Crusade Press in Tulsa, Okla.: *Communism, Hypnotism, and the Beatles* (1965), *Rhythm, Riots, and Revolution* (1966), and *The Beatles: A Study in Drugs, Sex, and Revolution* (1969). Richard J. Fogarty, a graduate of the Word of Life Bible Institute in Pottersville, N.Y., has continued this campaign against "atheistic" singers and songs in *Rock – The Quiet Revolution* (Schroon Lake, N.Y.: Word of Life Fellowship, 1972).

2. Jerome L. Rodnitzky, "The New Revivalism: American Protest Songs, 1945–1968," *South Atlantic Quarterly* 70 (Winter 1971):13–21; Hughson F. Mooney, "Rock as an Historical Phenomenon," *Popular Music and Society* 1 (Spring 1972):129–43.

3. William C. Shepard, "Religion and the Counter Culture – A New Religiosity," *Sociological Inquiry* 42 (1972):3–9.

4. William E. Wolfe, "Rock Music – Cubicle or Telstar," *Christian Home* 5 (October 1972):6.

5. The instructional methodology suggested herein should not be mistaken for "content analysis." The subjectivity inherent in this teaching technique is antithetical to Bernard Berelson's definition of "systematic and quantitative description of the manifest content of communication." See his *Content Analysis in Communication Research* (Glencoe, Ill.: Free Press, 1952), p. 18.

6. Alan Aldridge, comp., *The Beatles Illustrated Lyrics*, vols. 1 and 2 (New York: Delacorte, 1969, 1971); Bruce L. Chipman, ed., *Hardening Rock: An Organic Anthology of the Adolescence of Rock 'N Roll* (Boston: Little, Brown, 1972); Landon Gerald Dowdey, comp., *Journey to Freedom: A Case-book with Music* (Chicago: Swallow, 1969); Tom Glazer,

ed., *Songs of Peace, Freedom, and Protest* (Greenwich, Conn.: Fawcett, 1970); Richard Goldstein, ed., *The Poetry of Rock* (New York: Bantam, 1971); Louis M. Savary, ed., *Popular Song and Youth Today, Fifty Songs – Their Meaning and You* (New York: Association Press, 1971); and Stephanie Spinner, ed., *Rock Is Beautiful: An Anthology of American Lyrics, 1953–1968* (New York: Dell, 1970).

7. This aspect of American Protestant belief, particularly with respect to music employed in the religious framework, is historically documented by R. Serge Denisoff, "The Religious Roots of the American Song of Persuasion," *Western Folklore* 39 (1970):175–77.

8. Jerome L. Rodnitzky, "The New Revivalism: American Protest Songs, 1945–1968," *South Atlantic Quarterly* 70 (Winter 1971):16.

## Chapter 4

1. "The Black Aesthetic Imperative" in *The Black Aesthetic*, ed. Addison Gayle, Jr. (Garden City, N.Y.: Doubleday, 1972), p. 126.

2. From the song "Why I Sing the Blues," which appears in *The Poetry of Soul*, ed. A. X. Nicholas (New York: Bantam, 1971), p. 43.

3. Melville J. Herskovits, *The Myth of the Negro Past* (Boston: Beacon, 1958), pp. 261–91; LeRoi Jones (Imamu Amiri Baraka), *Blues People: Negro Music in White America* (New York: William Morrow, 1963), pp. 1–10, 17–49; Charles Keil, *Urban Blues* (Chicago: University of Chicago Press, 1966), pp. 30–49; Paul Oliver, *Savannah Syncopators: African Retentions in the Blues* (New York: Stein and Day, 1970); Eileen Southern, *The Music of Black Americans: A History* (New York: W. W. Norton, 1971), pp. 3–24; Ortiz M. Walton, "A Comparative Analysis of the African and Western Aesthetics," in *The Black Aesthetic*, ed. Addison Gayle, Jr. (Garden City, N.Y.: Doubleday, 1972), pp. 154–64; Eklin T. Sithole, "Black Folk Music," in *Rappin' and Stylin' Out: Communication in Urban Black America*, ed. Thomas Kochman (Urbana: University of Illinois Press, 1972), pp. 65–82; and J. H. Kwabena Nketia, "The Musical Heritage of Africa," in *Slavery, Colonialism, and Racism*, ed. Sidney W. Mintz (New York: W. W. Norton, 1974), pp. 151–61; Samuel Charters, *The Legacy of the Blues: Art and Lives of Twelve Great Bluesmen* (New York: Da Capo, 1975); Gerald W. Haslam, *Afro-American Oral Literature* (New York: Harper and Row, 1975); Ian Hoare, "Mighty, Mighty Spade and Whitey: Black Lyrics

and Soul's Interaction with White Culture," in *The Soul Book*, ed. Ian Hoare, Tony Cummings, Clive Anderson, and Simon Frith (New York: Dell, 1975), pp. 146–210; Harry Oster, comp., *Living Country Blues* (New York: Minerva Press, 1975); Gordon Stevenson, "Race Records: Victims of Benign Neglect in Libraries," *Wilson Library Bulletin* 50 (November 1975):224–32; Irene V. Jackson-Brown, "Afro-American Song in the Nineteenth Century: A Neglected Source," *Black Perspective in Music* 4 (April 1976):22–38; John P. Morgan and Thomas C. Tulloss, "The Jake Walk Blues: A Toxicologic Tragedy Mirrored in American Popular Song," *Annals of Internal Medicine* 85 (December 1976):804–808; and Lawrence W. Levine, *Black Culture and Black Consciousness: Afro-American Folk Thought from Slavery to Freedom* (New York: Oxford University Press, 1977).

4. For discussions of the most significant black recording companies see and hear the following: Atlantic: Charlie Gillett, *Making Tracks: Atlantic Records and the Growth of a Multi-Billion-Dollar Industry* (New York: E. P. Dutton, 1974); "Ahmet Ertegun Interview" and "Jerry Wexler Interview" in *The Rockin' 50's: The Decade That Transformed the Pop Music Scene*, written by Arnold Shaw (New York: Hawthorn Books, 1974), pp. 78–79, 83–86; *History of Rhythm and Blues, 1947–1967* (SD 8161-4/8193-4/8208-9) – 8 vols. (New York: Atlantic Recording Company, 1968 (vols. I–VI), and 1969 (vols. VII–VIII)); and *The Super Hits* (SD 501/8188/8203/8224/8274) – 5 vols. (New York: Atlantic Recording Company, 1967 (vol. I), 1968 (vols. II–III), and 1970 (vols. IV–V)); Chess: Peter Guralnick, *Feel Like Going Home: Portraits in Blues and Rock and Roll* (New York: Outerbridge and Dienstirey, 1971), pp. 180–202; *Pop Origins* (Chess 1544) (Chicago: Chess Records, n.d.); Willie Dixon, *I Am the Blues* (CS 9987) (New York: Columbia Records/CBS, Inc., n.d.); Howlin' Wolf, *Chester Burnett Aka Howlin' Wolf* (New York: Chess/Janus Records, 1972); The Moonglows, *Moonglows: Chess Rock 'N' Rhythm Series* – 1 vol. (Englewood Cliffs, N.J.: Chess Records, 1976); and Muddy Waters, *Folk Singer* (Chess 1483) (Chicago: Chess Recording Corporation, n.d.); Motown: Simon Frith, "You Can Make It If You Try: The Motown Story," in *The Soul Book*, eds. Ian Hoare, Tony Cummings, Clive Anderson, and Simon Frith (New York: Dell, 1975), pp. 39–73; Jon Landau, "Motown: The First Ten Years," in *It's Too Late to Stop*

*Now: A Rock and Roll Journal* (San Francisco: Straight Arrow Press, 1972), pp. 143–50; Rochelle Larkin, "Tales of Two Cities: Memphis and Motown," in *Soul Music!* (New York: Lancer, 1970), pp. 77–97; Joe McEwen and Jim Miller, "Motown," in *The Rolling Stone Illustrated History of Rock and Roll*, ed. by Jim Miller (New York: Random House, 1976), pp. 222–33; David Morse, *Motown and the Arrival of Black Music* (New York: Collier, 1971); Earl Paige et al., "Diana: A *Billboard* Special Supplement," *Billboard* (March 20, 1976), 72 pp.; Arnold Shaw, "Motown: The Detroit Sound," in *The World of Soul* (New York: Paperback Library, 1971), pp. 202–18; *Motown's Preferred Stock* (M6 881/2/3 SI) – 3 vols. (Hollywood, Calif.: Motown Record Corporation, 1977); Diana Ross and the Supremes, *Diana Ross and the Supremes Anthology* (M7 794 A3) (Hollywood, Calif.: Motown Record Corporation, 1974); Stevie Wonder, *Greatest Hits* (T 282/T6 313 SI) – 2 vols. (Detroit: Tamala Records, 1968 and 1971); SAVOY – *The Roots of Rock 'N' Roll* (SJL 2221) – 1 vol., 2 records (New York: Arista Records, 1977; Specialty: *This Is How It All Began: The Roots of Rock 'N' Roll as Recorded from 1945 to 1955 on Specialty Records* (SPS 2117/8 – 2 vols., 4 records (Hollywood, Calif.: Specialty Records, 1969 and 1970); STAX – Clive Anderson, "Memphis and the Sounds of the South," in *The Soul Book*, ed. by Ian Hoare, Tony Cummings, Clive Anderson, and Simon Frith (New York: Dell, 1975), pp. 74–145; Robert Palmer, "The Sound of Memphis," in *The Rolling Stone Illustrated History of Rock and Roll*, ed. Jim Miller (New York: Random House, 1976), pp. 202–205; *Wattstax: The Living Word* (STS 2 3010/18) – 2 vols., 4 records (Memphis: Stax Records, 1972 and 1973).

5. Russell Ames, "Protest and Irony in Negro Folksong," *Science and Society* 14 (Summer 1950):193–213; Samuel Charters, *The Poetry of the Blues* (New York: Oak Publications, 1963); Lloyd Miller and James K. Skipper, Jr., "Sounds of Protest: Jazz and the Militant Avant-Garde," in *Approaches to Deviance: Theories, Concepts, and Research Findings*, eds. Mark Lefton, James K. Skipper, Jr., and Charles H. McCaghy (New York: Appleton-Century-Crofts, 1968), pp. 129–40; Phyl Garland, *The Sound of Soul: The History of Black Music* (Chicago: Henry Regnery Company, 1969), pp. 3–79; Ulf Hannerz, *Soulside: Inquiries into Ghetto Culture and Community* (New York: Columbia University Press, 1969); Paul Oliver, *The Story of the Blues* (Radnor, Pa.: Chilton, 1969);

George H. Lewis, "Social Protest and Self Awareness in Black Popular Music," *Popular Music and Society* 2 (Summer 1973):327–33; and Michael Haralambos, *Right On: From Blues to Soul in Black America* (New York: Drake, 1975).

6. Chuck Berry, *The London Chuck Berry Sessions* (CH 60020) (New York: Chess/Janus Records, 1972); B. B. King, *B. B. King in London* (ABCX 730) (Los Angeles: ABC Records, 1971); Les McCann, *Live at Montreaux* (SD2 312) (New York: Atlantic Recording Corp., 1973); Les McCann and Eddie Harris, *Swiss Movement* (SD 1537) (New York: Atlantic Recording Corp., 1969); and Muddy Waters, *The London Muddy Waters Sessions* (CH 60013) (New York: Chess/Janus Records, 1972).

7. LeRoi Jones (Imamu Amiri Baraka), *Blues People: Negro Music in White America* (New York: William Morrow, 1963), pp. ix–x.

## Chapter 5

1. Charles T. Morris, "Oral History as a Classroom Tool," *Social Education* 32 (October 1968):546–49; David E. Bynum, "Oral Evidence and the Historian: Problems and Methods," *Journal of the Folklore Institute* (August/December 1971):82–84; Manfred J. Waserman, *Bibliography on Oral History* (New York: Oral History Association, 1971); Willa K. Baum, *Oral History for the Local Historical Society*, rev. ed., (Nashville: American Association for State and Local History, 1971); Larry Van Dyne, "Oral History: Sharecroppers and Presidents, Jazz and Texas Oil," *Chronicle of Higher Education* (December 24, 1973):9–10; William W. Moss, *Oral History Program Manual* (New York: Praeger, 1974); Alan Meckler and Ruth McMullin, eds., *Oral History Collection* (New York: Bowker, 1975); Studs Terkel, *Envelopes of Sound: Six Practitioners Discuss the Methods, Theory, and Practice of Oral History and Oral Testimony*, (New York: Precedent Pub., 1975); and John A. Neuenschwander, *Oral History as a Teaching Approach* (Washington, D.C.: National Education Association, 1976.)

2. Michael Lydon, "Chuck Berry Lives!" *Ramparts* 7 (December 1969):47–56; Griel Marcus, "Chuck Berry," in *The Rolling Stone Interviews* vol. 1 eds. Jann Wenner et al. (New York: Paperback Library, 1971), pp. 173–87; Carl Belz, "Chuck Berry: Folk Poet of the Fifties," in *The Story of Rock*, 2d ed. (New York: Harper and Row, 1972), pp.

61–66; Robert Christgau, "Chuck Berry: Eternal Rock and Roller," in *Any Old Way You Choose It: Rock and Other Pop Music, 1967–1973* (Baltimore: Penguin, 1973), pp. 140–48; B. Lee Cooper, "Review of *Chuck Berry's Golden Decade*," *History Teacher*, 8 (February 1975):300–301; *Chuck Berry—The Golden Decade* (New York: ARC Music, n.d.); and Robert Christgau, "Chuck Berry," in *The Rolling Stone Illustrated History of Rock and Roll*, ed. Jim Miller (New York: Random House, 1976), pp. 58–63.

3. Rochelle Larkin, "Ray Charles—That's All!" in *Soul Music!* (New York: Lancer Books, 1970), pp. 157–64; "Playboy Interview: Ray Charles," *Playboy* 17 (March 1970):67–82; Arnold Shaw, "Ray Charles: Soul Supreme," in *The World of Soul* (New York: Paperback Library, 1971), pp. 323–30; Sharon B. Mathis and Susan B. Weber, *Ray Charles* (New York: Crowell, 1973); Michael Lydon, "Ray Charles," in *Boogie Lightning* (New York: Dial, 1974), pp. 186–229; Tony Cummings, "The Gospel According to Ray Charles," in *The Soul Book*, eds. Ian Hoare, Tony Cummings, Clive Anderson, and Simon Frith (New York: Dell, 1975), pp.6–13; Ben Fong-Torres, "Ray Charles: The Rolling Stone Interview," in *What's That Sound? The Contemporary Music Scene from the Pages of "Rolling Stone"* (Garden City: N.Y.: Doubleday, 1976), pp. 264–88; Peter Guralnick, "Ray Charles," in *The Rolling Stone Illustrated History of Rock and Roll*, ed. Jim Miller (New York: Random House, 1976), pp. 110–13; and Joel Vance, "Remarkable Authority and Rekindling Vigor in Ray Charles' New 'True to Life,' " *Stereo Review* 40 (February 1978):112.

4. Doon Arbus, "James Brown Is Out of Sight," in *The Age of Rock: Sounds of The American Cultural Revolution*, ed. Jonathan Eisen (New York: Vintage Books, 1969), pp. 286–97; Mel Watkins, "The Lyrics of James Brown," in *Amistad 2*, eds. John A. Williams and Charles F. Harris (New York: Vintage Books, 1971), pp. 140–96; Albert Goldman, "James Brown—Black Power," in *Freakshow* (New York: Atheneum, 1971), pp. 66–70; George H. Lewis, "James Brown," in *Side-Saddle on the Gold Calf: Social Structure and Popular Culture in America*, ed. George H. Lewis (Pacific Palisades, Calif.: Goodyear Publishing Company, 1972), pp. 197–200; and Robert Palmer, "James Brown," in *The Rolling Stone Illustrated History of Rock and Roll*, ed. Jim Miller (New York: Random House, 1976), pp. 134–39.

5. Phyl Garland, "Aretha Franklin: Sister Soul," in *The Sound of Soul: The Story of Black Music* (New York: Pocket Books, 1969), pp. 158–67; Rochelle Larkin, "Aretha Franklin – Lady Soul," in *Soul Music!* (New York: Lancer, 1970), pp. 39–45; Richard Goldstein, "Aretha Arouses," in *Goldstein's Greatest Hits: A Book Mostly about Rock 'N' Roll* (Englewood Cliffs, N.J.: Prentice-Hall, 1970), pp. 164–65; Arnold Shaw, "Aretha Franklin: Lady Soul," in *The World of Soul* (New York: Paperback Library, 1971), pp. 316–22; Albert Goldman, "She Makes Salvation Seem Erotic – Aretha Franklin," in *Freakshow* (New York: Atheneum, 1971), pp. 76–79; John Landau, "Aretha Franklin and Ray Charles: Live at Fillmore West," in *It's Too Late to Stop Now: A Rock and Roll Journal* (San Francisco: Straight Arrow Books, 1972), pp. 171–73; James T. Olsen, *Aretha Franklin* (Mankato, Minn.: Creative Educational Society, 1974); Michael Lydon, "Aretha Franklin, in *Boogie Lightning* (New York: Dial, 1974), pp. 160–84; and Russell Gersten, "Aretha Franklin," in *The Rolling Stone Illustrated History of Rock and Roll*, ed. Jim Miller (New York: Random House, 1976), pp. 234–37.

6. The illustrations provided in the next few paragraphs are drawn from the following recordings: Les McCann and Eddie Harris, *Swiss Movement* (SD 1537) (New York: Atlantic Recording Corporation, 1969); Les McCann, *Comment* (SD 1547) (New York: Atlantic Record Corporation, 1969); Eddie Harris and Les McCann, *Second Movement* (SD 1583) (New York: Atlantic Recording Corporation, 1971); Roberta Flack, B. B. King, Curtis Mayfield, Herbie Mann, Les McCann, and Billy Eckstein, *Newport in New York '72: The Soul Sessions*, vol. 6 (CST 9028) (New York: Budda Records, 1972); and Les McCann, *Talk to the People* (SD 1619) (New York: Atlantic Recording Corporation, 1972); Les McCann, *Layers* (SD 1646) (New York: Atlantic Recording Corporation, 1973); Les McCann, *Live at Montreaux* (SD 2-312) (New York: Atlantic Recording Corporation, 1973); Les McCann, *Hustle to Survive* (SD 1679) (New York: Atlantic Recording Corporation, 1975); and Les McCann, *River High, River Low* (SD 1690) (New York: Atlantic Recording Corporation, 1976).

7. Beyond the field of history, however, some interesting studies on the nature and meaning of black nonverbal communication in the arts have been published: Lloyd Miller and James K. Skipper, Jr., "Sounds of Protest: Jazz and the Militant Avant-Garde," in *Approaches to Devi-*

*ance: Theories, Concepts, and Research Findings* (New York: Appleton-Century-Crofts, 1968), pp. 129–40; and Charles Keil, "Motion and Feeling through Music," in *Rappin' and Stylin' Out: Communication in Urban Black America*, ed. Thomas Kochman (Urbana: University of Illinois Press, 1972), pp. 83–100.

8. Note the speculative essay by Ralph J. Gleason, "The Education of the Jazz Virtuoso," in *The Creative College Student: An Unmet Challenge*, ed. Paul Heist (San Francisco: Jossey-Bass, 1968), pp. 84–98. A fascinating illustration of the interview technique applied to the study of jazz can be found in Nat Shapiro and Nat Hentoff, eds., *Hear Me Talkin' to Ya: The Story of Jazz as Told by the Men Who Made It* (New York: Dover, 1966).

9. B. Lee Cooper, "Popular Music, Oral History, and Les McCann," *Social Studies* 67 (May/June 1976):115–18.

10. Samuel Charters, *The Poetry of the Blues* (New York: Oak Publications, 1963); Claude Brown, "The Language of Soul," in *Black America: Accommodation and Confrontation in the Twentieth Century*, ed. Richard Resh (Lexington, Mass.: D. C. Heath, 1969), pp. 244–49; William R. Ferris, Jr., "Racial Repertoires among Blues Performers," *Ethnomusicology* 14 (September 1970):439–49; Dorothy Z. Seymour, "Black English," in *The American Language in the 1970's*, eds. Herman A. Estrin and Donald V. Mehus (San Francisco: Boyd and Fraser, 1971), pp. 136–43; Paul Oliver, *The Meaning of the Blues* (New York: Collier, 1972); and Geneva Smitherman, *Black Language and Culture: Sounds of Soul* (New York: Harper and Row, 1975).

**Chapter 6**

1. Arthur M. Schlesinger, Jr., *Violence: America in the Sixties* (New York: New American Library, 1968); Richard Hofstadter and Michael Wallace, eds., *American Violence: A Documentary History* (New York: Vintage Books, 1970); Richard Maxwell Brown, "Historical Patterns of Violence in America," in *Violence in America: Historical and Comparative Perspectives*, eds. Hugh Davis Graham and Ted Robert Gurr (New York: Bantam, 1970), pp. 45–84; and Henry Steele Commager, "The Roots of Lawlessness," *Saturday Review* (February 13, 1971):17–19ff.

2. David Brion Davis, "Violence in American Literature," in *Vio-*

*lence: Causes and Solutions*, eds. Renatus Hartogs and Eric Artzt (New York: Dell, 1970): 54–66; and Robert Jay Nash, *Bloodletters and Bad-men: A Narrative Encyclopedia of American Criminals from the Pilgrims to the Present* (New York: M. Evan, 1973).

3. Joe Morella and Edward Z. Epstein, *Rebels: The Rebel Hero in Films* (Secaucus, N.J.: Citadel Press, 1971).

4. Carl G. Jung, *Modern Man in Search of a Soul* trans. W. S. Dell and Cary G. Baynes (New York: Harcourt, Brace and World, 1933), pp. 74–94, 125–51; Karen Horney, *Our Inner Conflicts: A Constructive Theory of Neurosis* (New York: W. W. Norton, 1945), pp. 63–72, 191–216; Karen Horney, *The Neurotic Personality of Our Time* (New York: W. W. Norton, 1957), pp. 30–40, 162–229; Paul Roazen, *Freud: Political and Social Thought* (New York: Knopf, 1968), pp. 193–251; and Frederick S. Perls, *Ego, Hunger, and Aggression* (New York: Vintage Books, 1969), pp. 52–79.

5. Sheldon G. Levy, "Attitudes toward Political Violence," in *Assassination and Political Violence*, eds. James F. Kirkham, Sheldon G. Levy, and William J. Crotty (New York: Bantam, 1970), pp. 512–14; Robert L. Kahn, "Who Buys Bloodshed and Why", *Psychology Today* (June 1972):47–48ff; and Rollo May, *Power and Innocence: A Search for the Sources of Violence* (New York: W. W. Norton, 1972).

6. Elliot Aronson, *The Social Animal* (San Francisco: W. H. Freeman, 1972), p. 161.

7. Although many authors have described the characteristics of the "violent man" syndrome, the two specific sources employed in this study were: Anthony Hopkins, "Contemporary Heroism – Vitality in Defeat," in *Heroes of Popular Culture*, eds. Ray B. Browne, Marshall Fishwick, and Michael T. Harsden (Bowling Green, Ohio: Bowling Green State University Popular Press, 1972) pp. 113–23; and Robert Linder, *Rebel without a Cause* (New York: Grove Press, 1942), pp. 1–17.

8. Sol Stern, "Altamont: Pearl Harbor to the Woodstock Nation," in *Side Saddle on the Golden Calf*, ed. George H. Lewis (Pacific Palisades, Calif.: Goodyear Pub. Co., 1972): pp. 321–40; Michael Lydon, "The Rolling Stones – A Play in the Apocalypse," *Ramparts* (March 1970):28–53; and George Paul Csicsery, "Altamont, California: December 6, 1969," in *The Age of Rock/2: Sights and Sounds of the Ameri-*

*can Cultural Revolution*, ed. Jonathan Eisen (New York: Vintage Books, 1970), pp. 145–48.

9. George Grella, analyzing the power of the James Bond image on the American mind, contends, "He (Bond) lives the dreams of countless drab people, his gun ready, his honor intact, his morals loose: the hero of our anxiety-ridden, mythless age: the savior of our culture." See "James Bond: Culture Hero," in *Now and Tomorrow: The Rhetoric of Culture in Transition*, eds. Tom E. Kakonis and James C. Wilcox (Lexington, Mass.: D. C. Heath, 1971), p. 50.

10. See the description of the "race hero" in St. Clair Drake and Horace B. Cayton, *Black Metropolis* (New York: Harcourt and Brace, 1946). "Even conservative Negroes admire colored radicals who buck the white world. Preachers may oppose sin, but they will also express a sneaking admiration for the Negro criminal who decisively outwits white people. Even the quiet, well-disciplined family man may get a thrill when a 'bad Negro' blows his top and goes down with both guns blazing at the White Law." Also see William H. Friet and Price M. Cobbs, *Black Rage*, (New York: Bantam, 1968).

11. William C. Shepherd, "Religion and the Counter Culture – A New Religiosity," *Sociological Inquiry* 42 (1972):3–9.

12. Richard D. Carpenter has written, "Myths, far from being pretty stories from the past, are our principal way of objectifying and dramatizing our most essential and profound hopes and fears." See "007 and the Myth of the Hero," *Journal of Popular Culture* 1 (Fall 1967):88.

13. It is interesting to note Robert Warshow's analysis of the successful gangster as a prototype of the outsider – particularly with respect to the result of his successes. Warshow notes that "the very conditions of success make it impossible not to be alone, for success is always the accomplishment of an *individual* pre-eminence that must be imposed on others, in whom it automatically arouses hatred; the successful man is an outlaw. The gangster's whole life is an effort to assert himself as an individual, to draw himself out of the crowd, and he always dies *because* he is an individual; the final bullet thrusts him back, makes him, after all, a failure." See "The Gangster as Tragic Hero," in *Things in the Driver's Seat: Readings in Popular Culture*, ed. Harry Russell Huebel (Chicago: Rand McNally, 1972), p. 101.

14. This phenomenon has been thoroughly examined in several

books: John G. Burke, ed., *The New Technology and Human Values* (Belmont, Calif.: Wadsworth, 1966); Jack D. Douglas, ed., *Freedom and Tyranny: Social Problems in a Technological Society* (New York: Knopf, 1970); Thomas C. Cochran, *Social Change in America: The Twentieth Century* (New York: Harper and Row, 1972); Alvin Toffler, *Future Shock* (New York: Bantam, 1970); Charles A. Reich, *The Greening of America* (New York: Random House, 1970); and Theodore Toszak, *The Making of a Counter Culture* (Garden City, N.Y.: Anchor Books, 1969). Also see Harris Friedburg, "Bob Dylan: Psychohistorian of a Generation," *Chronicle of Higher Education* 8 (January 28, 1974):15–16.

## Chapter 7

1. Carl Belz, *The Story of Rock* (New York: Harper and Row, 1969); R. Serge Denisoff, *Solid Gold: The Popular Record Industry* (New Brunswick, N.J.: Transaction Books, 1975); Phyl Garland, *The Sound of Soul: The History of Black Music* (Chicago: Henry Regnery Company, 1969); Charlie Gillett, *The Sound of the City: The Rise of Rock and Roll* (New York: Outerbridge and Dienstfrey, 1970); Jerry Hopkins, *The Rock Story* (New York: New American Library, 1970); Mike Jahn, *Rock: From Elvis Presley to the Rolling Stones* (New York: Grosset and Dunlap, 1973); Jonathan Kamin, "Taking the Roll out of Rock 'n' Roll: Reverse Acculturation," *Popular Music and Society* 2 (Fall 1972):1–17; Richard A. Peterson and David G. Berger, "Cycles in Symbol Production: The Case of Popular Music," *American Sociological Review* 40 (April 1975):158–73; and Arnold Shaw, *The Rockin' 50's: The Decade That Transformed the Pop Music Scene* (New York: Hawthorn Books, 1974).

2. Joe Edwards,, comp., *Top 10's and Trivia of Rock and Roll and Rhythm and Blues, 1950–1973* (St. Louis: Blueberry Hill, 1974); Jim Quirin and Barry Cohen, comps., *Chartmasters' Rock 100: An Authoritative Ranking of the 100 Most Popular Songs for Each Year, 1956 through 1975* (Covington, La.: Chartmasters, 1975); Nat Shapiro, ed., *Popular Music: An Annotated Index of American Popular Songs*, vol. 1, 1950–59, vol. 3, 1960–64, and vol. 4, 1965–69 (New York: Adrian Press, 1967, 1973); Joel Whitburn, comp., *Record Research: Compiled from "Billboard" Magazine "Hot 100 Charts," 1955–1969* (Menomonee Falls,

Wis.: Record Research, 1970); and Joel Whitburn, comp., *Top Rhythm and Blues Records, 1949–1971* (Menomonee Falls, Wis.: Record Research, 1973).

3. Norm N. Nite, comp., *Rock On: The Illustrated Encyclopedia of Rock N' Roll* (New York: Crowell, 1974); *Lillian Roxon's Rock Encyclopedia* (New York: Grosset and Dunlap, 1969); and Irwin Stambler, comp., *Encyclopedia of Pop, Rock, and Soul* (New York: St. Martin's Press, 1974).

4. See the texts listed above by Joe Edwards, Joel Whitburn, Norm N. Nite, Lillian Roxon, and Irwin Stambler. Also see the bicentennial issue of *Billboard* magazine, published on July 4, 1976.

**Chapter 8**

1. Charlie Gillett, *The Sound of the City: The Rise of Rock and Roll* (New York: Outerbridge and Dienstfrey, 1970), p. i.

2. Ibid.

3. Karl E. Meyer, "Love Thy City: Marketing the American Metropolis," *Saturday Review* (April 28, 1979):16.

4. Stephen Holden, "Disco: The Medium Is the Message," *High Fidelity* (August 1979):105.

5. Donald Horton, "The Dialogue of Courtship in Popular Songs," *American Journal of Sociology* 62 (May 1957):569–78; James T. Carey, "Changing Courtship Patterns in the Popular Song," *American Journal of Sociology* 74 (May 1969):720–31; Patricia Freudiger, "Love Lauded and Love Lamented: Men and Women in Popular Music," *Popular Music and Society* 6 (1978):1–10; and Julia A. Heath, "Courtship Patterns Expressed in Popular Songs" (paper presented at the 8th National Convention of the Popular Culture Association, Cincinnati, Ohio, April 20, 1978).

6. Keith Swanwick, *Popular Music and the Teacher* (New York: Pergamon, 1968); David E. Morse, "Avant-Rock in the Classroom," *English Journal* 58 (February 1969):196–200ff.; Eric P. Johnson, "The Use of Folk Songs in Education: Some Examples of the Use of Folk Songs in the Teaching of History, Geography, Economics, and English Literature," *The Vocational Aspect of Education* 21 (Summer 1969):89–94; Sharon I. Ritt, "Using Music to Teach Reading Skills in Social Studies," *Reading Teacher* 27 (March 1974):594–601; Anne W.

Lyons, "Creative Teaching in Interdisciplinary Humanities: The Human Values in Pop Music," *Minnesota English Journal* 10 (Winter 1974):23–31; B. Lee Cooper, "Teaching American History through Popular Music," *AHA Newsletter* 14 (October 1976):3–5; Graham Vulliamy and Ed Lee, eds., *Pop Music in School* (Cambridge: Cambridge University Press, 1976); B. Lee Cooper, "Folk History, Alternative History, and Future History," *Teaching History: A Journal of Methods* 2 (Spring 1977):58–62; Robert H. Reid, "Philosophy Teacher Tunes in Students with Rock Music," *Cleveland Plain Dealer* (February 20, 1977):20; B. Lee Cooper, "Popular Culture: Teaching Problems and Challenges," in *Popular Culture and the Library: Current Issues Symposium II*, ed. Wayne A. Wiegand (Lexington: University of Kentucky, 1978), pp. 10–26; B. Lee Cooper, "Women's Studies and Popular Music: Using Audio Resources in Social Studies Instruction," *History and Social Science Teacher* 14 (Fall 1978):29–40; B. Lee Cooper "Contemporary Singers as Subjects for Biographical Study," *Library-College Experimenter* 5 (May 1979):13–28; and B. Lee Cooper, "Popular Music: An Untapped Resource for Teaching Contemporary Black History," *Journal of Negro Education* 48 (Winter 1979):20–36.

## Chapter 9

1. Arnold Shaw, *The Rock Revolution* (New York: Paperback Library, 1969), p. 26.

2. Ian Hoare, "Mighty, Mighty Spade and Whitey: Black Lyrics and Soul's Interaction with White Culture," in *The Soul Book*, eds. Ian Hoare, Tony Cummings, Clive Anderson, and Simon Frith (New York: Dell, 1975), pp. 185–86.

3. Mike Jahn, *The Story of Rock: From Elvis Presley to the Rolling Stones* (New York: Quadrangle/New York Times Book Company, 1973), p. 146.

4. Paul Oliver, *The Story of the Blues* (Radnor, Penn.: Chilton, 1969), p. 166.

5. Russell B. Nye, "Let the People Sing–Popular Music," in *The Unembarrassed Muse: The Popular Arts in America* (New York: Dial, 1970), pp. 305–59; Ray B. Browne, "Forward," *Popular Music and Society* 1 (Fall 1971): 2; B. Lee Cooper, "Popular Songs as Oral History: Teaching Black History through Contemporary Audio Resources,"

*International Journal of Instructional Media* 5 (1977–78): 185–95; B. Lee Cooper, "Record Revivals as Barometers of Social Change: The Historical Use of Contemporary Audio Resources," *The JEMF Quarterly* 14 (Spring 1978): 38–44; and R. Serge Denisoff, "Introduction," in *Sing a Song of Social Significance* (Bowling Green, Ohio: Bowling Green University Popular Press, 1972), pp. ix–xii.

6. A few black singers/songwriters such as Chuck Berry and Fats Domino succeeded in establishing themselves as distinctive song stylists on Chess Records and Imperial Records, respectively. In contrast to the Berry/Domino situation, however, black rocker Little Richard of Specialty Records faced insurmountable "cover" challenges on his recordings of "Tutti Frutti," "Long Tall Sally," and "Rip It Up" from three of the top white pop stars of the mid-1950s — Pat Boone on Dot Records, Bill Haley and the Comets on Decca Records, and Elvis Presley on RCA Victor Records.

7. Chris Albertson, "Treasures from the Atlantic Archives: Six Volumes of the Blues," *Stereo Review* 31 (August 1973):92–93; Carl Belz, "Early Rock: Crossovers and Covers," in *The Story of Rock*, 2d ed. (New York: Harper and Row, 1972), pp. 25–30; Steve Chapple and Reebee Garofalo, "Black Roots, White Fruits: Racism in the Music Industry," in *Rock 'n' Roll Is Here to Pay: The History and Politics of the Music Industry* (Chicago: Nelson-Hall, 1977), pp. 231–67; Tony Cummings, "Roots, Forerunners, and Originators," in *The Soul Book*, eds. Ian Hoare, Tony Cummings, Clive Anderson, and Simon Frith (New York: Dell, 1976), pp. 1–38; Charlie Gillett, *The Sound of the City: The Rise of Rock and Roll* (New York: Outerbridge and Dienstfrey, 1970), pp. 21–131; Jonathan Kamin, "Taking the Roll Out of Rock 'N' Roll: Reverse Acculturation," *Popular Music and Society* 2 (Fall 1972):1–17; Arnold Shaw, *The Rock Revolution* (New York: Paperback Library, 1969), pp. 26–54; Arnold Shaw, *Honkers and Shouters, The Golden Years of Rhythm and Blues* (New York: Collier, 1978); and Joel Vance, "Rock 'n' Roll Roots on Savoy Records," *Stereo Review* 39 (November 1977):112.

8. Alan Beckett and Richard Merton, "Stones/Comment," in *The Age of Rock: Sounds of the American Cultural Revolution*, ed. Jonathan Eisen (New York: Vintage Books, 1969), pp. 109–17; John M. Hellmann, Jr., "'I'm a Monkey': The Influence of the Black American Blues Argot on the Rolling Stones," *Journal of American Folklore* 86

(October-December 1973):367–73; and Mike Jahn, "Berryized Beatles, Beatlized Monkees, Unmonkeed Dolenz, Jones . . ." *High Fidelity* 26 (October 1976):96–97.

9. Claude Brown, "The Language of Soul," in *Black America: Accommodation and Confrontation in the Twentieth Century*, ed. Richard Resh (Lexington, Mass.: D. C. Heath, 1969), pp. 244–49; Ulf Hannerz, "The Meaning of 'Soul,' " and William L. O'Neill, "The Counter-Culture," in *The Private Side of American History: Readings in Everyday Life*, vol. 2, ed. Thomas R. Frazier (New York: Harcourt Brace Jovanovich, 1975), pp. 336–47 and 308–35; Roderick Nash, "Bob Dylan," in *From These Beginnings: A Biographical Approach to American History* (New York: Harper and Row, 1973), pp. 512–41; and Jerome L. Rodnitzky, "The New Revivalism: American Protest Songs since 1945," in *American Vistas, 1877 to the Present*, 2d ed., eds. Leonard Dinnerstein and Kenneth T. Jackson (New York: Oxford University Press, 1975), pp. 323–31.

## Chapter 10

1. Examples of the newspapers that have featured stories on the Audio Center include: " 'Eavesdropping' New Feature at University's Unusual Audio Studio," (Bowling Green, Ohio) *Daily Sentinel-Tribune* (July 23, 1968):2; "Gypsy, Elvis, 007 Are Now Part of Bowling Green's Curriculum," *Cleveland Plain Dealer* (July 4, 1969):p.p.; Norman Mark, "What You'd Throw Away Fills Culture Center," *Buffalo* (New York) *Evening News* (December 27, 1969):B-5; Robert Cross, "Batman — Ph.D.," *Chicago Tribune Magazine* (October 26, 1969):72–78; Bill Marvel, "That Calendar? Grist for Scholars?" *National Observer* 9 (July 20, 1970):22; Glenn Waggoner, "Pop Music Lover Plays All Day in Job as BGSU Audio Center Head," *Toledo* (Ohio) *Blade* (August 19, 1971):n.p.; John S. Brecher, "Is Clyde McCoy a Piece of History? Maybe So. But Again, Maybe Not," *Wall Street Journal* (September 12, 1972):1,36; Adele U. Schweller, "Popular Culture Center a Leader," *Dayton* (Ohio) *Leisure Magazine* (February 20, 1972):4–5; and Frances Sullivan, "Bowling Green's Pop Culture Attic," *Toledo* (Ohio) *Blade Sunday Magazine* (March 3, 1974):6–9.

2. The proceedings of this symposium, which was organized by Dr.

Wayne A. Wiegand and sponsored by the College of Library Science, are reported in *Popular Culture and the Library: Current Issues Symposium II* (Lexington: University of Kentucky, 1978).

3. "Audio Center Opened at University Library," *Bowling Green Alumni Bulletin* 54 (September-October 1968):6. The most recent university report on the ten-year development of the Audio Center can be found in Bruce Dudley, "Comic Books and Rock 'N' Roll: The Artifacts of Our Society," *At Bowling Green: News For Alumni* 8 (February 1978):3–7.

4. Circulation statistics for the Audio Center are provided by Mr. Schurk in his "Annual Report to the Director of Libraries." The Audio Center Director shared photocopies of these reports from May 30, 1968, through August 15, 1977, with the author.

5. William L. Schurk, "The Popular Culture Library at Bowling Green State University," in *Popular Culture and the Library: Current Issues Symposium II*, ed. Wayne A. Wiegand (Lexington: University of Kentucky, 1978), pp. 53–59.

6. William L. Schurk, "Recommended Popular Records for a Non-Classical Record Library," in *Selected Recordings and Publications in the Popular Music Field*, ed. William Ivey (Nashville: Country Music Foundation Press, 1975), pp. 1–9.

7. William L. Schurk and Ray B. Browne, "The Popular Culture Library and Audio Center—Bowling Green State University," pamphlet (Bowling Green, Ohio: Center for the Study of Popular Culture, n.d.).

8. Mr. Schurk was unable to locate either the author or title of this anthology.

9. It should be noted that Bowling Green State University is one of the nine academic libraries that contribute information on an annual catalog basis to the *Music, Books on Music, and Sound Recordings* catalog issued by the Library of Congress. The other institutions that provide audio data to Washington, D.C., are: University of Toronto, Stanford University, University of Chicago, University of North Carolina, Oberlin College, Ohio State University, Harvard University, and the University of Illinois.

10. Roy Bongartz, "Center for Popular Culture," *Nation* (September 17, 1973):239–42.

11. Mr. Schurk neglected to mention one of his most publicized record acquisition coups. In September 1973 he purchased the entire stock of a Springfield, Ohio, company called the Record Shop, (*BG News*, 57 [October 9, 1973]:3, and Edward Morris, "America's Biggest Jukebox," *The Press* 3 [January 1978]: pp. 1, 4). He also failed to mention the large number of used 45 r.p.m. jukebox records which were annually donated to the Audio Center by the Ohio Vending Company. Finally, although commenting on the gifts from individual radio personalities, he neglected to note that various nearby stations — WMGS and WOHO, for example — regularly channel promotional recordings to the Audio Center. See Edward Morris, "Bowling Green U.'s Keen Audio Center," *Billboard* 87 (December 20, 1975):27.

12. To illustrate Mr. Schurk's warning in a humorous fashion, the "grading system" developed by record dealer Richard A. Bass to describe the condition of his auction discs is reproduced below:

N — New

VG — Very good, excellent (like new to very minor surface scratches that are inaudible)

G + — Good (minor scratches that are only slightly noticeable if at all)

G – – Good (noticeable scratches but music predominates)

F — Fair (extensive scratches — music and scratches fight it out)

P — Poor (very extensive scratches — scratches blot out most of the music, may skip)

See "Auction #17 — Blues, R&B, Soul, Rockabilly, R&R, C&W, and Black Vocal Groups 45's, 78's, and Lp's" (Postal date May 28, 1978), mailed to B. Lee Cooper by Richard A. Bass, 915 York St., Oakland, CA 94610.

13. A fine story on the Audio Center's bootleg record resources was published in *BG News* under the title "Bootleg Cuts Available." Unfortunately, the photocopy of this essay which I secured from Mr. Schurk lacks both a publication date and a page number. Among the specific bootleg albums cited by Chris Flowers, the author of the student newspaper article, were: The Beatles' *Kum Back*, Bob Dylan's *Great White Wonder*, and Crosby, Stills, and Nash's *Wooden Nickel* in addition to untitled discs by the Band, Jethro Tull, and the Rolling Stones.

14. Published in Menomonee Falls, Wisconsin, by Record Research, Inc., Joel C. Whitburn's *Billboard* chart data have become the

key scholarly reference for chronicling the rise and fall of popular recordings. The different sets of listings provided by Whitburn include: *Top Pop ("Hot 100") Records, 1955–1972* (1973), *Top Pop Records, 1940–1955* (1973), *Top LP Records, 1945–1972* (1973), *Top Country & Western Records, 1949–1971* (1972), *Top Rhythm & Blues ("Soul") Records, 1949–1971* (1972), and *Top Easy Listening Records, 1961–1974* (1975). These basic chronological listings are updated annually through supplementary booklets.

15. Schurk, "Annual Report to the Director of Libraries" (1968–77). See footnote 4.

16. Gordon Stevenson, "Race Records: Victims of Benign Neglect in Libraries," *Wilson Library Bulletin*, 50 (November 1975):224–32. Also see two other Stevenson essays: "Popular Culture and the Public Library," in *Advances in Librarianship – VII*, eds. Melvin J. Voight and Michael H. Harris (New York: Academic Press, 1977), pp. 177–229, and "The Wayward Scholar: Resources and Research in Popular Culture," *Library Trends* 25 (April 1977):779–818.

17. The popular-culture movement has been criticized by a variety of academicians including Dwight MacDonald, Russell Kirk, and William Gass. And beyond the realm of academia, many theologians, politicians, journalists, and businessmen have condemned the study of contemporary film, television, radio, and popular music as "faddism." Nonetheless, popular-culture studies have received positive attention from a broad spectrum of teachers, writers, lecturers, and research specialists including Carl Bode, Leslie A. Fiedler, Russel B. Nye, Marshall Fishwick, John Cawelti, Fred E. H. Schroeder, Susan Sontag, Roderick Nash, David Noble, Jerome Rodnitzky, Ray B. Browne, David Madden, Arthur Berger, Richard A. Peterson, David Feldman, Paul M. Hirsch, Marshall McLuhan, Roger B. Rollin, Gordon Stevenson, and R. Serge Denisoff.

### Chapter 11

1. "Audio Center Opened at University Library," *Bowling Green Alumni Bulletin* 54 (September-October 1968):6; Chris Flowers, "Bootleg Cuts Available," *BG News* 55 (November 3, 1970):4; Bill Marvel, "*That* Calendar? Grist for Scholars?" *National Observer* 9 (July 20, 1970):22; John S. Brecher, "Is Clyde McCoy a Piece of History?

*Maybe* So. But Again, Maybe Not," *Wall Street Journal* (September 12, 1972):1, 36; Roy Bongartz, "Center for Popular Culture," *Nation* (September 17, 1973):239–42; Patricia L. Sinn, "Audio Center Grows, Changes," *BG News* (April 17, 1975):7; Edward Morris, "Bowling Green U.'s Keen Audio Center," *Billboard* (December 20, 1975):27; William L. Schurk, "The Popular Culture Library at Bowling Green State University," in *Popular Culture and the Library: Current Issues Symposium II*, ed. Wayne A. Wiegand (Lexington: University of Kentucky, College of Library Science, 1978), pp. 53–59; Edward Morris, "America's Biggest Jukebox," *The Press* 3 (January 1978):1, 4; Bruce Dudley, "Comic Books and Rock 'N' Roll: The Artifacts of Our Society," *At Bowling Green: News for Alumni* 8 (February 1978):3–7; and "The Popular Culture Library and Audio Center–Bowling Green State University" (Bowling Green, Ohio: Center for the Study of Popular Culture, n.d.).

2. Gordon Stevenson, ed., "Trends in Archival and Reference Collections of Recorded Sound," *Library Trends* 21 (July 1972): entire issue; Gordon Stevenson, "Sound Recordings," in *Advances in Librarianship – Vol. V* (New York: Academic Press, 1975), pp. 279–320; Gordon Stevenson, "The Wayward Scholar: Resources and Research in Popular Culture," *Library Trends* 25 (April 1977):779–818; and Gordon Stevenson, "Popular Culture and the Public Library," *Advances in Librarianship – Vol. VII* (New York: Academic Press, 1977), pp. 177–229.

3. Frank Hoffmann, "Popular Music Collections and Public Libraries," *Southeastern Librarian* 23 (Winter 1974):26–31; Gordon Stevenson, "Discography: Scientific, Analytical, Historical, and Systematic," *Library Trends* 21 (July 1972):101–35; Gordon Stevenson, "Standards for Bibliographies of Discographies," *Reference Quarterly* 15 (Summer 1976):309–16; Andrew Armitage and Dean Tudor, comps., *Annual Index to Popular Music Record Reviews – 1972* (Metuchen, N.J.: Scarecrow Press, 1973); Dean Tudor and Andrew Armitage, "Best Popular Records of 1975," *Previews* 4 (May 1976):10–15; Christopher May, "A Basic List of Rock Records," *BRIO* (United Kingdom Branch of the International Association of Music Libraries) 13 (Autumn 1976):34–38; Charles Miron, comp., *Rock Gold: All the Hit Charts from 1955 to 1976* (New York: Drake, 1977); Stephen Nugent and Charlie

Gillett, comps., *Rock Almanac: Top Twenty American and British Singles and Albums of the '50's, '60's, and '70's* (Garden City, N.Y.: Anchor Press/Doubleday, 1976); Clive Solomon, comp., *Record Hits: The British Top 50 Charts, 1954–1976* (London: Omnibus Press, 1977); Helmat Rosner, "A Basic Collection of Pop Music? Many Problems and a Gracious Suggestion," *Buch und Bibliographie* 26 (March 1974):157–59; Ulrich Raschke, "One Hundred Times Pop Music: Concrete Advice for the Construction of a Basic Collection," *Buch und Bibliographia* 27 (July-August 1975):661–82ff.; and Detlef Schwarz, "The Characteristics of Pop Music: History, Inventory, Theory and Analysis," *Buch und Bibliographia* 27 (October 1975):958–62.

## Chapter 12

1. Exceptions to this generalization are: Gordon Stevenson, "Race Records: Victims of Benign Neglect in Libraries," *Wilson Library Bulletin* 50 (November 1975):223–32; Gordon Stevenson, "Sound Recordings," in *Advances in Librarianship*, vol. 5 (New York: Academic Press, 1975), pp. 279–320; Gordon Stevenson, "The Wayward Scholar: Resources and Research in Popular Culture," *Library Trends* 25 (April 1977):779–818; and Gordon Stevenson, "Popular Culture and the Public Library," in *Advances in Librarianship*, vol. 7 (New York: Academic Press, 1977), pp. 177–229.

2. B. Lee Cooper, "Teaching Contemporary History from an Audio Perspective – 'The Image of American Society in Popular Music,'" *Library-College Experimenter* 2 (November 1976):22–34.

3. Frank Hoffmann, "Popular Music Collections and Public Libraries." *Southeastern Librarian* 23 (Winter 1974):26–31; Christopher May, "A Basic List of Rock Records," *BRIO* 13 (Autumn 1976):34–38; Jim O'Connor, "A Rock and Roll Discography," *School Library Journal* 22 (September 1975):21–24; Michael Olds, "From Sargeant Pepper to Captain Fantastic: A Basic Rock Collection," *Hoosier School Libraries* 16 (December 1976):17–19; and Ulrich Raschke, "One Hundred Times Pop Music: Concrete Advice for the Construction of a Basic Collection," *Buch und Bibliographie* 27 (July-August 1975):661–82.

4. Undated letter from Charles Briefer, manager of Columbia Records' Library Subscription Services, located at 51 West 52d St. New

York, NY 10019, addressed to the "College Librarian" at Newberry College in Newberry, South Carolina.

5. Friedrich Summan and Manfred Jagnow, "A Basic Collection of Rock 'N' Roll Records and Tape Cassettes," *Buch und Bibliographie* 27 (July-August 1975), p. 683.

6. Ulrich Raschke, "One Hundred Times Pop Music, . . ." p. 662.

7. Irwin Stambler, "Twenty Years of Rock 'N' Soul: A Casual Summary," in *Encyclopedia of Pop, Rock, and Soul*, comp. Irwin Stambler (New York: St. Martin's Press, 1974), p. 13.

8. R. Serge Denisoff, *Solid Gold: The Popular Record Industry* (New Brunswick: N.J.: Transaction Books, 1975), p. 39.

9. Carl Belz, *The Story of Rock*, 2d ed. (New York: Harper and Row, 1972), p. vii.

# Selected Bibliography

Belz, Carl. *The Story of Rock,* 2d ed. New York: Harper and Row, 1972.

Benedict, Brad, and Linda Barton, comps. *Phonographics: Contemporary Album Covert Art and Design.* New York: Collier, 1977.

Braun, D. Duane. *Toward a Theory of Popular Culture: The Sociology and History of American Music and Dance, 1920–1968.* Ann Arbor, Mich.: Ann Arbor Publishers, 1969.

Broven, John. *Walking to New Orleans: The Story of New Orleans Rhythm and Blues.* Bexhill-on-Sea, Sussex: Blues Unlimited, 1974.

Chapple, Steve, and Reebee Garofalo. *Rock 'N' Roll Is Here to Pay: The History and Politics of the Music Industry.* Chicago: Nelson-Hall, 1977.

Charters, Samuel B. *The Bluesmen.* New York: Oak Publications, 1967.

_____. *The Country Blues.* New York: Da Capo, 1976.

_____. *The Legacy of the Blues: Art and Lives of Twelve Great Bluesmen.* New York: Da Capo, 1975.

_____. *The Poetry of the Blues.* New York: Oak Publications, 1963.

Christgau, Robert. *Any Old Way You Choose It: Rock and Other Pop Music, 1967–1973.* Baltimore: Penguin, 1973.

Cone, James H. *The Spirituals and the Blues: An Interpretation.* New York: Seabury, 1972.

Cousins, Eddie, and Linda Cousins. *Traveling with the Blues: American Bluesmen in England, 1973: A Photographic Survey.* Liverpool: Blues Gospel Research Library, 1974.

Davis, Clive, with James Willwerth. *Clive: Inside the Record Business.* New York: William Morrow, 1974.

Davis, Lloyd, Ron Davis, and Marvin Davis. *Collectors Price Guide to 45 R.P.M. Picture Sleeves*. Ashland, Oreg.: Independent Printing Company, 1977.

Denisoff, R. Serge, *Great Day Coming: Folk Music and the American Left*. Baltimore: Penguin, 1971.

———. *Sing a Song of Social Significance*. Bowling Green, Ohio: Bowling Green University Popular Press, 1972.

———. *Solid Gold: The Popular Record Industry*. New Brunswick, N.J.: Transaction Books, 1975.

——— and Richard A. Peterson, eds. *The Sounds of Social Change: Studies in Popular Culture*. Chicago: Rand McNally, 1972.

DeTurk, David A. and A. Poulin, Jr., eds. *The American Folk Scene: Dimensions of the Folksong Revival*. New York: Dell, 1967.

Dexter, Dave, Jr. *Playback: A Newsman/Record Producer's Hits and Misses from the Thirties to the Seventies*. New York: Billboard Publications, 1976.

Dufty, David, and John Anthony Scott. "How to Use Folk Songs" (No. 25). Washington, D.C.: National Council for the Social Studies, 1969.

Eisen, Jonathan, ed. *The Age of Rock: Sounds of the American Cultural Revolution*. New York: Vintage Books, 1969.

———, ed. *The Age of Rock – 2: Sights and Sounds of the American Cultural Revolution*. New York: Vintage Books, 1970.

———, ed. *Altamont: The Death of Innocence in the Woodstock Nation*. New York: Avon, 1970.

———, ed. *Twenty-Minute Fandangos and Forever Changes: A Rock Bazaar*. New York: Vintage Books, 1971.

Eliot, Marc. *Death of a Rebel – Phil Ochs and a Small Circle of Friends*. Garden City, N.Y.: Anchor Books, 1979.

Engel, Edward R. *White and Still All Right! A Collection of "White Group" Histories of the 50's and Early 60's*. New York: Crackerjack Press, 1977.

Escott, Colin, and Martin Hawkins. *Catalyst*. London: Aquarius, 1975.

Ewen, David. *All the Years of American Popular Music*. Englewood Cliffs, N.J.: Prentice-Hall, 1977.

*Exploring the World of EMI Music: A Billboard Advertising Supplement*. Los Angeles: Billboard Publications, 1979.

Fawcett, Anthony. *California Rock/California Sound*. Danbury, N.H.: Reed, 1978.

Ferris, William. *Blues from the Delta*. Garden City, N.Y.: Anchor Books/Doubleday, 1979.

Fong-Torres, Ben, ed. *The Rolling Stone Interviews* (vol. 2). New York: Warner Paperback Library, 1973.

———. *The Rollings Stone Rock 'N' Roll Reader*. New York: Bantam, 1974.

_____. *What's That Sound? The Contemporary Music Scene from the Pages of "Rolling Stone."* Garden City, N.Y.: Doubleday, 1976.

Gabree, John. *The World of Rock.* Greenwich, Conn.: Fawcett, 1968.

Garland, Phyl. *The Sound of Soul: The History of Black Music.* Chicago: Henry Regnery Company, 1969.

Garon, Paul. *Blues and the Poetic Spirit.* London: Eddison Press, 1975.

Gillett, Charlie. *Making Tracks: Atlantic Records and the Growth of a Multi-Billion-Dollar Industry.* New York: E. P. Dutton, 1974.

_____. *The Sound of the City: The Rise of Rock and Roll.* New York: Outerbridge and Dienstfrey, 1970.

Gleason, Ralph J. *The Jefferson Airplane and the San Francisco Sound.* New York: Ballantine, 1969.

Golden, Bruce. *The Beach Boys: Southern California Pastoral.* San Bernadino, Calif.: Borgo Press, 1976.

Goldman, Albert. *Freakshow.* New York: Atheneum, 1971.

Goldrosen, John. *Buddy Holly: His Life and Music.* New York: Quick Fox, 1979.

Goldstein, Richard. *Goldstein's Greatest Hits: A Book Mostly about Rock 'n Roll.* Englewood Cliffs, N.J.: Prentice-Hall, 1970.

Gray, Michael. *Song and Dance Man: The Art of Bob Dylan.* New York: E. P. Dutton, 1972.

Green, Douglas. *Country Roots: The Origins of Country Music.* New York: Hawthorn Books, 1976.

Grissim, John. *Country Music: White Man's Blues.* New York: Paperback Library, 1970.

Groia, Philip. *They All Sang on the Corner: New York City's R & B Vocal Groups of the 1950's.* Setauket, N.Y.: Edmond Pub. Co., 1974.

Guralnick, Peter. *Feel Like Going Home: Portraits in Blues and Rock 'N' Roll.* New York: Outerbridge and Dienstfrey, 1971.

Haralambos, Michael. *Right On: From Blues to Soul in Black America.* New York: Drake, 1975.

Heilbut, Tony. *The Gospel Sound: Good News and Bad Times.* New York: Simon and Schuster, 1971.

Hemphill, Paul. *The Nashville Sound: Bright Lights and Country Music.* New York: Simon and Schuster, 1970.

Herdeg, Walter, ed. *Graphis: Record Covers — The Evolution of Graphics Reflected in Record Packaging.* Zurich, Switzerland: Graphis Press, 1974.

Hirsch, Paul, and James W. Carey, eds. *Communication and Culture: Humanistic Models in Research.* Beverly Hills, Calif.: Sage, 1978.

Hoare, Ian, Tony Cummings, Clive Anderson, and Simon Frith. *The Soul Book.* New York: Dell, 1976.

Hoover, Cynthia A. *Music Machines — American Style.* Washington, D.C.: National Museum of History and Technology — Smithsonian Institution Press, 1971.

Hopkins, Jerry. *Elvis: A Biography.* New York: Warner Paperback Library, 1971.

————. *Festival! The Book of American Music Celebrations.* New York: Collier, 1970.

————. *The Rock Story.* New York: New American Library, 1970.

Jahn, Mike. *Rock: From Elvis Presley to the Rolling Stones.* New York: Grosset and Dunlap, 1973.

Jenkinson, Philip, and Alan Warner. *Celluloid Rock: Twenty Years of Movie Rock.* London: Lorrimer Publishing, 1974.

Jones, LeRoi. *Blues People: Negro Music in White America.* New York: William Morrow, 1963.

Karshner, Roger. *The Music Machine.* Los Angeles: Nash, 1971.

Keil, Charles. *Urban Blues.* Chicago: University of Chicago Press, 1966.

Kline, F. Gerald, and Peter Clarke, eds. *Mass Communications and Youth: Some Current Perspectives.* Beverly Hills, Calif.: Sage, 1971.

Krivine, J. *Juke Box Saturday Night.* Secaucus, N.J.: Chartwell, 1977.

Landau, Jon. *It's Too Late to Stop Now: A Rock and Roll Journal.* San Francisco: Straight Arrow Books, 1972.

Leaf, David. *The Beach Boys and the California Myth.* New York: Grosset and Dunlap, 1978.

Lepri, Paul. *The New Haven Sound, 1946–1976.* New Haven, Conn.; United Printing Services, 1977.

Levine, Lawrence W. *Black Culture and Black Consciousness: Afro-American Folk Thought from Slavery to Freedom.* New York: Oxford University Press, 1977.

Lewis, George, ed. *Side-Saddle on the Golden Calf.* Pacific Palisades, Calif.: Goodyear Pub. Co., 1972.

Lichter, Paul. *The Boy Who Dared to Rock: The Definitive Elvis.* Garden City, N.Y.: Dolphin, 1978.

Lydon, Michael. *Boogie Lightning.* New York: Dial, 1974.

————. *Rock Folk: Portraits from the Rock 'N' Roll Pantheon.* New York: Dial, 1971.

Mabey, Richard. *The Pop Process.* London: Hutchinson Educational, 1969.

McGregor, Craig, ed. *Bob Dylan: A Retrospective.* New York: William Morrow, 1972.

Malone, Bill C. *Country Music, U.S.A.: A Fifty Year History.* Austin: University of Texas, 1968.

———. and Judy McCulloh, eds. *Stars of Country Music: Uncle David Macon to Johnny Rodriguez.* Urbana: University of Illinois Press, 1975.

Marcus, Greil. *Mystery Train: Images of America in Rock 'n Roll Music.* New York: E. P. Dutton, 1975.

———, ed. *Rock and Roll Will Stand.* Boston: Beacon, 1969.

Marks, J. *Rock and Other Four Letter Words.* New York: Bantam, 1968.

May, Chris, and Tim Phillips. *British Beat.* London: Socion, 1974.

Mellers, Wilfrid. *Music in a New Found Land: Themes and Developments in the History of American Music.* London: Barrie and Rickliff, 1964.

———. *Twilight of the Gods: The Music of the Beatles.* New York: Schirmer, 1973.

Meltzer, Richard. *The Aesthetics of Rock.* New York: Something Else Press, 1970.

Millar, Bill. *The Drifters: The Rise and Fall of the Black Vocal Group.* New York: Collier, 1971.

Miller, Jim, ed. *The Rolling Stone Illustrated History of Rock And Roll.* New York: Random House, 1976.

Morse, David. *Motown and the Arrival of Black Music.* New York: Collier, 1971.

*Music/Records/200: Billboard's July 4, 1976 Spotlight on America.* New York: Billboard Publications, 1976.

Nanry, Charles, ed. *American Music: From Storyville to Woodstock.* New Brunswick, N.J.: Transaction Books, 1972.

Nassour, Ellis, and Richard Broderick. *Rock Opera: The Creation of Jesus Christ Superstar From Record Album to Broadway Show to Motion Picture.* New York: Hawthorne Books, 1973.

Neff, Robert, and Anthony Connor, comps. *Blues.* Boston: Godine, 1975.

Nye, Russel B. *The Unembarrassed Muse: The Popular Arts in America.* New York: Dial, 1970.

Oakley, Giles. *The Devil's Music: A History of the Blues.* New York: Harcourt Brace Jovanovich, 1978.

Oliver, Paul. *Aspects of the Blues Tradition.* New York: Oak Publications, 1970.

———. *Conversations with the Blues.* New York: Horizon Press, 1965.

———. *The Meaning of the Blues.* New York: Collier, 1972 (1960).

———. *The Story of the Blues.* London: Chilton, 1969.

Orloff, Katherine. *Rock 'N' Roll Woman.* Los Angeles: Nash, 1974.

Oster, Harry, comp. *Living Country Blues.* New York: Minerva Press, 1975.

Oxtoby, David, edited by David Sandison. *Rockvisions: The Art of David Oxtoby*. New York: E. P. Dutton, 1978.

Paige, Earl, ed. *Black Magic — A Genealogy of Sound. A Billboard Spotlight*. Los Angeles: Billboard Publications, 1979.

Palmer, Tony. *All You Need Is Love: The Story of Popular Music*. New York: Grossman, 1976.

Peck, Ira, ed. *The New Sound*. New York: Scholastic Book Services, 1966.

Peellaert, Guy, and Nik Cohn. *Rock Dreams*. New York: Popular Library, 1973.

Peterson, Richard A., ed. *The Production of Culture*. Beverly Hills, Calif.: Sage, 1976.

*Playboy's Music Scene*. Chicago: Playboy, 1972.

Pollock, Bruce. *In Their Own Words: Twenty Successful Song Writers Tell How They Write Their Songs*. New York: Collier, 1975.

Pollock, Bruce, and John Wagman. *The Face of Rock and Roll: Images of a Generation*. New York: Holt, Rinehart and Winston, 1978.

Editors of Ramparts, eds. *Conversations with the New Reality: Readings in the Cultural Revolution*. San Francisco: Canfield Press, 1971.

Reid, Robert. "Music and Social Problems" (A Poster Series). Portland, Maine: J. Weston Walch, 1971.

Rivelli, Pauline, and Robert Levin, eds. *The Rock Giants*. New York: World, 1970.

Robinson, Richard. *Pop, Rock, and Soul*. New York: Pyramid, 1972.

———. *Rock Revolution*. New York: Popular Library, 1976.

——— and Andy Zwerling. *The Rock Scene*. New York: Pyramid, 1971.

Rodnitzky, Jerome L. *Minstrels of the Dawn: The Folk-Protest Singer as a Cultural Hero*. Chicago: Nelson-Hall, 1976.

Editors of Rolling Stone, comps. *The Rolling Stone Interviews*. New York: Paperback Library, 1971.

———, eds. *The Rolling Stone Record Review*. New York: Pocket Books, 1971.

———, eds. *The Rolling Stone Record Review (Vol. II)*. New York: Pocket Books, 1974.

Rowe, Mike. *Chicago Breakdown*. New York: Drake, 1975.

Rust, Brian. *The American Record Label Book: From the 19th Century through 1942*. New Rochelle, N.Y.: Arlington, 1978.

Saleh, Dennis, ed. *Rock Art: The Golden Age of Record Album Covers*. New York: Comma Books, 1978.

Sander, Ellen. *Trips: Rock Life in the Sixties*. New York: Scribner's, 1973.

Sarlin, Bob. *Turn It Up (I Can't Hear the Words): The Best of the New Singer/ Song Writers.* New York: Simon and Schuster, 1973.

Schiffman, Jack. *Uptown — The Story of Harlem's Apollo Theatre.* New York: Cowles, 1971.

Scott, John Anthony. *The Ballad of America: The History of the United States in Song and Story.* New York: Bantam, 1966.

Shaw, Arnold. *Honkers and Shouters: The Golden Years of Rhythm and Blues.* New York: Collier, 1978.

———. *Rock Revolution.* New York: Crowell-Collier, 1969.

———. *The Rockin' 50's: The Decade That Transformed the Pop Music Scene.* New York: Hawthorn Books, 1974.

———. *The World of Soul.* New York: Paperback Library, 1971.

Smitherman, Geneva. *Black Language and Culture: Sounds of Soul.* New York: Harper and Row, 1975.

Somma, Robert, ed. *No One Waved Good-Bye: A Casualty Report on Rock and Roll.* New York: Outerbridge and Dienstfrey, 1971.

Southern, Eileen. *The Music of Black Americans: A History.* New York: W. W. Norton, 1971.

———, ed. *Readings in Black American Music.* New York: W. W. Norton, 1971.

Spitz, Robert Stephen. *The Making of Superstars: Artists and Executives of the Rock Music Business.* Garden City, N.Y. Anchor Books/Doubleday, 1978.

Stampler, Irwin. *Guitar Years: Pop Music from Country and Western to Hard Rock.* Garden City, N.Y.: Doubleday, 1970.

Stokes, Geoffrey. *Starmaking Machinery: Inside the Business of Rock and Roll.* New York: Vintage Books, 1976.

Thorgerson (Hipgnosis), Storm, and Roger Dean, eds. *Album Cover Art.* Surrey, Eng.: A Dragon's World Book, 1977.

Tobler, John. *Guitar Heroes.* New York: St. Martin's Press, 1978.

Titon, Jeff Todd. *Early Downhome Blues: A Musical and Cultural Analysis.* Urbana: University of Illinois Press, 1977.

Tosches, Nick. *Country: The Biggest Music in America.* New York: Stein and Day, 1977.

Vassal, Jacques. *Electric Children: Roots and Branches of Modern Folkrock.* New York: Taplinger, 1976.

Vulliamy, Graham, and Ed Lee, eds. *Pop Music in School.* Cambridge: Cambridge University Press, 1976.

Whetmore, Edward Jay. *Mediamerica: Form, Content, and Consequence of Mass*

*Communication*. Belmont, Calif.: Wadsworth, 1979.

Whitcomb, Ian. *After the Ball: Pop Music from Rag to Rock*. Baltimore: Penguin, 1972.

Wiegand, Wayne A., ed. *Popular Culture and the Library: Current Issues Symposium II*. Lexington: University of Kentucky, 1978.

Williams, Paul. *Outlaw Blues: A Book of Rock Music*. New York: E. P. Dutton, 1969.

Yorke, Ritchie. *The History of Rock 'N' Roll*. New York: Methuen, 1976.


## ARTICLES AND RECORD REVIEWS

Abramson, Rudy. " 'Take This Job . . .' – A Timely Symbol." *The* (Columbia, South Carolina) *State* (March 27, 1978):1, 4.

Ackerman, Paul. "A Look at the Record Industry 25 Years Ago as the Old Generation Yielded to the New." *Billboard* (January 3, 1976):11, 47.

———. "The Poetry and Imagery of Country Songs." *Billboard* (March 18, 1978): CMA 22, 42.

Albert, Werner G. "Dimensionality of Perceived Violence in Rock Music: Musical Intensity and Lyrical Violence Content." *Popular Music and Society* 6 (1978):27,38.

Ames, Russell. "Implications of Negro Folk Songs." *Science and Society* 4 (Spring 1951):163–73.

———. "Protest and Irony in Negro Folksongs." *Science and Society* 14 (Summer 1950):193–213.

Averill, Patricia. "How to Teach the Rock and Roll Generation What They Don't Know." *Popular Culture Methods* 3 (Spring 1976):31–36.

Barbieri, Richard E. "Resources for the Study of Popular Culture." *English Journal* 65 (March 1976):35–40.

Barker, John W. "Music – The Forgotten Art." *Network News Exchange* 3 (1978):19–21.

Becker, Howard S. "The Professional Dance Musician and His Audience." *American Journal of Sociology* 62 (September 1961):136–44.

Belz, Carl I. "Popular Music and the Folk Tradition." *Journal of American Folklore* 80 (April-June 1967):130–42.

Browne, Ray B. "The Uses of Popular Culture in the Teaching of American History." *Social Education* 36 (January 1972):49–53.

Byrd, Donald. "The Meaning of Black Music." *Black Scholar* 3 (Summer 1972):28–31.

Campbell, Gregg M. "Bob Dylan and the Pastoral Apocalypse." *Journal of Popular Culture* 8 (Spring, 1975):696–707.

Cantrick, Robert B. "The Blind Men and the Elephant: Scholars on Popular Music." *Ethnomusicology* 9 (May 1965):100–14.

Carey, James T. "Changing Courtship Patterns in the Popular Song." *American Journal of Sociology* 74 (May 1969):720–31.

————. "The Ideology of Autonomy in Popular Lyrics: A Content Analysis." *Psychiatry* 32 (May 1969):150–64.

Castleman, Harry, and Wally Podrazik. "The Case of the Belittled Beatles Tapes." *Stereo Review* 39 (November 1977):66–68.

Cawelti, John G. "Popular Culture's Coming-of-Age." *Journal of Aesthetic Education* 10 (July-October 1976):165–82.

Chenoweth, Lawrence. "The Rhetoric of Hope and Despair: A Study of the Jimi Hendrix Experience and the Jefferson Airplane." *American Quarterly* 23 (Spring 1971):25–45.

Christianson, Nora D. "Teaching American History through Its Period Music." *Social Studies* 40 (April 1949):156–65.

Christgau, Robert. "Rock Critics." *Harper's* (September 1969):24–28.

Cohen, John. "The Folk Music Interchange: Negro and White." In *The American Folk Scene: Dimensions of the Folksong Revival,* ed. David A. DeTurk and A. Poulin, Jr. New York: Dell, 1967. Pp. 59–66.

Cohen, Mitch. "Rockcinema—The First 21 Years, 1955–1976." *Phonograph Record Magazine* 6 (August 1976):1, 36–43.

Cohn, William H. "Popular Culture and Social History." *Journal of Popular Culture* 11 (Summer 1977):167–79.

Cole, Richard. "Top Songs of the Sixties: A Content Analysis of Popular Lyrics." *American Behavioral Scientist* 14 (January-February 1971):389–400.

Cooper, B. Lee. "Beyond Flash Gordon and 'Star Wars': Science Fiction and History Instruction." *Social Education* 42 (May 1978):392–97.

————. "Contemporary Singers as Subjects for Biographical Study." *Library-College Experimenter* 5 (May 1979):13–28.

————. "Examining Social Change through Contemporary History: An Audio Media Proposal." *History Teacher* 6 (August 1973):523–34.

————. "Exploring the Future through Contemporary Music," *Media and Methods* 12 (April 1976):32–35ff.

————. "Folk History, Alternative History, and Future History." *Teaching History: A Journal of Methods* 2 (Spring 1977):58–62.

————. "Futurescope," *Audiovisual Instruction* 21 (January 1976):42–48.

————. "The Image of the Black Man: Contemporary Lyrics as Oral History." *Journal of the Interdenominational Theological Center* 5 (Spring 1978):105–22.

_____. "The Image of the Outsider in Contemporary Lyrics." *Journal of Popular Culture* 12 (Summer 1978):168–78.

_____. "Images of the Future in Popular Music: Lyrical Comments on Tomorrow." *Social Education* 39 (May 1975):276–85.

_____. "Jerry Lee Lewis and Little Richard: Career Parallels in the Lives of the Court Jesters of Rock 'N' Roll." *Music World and Record Digest* 46 (May 23, 1979):6.

_____. "Oral History, Popular Music, and Les McCann." *Social Studies* 67 (May/June 1976):115–18.

_____. "Popular Culture: Teaching Problems and Challenges." In *Popular Culture and the Library,* edited by Wayne A. Wiegand. Lexington: University of Kentucky, 1978. Pp. 10–26.

_____. "Popular Music: A Creative Teaching Resource." *Audiovisual Instruction* 24 (March 1979):37–43.

_____. "Popular Music: An Untapped Resource for Teaching Contemporary Black History." *Journal of Negro Education* 48 (Winter 1979):20–36.

_____. "Popular Music and Academic Enrichment in the Residence Hall." *NASPA Journal* 11 (Winter 1974):50–57.

_____. "Popular Music, Science Fiction, and Controversial Issues: Sources for Reflective Thinking." *History and Social Science Teacher* 12 (Fall 1976):31–45.

_____. "Record Revivals as Barometers of Social Change: The Historical Use of Contemporary Audio Resources." *JEMF Quarterly* 14 (Spring 1978):38–44.

_____. "Review of *American Graffiti,*" *History Teacher* 7 (February 1974):283–84.

_____. "Review of *Chuck Berry's Golden Decade.*" *History Teacher* 8 (February 1975):300–301.

_____. "Rock Music and Religious Education: A Proposed Synthesis." *Religious Education* 70 (May-June 1975):289–99.

_____. "Social Change, Popular Music and the Teacher." *Social Education* 37 (December 1973):776–81, 793.

_____. "Teaching American History Through Popular Music." *AHA Newsletter* 14 (October 1976):3–5.

_____. "Teaching Contemporary History from an Audio Perspective – 'The Image of American Society in Popular Music,'" *Library-College Experimenter* (November 1976):22–34.

_____. "The Traditional and Beyond: Resources for Teaching Women's Studies." *Audiovisual Instruction* 22 (December 1977):14–18ff.

_____. "Women's Studies and Popular Music: Using Audio Resources in Social Studies Instruction." *History and Social Science Teacher* 14 (Fall 1978):29–40.

_____ and Larry S. Haverkos. "The Image of American Society in Popular Music: A Search for Identity and Values." *Social Studies* 64 (December 1973):319–32.

_____ and Verdan D. Traylor. "Establishing Rock Standards: The Practice of Record Revivals in Contemporary Music, 1953–1977." *Goldmine* 36 (May 1979):37–38.

_____. "Liberal Education and Technology in Small Colleges: Popular Music and the Computer." *International Journal of Instructional Media* 7 (1979–80):25–35.

Coppage, Noel. "In Country Music, the Play on Words, Words, Words Is the Thing," *Stereo Review* (July 1975):54–56.

_____. "Music and TV." *Stereo Review* (June 1976):64–68.

_____. "Phil Ochs and the Death of Innocence." *Stereo Review* (April 1977):104.

Cowan, Paul. "Paul Simon: The Odysseus of Urban Melancholy." *Rolling Stone* (July 1, 1976):50–59.

Culkin, John. "Why the Arts?" *Media and Methods* 13 (October 1976):52–53.

Danker, Frederick E. "Folksongs in the High School Classroom." *Sing Out!* 13 (February/March 1963):16–17.

_____. "The Repertory and Style of a Country Singer: Johnny Cash." *Journal of American Folklore* 85 (October/December 1972):309–29.

Davis, Evan. "The Psychological Characteristics of Beatle Mania." *Journal of the History of Ideas* 30 (April/June 1969):273–80.

Dean, Maury. "Wo-Uh-Ho Peggy Sue: Exploring a Teenage Queen Linguistically." *Popular Music and Society* 2 (Spring 1973):244–54.

Denisoff, R. Serge. "Content Analysis: The Achilles Heel of Popular Culture?" *Journal of Popular Culture* 9 (Fall 1975):456–60.

_____. "Folk-Rock: Folk Music, Protest, or Commercialism?" *Journal of Popular Culture* 3 (Fall 1969):214–30.

_____. "Massification and Popular Music: A Review." *Journal of Popular Culture* 9 (Spring 1976):886–94.

_____. "Nashville Rebels: Myth or Reality." *Popular Music and Society* 5 (1977):79–88.

_____. "Protest Songs: Those on the Top Forty and Those of the Streets." *American Quarterly* 22 (Winter 1970):807–23.

_____. "A Short Note on Studying Popular Culture." *Popular Culture Methods* 1 (August 1972):2–5.

_____. "Songs of Persuasion: A Sociological Analysis of Urban Propaganda

Songs." *Journal of American Folklore* 79 (October-December 1966):581–89.

_____ and Fandray, David. " 'Hey, Hey Woody Guthrie I Wrote You a Song'; The Political Side of Bob Dylan." *Popular Music and Society* 5 (1977):31–42.

_____. and Levine, Mark H. "The One Dimensional Approach to Popular Music: A Research Note" *Journal of Popular Culture* 4 (Spring 1971):911–19.

_____ and Richard A. Peterson. "Theories of Culture, Music; and Society." In *The Sounds of Social Change: Studies in Popular Culture*. Chicago: Rand McNally, 1972. Pp. 1–12.

Denzin, Norman K. "Problems in Analyzing Elements of Mass Culture: Notes on the Popular Song and Other Artistic Productions." *American Journal of Sociology* 65 (May 1970):1035–38.

"Dylan-Hard Rain." *Media and Methods* 13 (September 1976):34–35.

Ertegun, Nesuhi. "It's Just Thievery, Mr. Goh." *Billboard* (May 12, 1979):16.

Etzkorn, K. Peter. "The Relationship between Musical and Social Patterns in American Popular Music." *Journal of Research in Music Education* 12 (Winter 1964):279–86.

Evans, David. "From Contributors—Afro-American Folklore." *Journal of American Folklore* 86 (October-December 1973):413–34.

_____. "Techniques of Blues Composition among Black Folksingers." *Journal of American Folklore* 87 (July/September 1974):240–49.

Farley, M. Foster. "Music and Liberty." *Musical Heritage Review* 1 (November 21, 1977):16–18ff.

Feldman, David. "How to Teach Students About Something They Already Know More About than You Do: Some Approaches to Teaching Rock Music." *Popular Culture Methods* 3 (Spring 1976):22–31.

Ferrandino, Joe. "Rock Culture and the Development of Social Consciousness." In *Side-Saddle on the Golden Calf*, ed. George H. Lewis. Pacific Palisades, Calif.: Goodyear Publishing Company, 1972. Pp. 263–90.

Flippo, Chet. "The History of *Rolling Stone*—A Three-Part Study." *Popular Music and Society* 3 (1974):159–88, 258–80, and 281–98.

_____. "Phil Ochs, Troubadour, Dead: 'He Was A Child of the 60s." *Rolling Stone* (May 20, 1976):213–15.

Ford, Larry. "Geographical Factors in the Origin, Evolution, and Diffusion of Rock and Roll Music." *Journal of Geography* 70 (November 1971):455–64.

Fox, William S., and James D. Williams. "Political Orientation and Music Preferences among College Students." *Public Opinion Quarterly* 38 (Fall 1974):352–71.

Fox, William S., and Michael H. Wince. "Feminist Attitudes and Preferences for a Feminist 'Message' Song: A Research Note." *Popular Music and Society* 4 (1975):156–69.

Freudiger, Patricia. "Love Lauded and Love Lamented: Men and Women in Popular Music." *Popular Music and Society*, 6 (1978):1–10.

Friedberg, Harris. "Bob Dylan: Psychohistorian of a Generation." *Chronicle of Higher Education* 8 (January 28, 1974):15–16.

Gabree, John. "The Roots of Rock: Rhythm and Blues." In *Music '69: The 14th Annual down beat Yearbook*. Chicago: down beat magazine, 1969. Pp. 16–19ff.

Gantz, Walter, Howard M. Gartenberg, Martin L. Pearson, and Seth O. Schiller. "Gratifications and Expectations Associations with Pop Music among Adolescents." *Popular Music and Society* 6 (1978):81–89.

Gillett, Charlie. "Just Let Me Hear Some of That Rock and Roll Music." *Urban Review* 1 (December 1966):11–14.

Ginsburg, David D. "Rock Is a Way of Life: The World of Rock 'N' Roll Fanzines and Fandom." *Serials Review* (January/March 1979):29–46.

Gleason, Ralph J. "The Education of the Jazz Virtuoso." In *The Creative College Student: An Unmet Challenge*, ed. Paul Heist. San Francisco: Jossey-Bass, 1968. Pp. 84–98.

————. "Like a Rolling Stone." *American Scholar* 36 (Autumn 1967):555–63.

————."The Times They Are A-Changin,' " *Ramparts* (April 1965):36–48.

Goldberg, Steven. "Bob Dylan and the Poetry of Salvation." *Saturday Review* (May 30, 1970):43–46ff.

Goldman, Albert. "The Emergency of Rock." In *New American Review* #3, ed. Theodore Solotaroff. New York: New American Library, 1968. Pp. 118–39.

Goldstein, Richard. "Wiggy Words That Feed Your Mind." In *The Whole Idea Catalog: College Writing Projects*, ed. Idelle Sullens. New York: Random House, 1971. Pp. 401–5.

Graustark, Barbara, with Janet Huck, Peggy Clausen, and Ronald Henkoff. "Disco Takes Over." *Newsweek* (April 2, 1979):56–64.

Greenway, John. "Folk Songs as Socio-Historical Documents." *Western Folklore* 19 (January 1960):1–9.

Grendysa, Pete. "The Forty Year War: The Story of the Music Licensing Societies." *Goldmine* 32–34 (January/February/March 1979):25–26, 22–23, and 30–31.

Griffith, Asheley R., and Kerrin Griffith. "Elvis Presley." *Stereo Review* 37 (July 1976):76–80.

Gritzner, Charles F. "Country Music: A Reflection of Popular Culture." *Journal of Popular Culture* 11 (Spring 1978):857–64.

Gruver, Rod. "The Blues as Poetry." In *Music '69: The 14th Annual down beat Yearbook*. Chicago: down beat magazine, 1969. Pp. 38–41.

Haralambos, Michael. "Soul Music and Blues: Their Meaning and Relevance in Northern United States Black Ghettos." In *Afro-American Anthropology*, ed. Norman E. Whitten, Jr., and John F. Szwed. New York: Free Press, 1970. Pp. 367–84.

Harmon, James E. "Meaning in Rock Music: Notes toward a Theory of Communication." *Popular Music and Society* (Fall 1972):18–32.

Hecht, Michael L. "Rock-Tongue." In *Language: Concepts and Processes*, ed. Joseph A. DeVito. Englewood Cliffs, N.J.: Prentice-Hall, 1973. Pp. 221–28.

Heckman, Don. "Black Music and White America." In *Black America*, ed. John F. Szwed. New York: Basic Books, 1970. Pp. 158–70.

Hellmann, John M. Jr. " 'I'm a Monkey': The Influence of the Black American Blues Argot on the Rolling Stones." *Journal of American Folklore* 86 (October-December 1973):367–73.

Henderson, Floyd M. "The Image of New York City in American Popular Music of 1890–1970." *New York Folklore Quarterly* 30 (December 1974):267–78.

Hesbacher, Peter. "Contemporary Popular Music: Directions for Further Research." *Popular Music and Society* 2 (Summer 1973):297–310.

_____. "Sound Exposure in Radio: The Misleading Nature of the Station Playlist." *Popular Music and Society* 3 (1974):189–201.

_____, Nancy Clasby, H. Gerald Clasby, and David G. Berger. "Solo Female Vocalists: Some Shifts in Stature and Alterations in Song." *Popular Music and Society* 5 (1977):1–16.

_____, Robert Downing, and David G. Berger. "Sound Recording Popularity Charts: A Useful Tool for Music Research—A Two-Part Study." *Popular Music and Society* 4 (1975):3–18, 86–99.

_____. Robert Rosenow, Bruce Anderson, and David G. Berger. "Radio Programming: Relating Ratings to Revenues in a Major Market." *Popular Music and Society* 4 (1975):208–25.

Hey, Kenneth R. "I Feel a Change Comin' On: The Counter-Cultural Image of the South in Southern Rock 'N' Roll." *Popular Music and Society* 5 (1977):93–99.

_____. " 'I'll Give It a 95': An Approach to the Study of Early Rock 'N' Roll." *Popular Music and Society* 3 (Summer 1974):315–28.

Heyman, Scott. "And Music." *Music Educators Journal* 54 (May 1968):35–38.

Hirsch, Paul M. "Sociological Approaches to the Pop Music Phenomenon." *American Behavioral Scientist* 14 (January-February 1971):371-88.

Hirsch, Paul, John Robinson, Elizabeth Keogh Taylor, and Stephen B. Witney. "The Changing Popular Song: An Historical Overview." *Popular Music and Society* 1 (Winter 1972):83-93.

Hoffmann, Frank. "Popular Music Collections and Public Libraries." *Southeastern Librarian* 23 (Winter 1974): 26-31.

Horton, Donald. "The Dialogue of Courtship in Popular Song." *American Journal of Sociology* 62 (May 1957):569-78.

Janeti, Joseph. "Folk Music's Affair with Popular Culture: A Redefinition of the 'Revival.' " In *New Dimensions in Popular Culture*, ed. Russel B. Nye. Bowling Green, Ohio: Bowling Green University Popular Press, 1972. Pp. 224-35.

Jefferson, Margo. "Ripping Off Black Music." *Harper's* (January 1973):40-45.

Johnson, Eric P. "The Use of Folk Songs in Education: Some Examples of the Use of Folk Songs in the Teaching of History, Geography, Economics, and English Literature." *Vocational Aspect of Education* 21 (Summer 1969):89-94.

Johnstone, John, and Elihu Katz. "Youth and Popular Music: A Study of the Sociology of Taste." *American Journal of Sociology* 62 (May 1957):563-68.

Josephs, Norman A. "Reflections on Teaching American Popular Music in Britain . . ." *Popular Music and Society* 6 (1979):229-33.

Kamin, Jonathan. "Parallels in the Social Reactions to Jazz and Rock," *Journal of Jazz Studies* 2 (December 1974):95-125.

———. "Taking the Roll out of Rock 'N' Roll: Reverse Acculturation." *Popular Music and Society* 2 (Fall 1972):1-17.

———. "The White R&B Audience and the Music Industry, 1952-1956." *Popular Music and Society* 4 (1975):170-87.

"Keeping Up with Rock 'N' Roll." *Ohio Schools* 50 (February 25, 1972):21.

Kermode, Frank, Stephen Spender, and Art Kane. "Bob Dylan: The Metaphor at the End of the Funnel." *Esquire* (May 1972):109-18ff.

King, Woodie, Jr. "Searching for Brothers Kindred: Rhythm and Blues of the 1950's." *Black Scholar* 6 (November 1974):19-30.

Lees, Gene. "ZPG and Tomorrow's LPs." *Saturday Review* (November 11, 1975:45-48.

Levine, Mark H., and Thomas J. Harig. "The Role of Rock: A Review and Critique of Alternative Perspectives on the Impact of Rock Music." *Popular Music and Society* 4 (1975):195-207.

Lewis, George H. "Country Music Lyrics." *Journal of Communication* 26 (Autumn 1976):37–40.

_____. "Cultural Socialization and the Development of Taste Cultures and Culture Classes in American Popular Music: Existing Evidence and Proposed Research Directions." *Popular Music and Society* 4 (1975): 226–41.

_____. "Popular Music and Research Design: Methodological Alternatives." *Popular Music and Society* 1 (Winter 1972):108–15.

_____. "Social Class and Cultural Communication: An Analysis of Song Lyrics." *Popular Music and Society* 5 (1977):23–30.

_____. "Social Protest and Self Awareness in Black Popular Music." *Popular Music and Society* 2 (Summer 1973):327–33.

Linton, David S. "Rock and the Media." *Media and Methods* 13 (October 1976):56–59.

Lund, Jens. "Country Music Goes to War: Songs for the Red-Blooded American." *Popular Music and Society* 1 (Summer 1972):210–30.

_____ and R. Serge Denisoff. "The Folk Music Revival and the Counter Culture." *Journal of American Folklore* 84 (October/December 1971):394–405.

Lyons, Anne W. "Creative Teaching in Interdisciplinary Humanities: The Human Values in Pop Music." *Minnesota English Journal* 10 (Winter 1974):23–31.

McCaghy, Charles H., and R. Serge Denisoff. "Pirates and Politics: An Analysis of Interest Group Conflict." In *Deviance, Conflict, and Criminality*, ed. R. Serge Denisoff and Charles H. McCaghy. Chicago: Rand McNally, 1973. Pp. 297–309.

McCutcheon, Lynn. "Unsung Heroes Who Also Sang." *Negro History Bulletin* 36 (January 1973):9–11.

Madori, Peter J. "Filling the Moral Vacuum." *Billboard* (May 26, 1979):20.

Magarell, Jack. ". . . First Try Rock, Pop, and All That Jazz." *Chronicle of Higher Education* 14 (August 15, 1977):3.

Mayer, Ira. "Small Labels Have a Lot to Offer in Folk, Jazz, and Blues." *Stereo Review* (January 1977):74–78.

Melnick, Mimi Clar. " 'I Can Peep through Muddy Water and Spy Dry Land': Boasts in the Blues." In *Folklore International: Essays in Traditional Literature, Belief, and Custom in Honor of Wayland Debs Hand*, ed. D. K. Wilgus, with the assistance of Carol Sommer. (Hatboro, Pa.: Folklore Associates, 1967. Pp. 139–49.

Metcalfe, Ralph H., Jr. "The Western Roots of Afro-American Music." *Black Scholar* 1 (June 1970):16–25.

Miller, Lloyd, and James K. Skipper, Jr. "Sounds of Protest: Jazz and the Militant Avant-Garde." In *Approaches to Deviance: Theories, Concepts, and Research Findings*, ed. Mark Lefton, James K. Skipper, Jr., and Charles H. McCaghy. New York: Appleton-Century-Crofts, 1968. Pp. 129–40.

Mitz, Rick. "Who Writes All Those Rock Lyrics? *Stereo Review* 38 (February 1977):60–63.

Mohrmann, G. P., and F. Eugene Scott. "Popular Music and World War II: The Rhetoric of Continuation." *Quarterly Journal of Speech* (February 1976):145–56.

Mooney, Hughson F. "Just before Rock: Pop Music 1950–1953 Reconsidered." *Popular Music and Society* 3 (1974):65–108.

————. "Popular Music Since the 1920's: The Significance of Shifting Taste." *Popular Music and Society* 1 (Spring 1972):129–43.

————. "Rock as an Historical Phenomenon." *Popular Music and Society* 1 (Spring 1972):129–43.

————. "Songs, Singers, and Society." *American Quarterly* 6 (Fall 1954):221–32.

Moonoogian, George. "Elvis and the Originals." *Record Exchanger* 3 (1973):16.

Morgan, John P., and Thomas C. Tulloss. "The Jake Walk Blues: A Toxicologic Tragedy Mirrored in American Popular Music." *Annals of Internal Medicine* 85 (December 1976):804–808.

Morse, David E. "Avant-Rock in the Classroom." *English Journal* 58 (February 1969):196–200ff.

Mosher, Harold F., Jr. "The Lyrics of American Pop Music: A New Poetry." *Popular Music and Society* 1 (Spring 1972):167–76.

Murphy, Karen, and Ronald Gross. "All You Need Is Love, Love Is All You Need." In *Pop Culture in America*, ed. David Manning White. New York: Quadrangle, 1970. Pp. 205–21.

Murray, Donald C. "James Baldwin's 'Sonny's Blues': Complicated and Simple." *Studies in Short Fiction* 14 (Fall 1977):353–57.

"Nine Ways of Looking at the Beatles, 1963–1973." *Stereo Review* 30 (February 1973):56–63.

O'Neill, Catherine. "Making Music for the Movies." *Chronicle of Books and Arts* 18 (July 9, 1979):14–15.

Otto, John S., and Augustus M. Burns. "Black and White Cultural Interaction in the Early Twentieth Century South: Race and Hillbilly Music." *Phylon* 35 (December 1974):407–17.

————. "The Use of Race and Hillbilly Recordings as Sources for Historical

Research: The Problem of Color Hierarchy among Afro-Americans in the Early Twentieth Century." *Journal of American Folklore* 85 (October/December 1972):344–55.

Parker, Charles. "Pop Song—The Manipulated Ritual." In *The Black Rainbow: Essays on the Present Breakdown of Culture,* ed. Peter Abbs. London: Heimemann Educational Books, 1975. Pp. 134–67.

Peterson, Richard A., "Disco!" *Chronicle Review* 17 (October 2, 1978):26–27.

———. "Single-Industry Firm to Conglomerate Synergistics: Alternative Strategies for Selling Insurance and Country Music." In *Growing Metropolis: Aspects of Development in Nashville,* ed. James Blumstein and Benjamin Walter. Nashville: Vanderbilt University Press, 1975. Pp. 341–57.

Peterson, Richard A., and David G. Berger. "Cycles in Symbol Production: The Case of Popular Music." *American Sociological Review* 40 (April 1975):158–73.

———. "Entrepreneurship in Organizations: Evidence from the Popular Music Industry." *Administrative Science Quarterly* 16 (March 1971):97–106.

———. "Three Eras in the Manufacture of Popular Music Lyrics." In *The Sounds of Social Change: Studies in Popular Culture,* ed. R. Serge Denisoff and Richard Peterson. Chicago: Rand McNally, 1972. Pp. 282–303.

Peterson, Richard A., and Russell B. Davis, Jr. "The Contemporary American Radio Audience." *Popular Music and Society* 3 (Summer 1974):299–313.

Poirier, Richard. "Learning from the Beatles." *Partisan Review* 34 (Fall 1967):526–46.

Pollock, Bruce. "Paul Simon: Survivor from the Sixties." *Saturday Review* (June 12, 1976):43–44ff.

"Popular Culture in the English Classroom." *English Journal* 66 (March 1976):28–88.

Reid, Robert H. "Philosophy Teacher Tunes in Students with Rock Music." *Cleveland Plain Dealer* (February 20, 1977):20.

Reinartz, Kay F. "The Paper Doll: Images of American Woman in Popular Songs." In *Women: A Feminist Perspective,* ed. Jo Freeman. Palo Alto, Calif.: Mayfield, 1975. Pp. 293–308.

Rieger, Jon H. "The Coming Crisis in the Youth Music Market." *Popular Music and Society* 4 (1975):19–35.

Riesman, David. "Listening to Popular Music." *American Quarterly* 2 (Winter 1950):359–71.

Ritt, Sharon I. "Using Music to Teach Reading Skills in Social Studies." *Reading Teacher* 27 (March 1974):594–601.

Robinson, John R., and Paul Hirsch. "It's the Sound That Does It." *Psychology Today* 3 (October 1969):42–45.

Robinson, John P., Robert Pilskaln, and Paul Hirsch. "Protest Rock and Drugs." *Journal of Communication* 26 (Autumn 1976):125–36.

Rodnitzky, Jerome L. "The Decline of Contemporary Protest Music." *Popular Music and Society* 1 (Fall 1971):44–50.

———. "The Evolution of the American Protest Song." *Journal of Popular Culture* 3 (Summer 1969):35–45.

———. "The New Revivalism: American Protest Songs, 1945–1968." *South Atlantic Quarterly* 70 (Winter 1971):13–21.

———. "Popular Music in American Studies." *History Teacher* 7 (August 1974):503–10.

———. "Songs of Sisterhood: The Music of Women's Liberation." *Popular Music and Society* 4 (1975):77–85.

Rosenstone, Richard A. " 'The Times They Are A-Changing': The Music of Protest." *Annals of the American Academy of Political and Social Science* 381 (March 1969):131–44.

Russell, Wayne. "Blue Suede Shoes: Analysis of a Rock Classic." *Record Digest* 2 (February 1, 1979):39–40.

Sanjek, Russell. "The War on Rock." In *Music '72: The 17th Annual down beat Yearbook*. Chicago: down beat magazine, 1972. Pp. 16–19ff.

Seidman, Laurence I. " 'Get on the Raft with Taft' and Other Musical Treats." *Social Education* 40 (October 1976):436–37.

———. "Teaching about the American Revolution through Its Folk Songs." *Social Education* (November 1973):653–64.

Sievert, William A. "For Every Bob Dylan, a Joni Mitchell." *Chronicle of Higher Education* 11 (January 12, 1976):17.

Skipper, James K. "How Popular Is Popular Music? Youth and Diversification of Musical Preferences." *Popular Music and Society* 2 (Winter 1973):145–54.

Snyder, Robert. "Cover Records: What? When? And Why?" *Record Digest* 1 (July 1, 1978):3–18.

Stevenson, Gordon. "Popular Culture and the Public Library." In *Advances in Librarianship – Vol. VII*, ed. Melvin J. Voight and Michael H. Harris. New York: Academic Press, 1977. Pp. 177–229.

———. "Race Records: Victims of Benign Neglect in Libraries." *Wilson Library Bulletin* 50 (November 1975):224–32.

———. "The Wayward Scholar: Resources and Research in Popular Culture." *Library Trends* 25 (April 1977):779–818.

Sutherland, Sam. "Jerry Wexler: Producer with a Fan's Passion." *High Fidelity* 27 (August 1978):101–5.

Szwed, John F. "Negro Music: Urban Renewal." In *Our Living Traditions: An Introduction to American Folklore*, ed. Tristram Potter Coffin. New York: Basic Books, 1968. Pp. 272–82.

Tamke, Susan S. "Oral History and Popular Culture: A Method for the Study of the Experience of Culture." *Journal of Popular Culture* 11 (Summer 1977):267–79.

Taylor, A. J. W. "Beatlemania – The Adulation and Exuberance of Some Adolescents." In *Sociology and Everyday Life*, ed. Marcello Truzzi. Englewood Cliffs, N.J.: Prentice-Hall, 1968. Pp. 161–70.

Thorpe, Peter. "I'm Movin' On: The Escape Theme in Country and Western Music." *Western Humanities Review* 24 (Autumn 1970):307–18.

Titon, Jeff. "Autobiography and Blues Texts." *JEMF Quarterly* 6 (Summer 1970):79–82.

————. "Thematic Pattern in Downhome Blues Lyrics: The Evidence on Commercial Phonograph Records since World War II." *Journal of American Folklore* 90 (July/September 1977):316–30.

Vance, Joel. "Review of Jake Walk Blues." *Stereo Review* 40 (June 1978):116.

Vulliamy, Graham. "A Re-assessment of the 'Mass Culture' Controversy: The Case of Rock Music." *Popular Music and Society* 4 (1975):130–55.

Wallenstein, Barry. "Leonard Cohen and the Poets of Rock." *Chronicle of Higher Education* 13 (January 17, 1977):18.

Wanzenried, John, and Vincent DiSalvo. "Intensional and Extension Orientations in Rock and Roll Music." *ETC: A Review of General Semantics* 32 (March 1975):31–42.

Wanzenried, John, and Robert Henley Woody. "Country and Western Song Lyrics: Intensional and Extensional Orientations." *Popular Music and Society* 5 (1977):89–92.

Watts, Michael. "The Call and Response of Popular Music: The Impact of American Pop Music in Europe." In *Superculture: American Popular Culture and Europe*, ed. C. W. E. Bigsby. Bowling Green, Ohio: Bowling Green University Popular Press, 1975. Pp. 123–39.

Wells, John. "Bent Out of Shape from Society's Pliers: A Sociological Study of the Grotesque in the Songs of Bob Dylan." *Popular Music and Society* 6 (1978):27–38.

Wenner, Jann, et al. "Ralph J. Gleason in Perspective." *Rolling Stone* (July 17, 1975):39–49.

Wilgus, D. K. "Country-Western Music and the Urban Hillbilly." *Journal of American Folklore* 83 (April/June 1970):157–79.

Willis, Ellen. "Rock, etc.: But Now I'm Gonna Move." *New Yorker* (October 23, 1971):168–75.

Wright, David. "Rock Music, Media, and the Counter Culture." In *New Dimensions in Popular Culture*, ed. Russel B. Nye. Bowling Green, Ohio: Bowling Green University Popular Press, 1962. Pp. 211–23.

Wulffson, Don L. "Music to Teach Reading." *Journal of Reading* 14 (December 1970):179–82.

"Youth Music – A Special Report." *Music Educator's Journal* 56 (November 1969):43–73.


## ENCYCLOPEDIAS, DISCOGRAPHIES, AND POPULAR MUSIC CHARTS

Anthonissen, Juul, et al. "Black Music Discography." *Billboard* (June 9, 1979):BM30, 39–41.

Berry, Peter E. ". . . *And the Hits Just Keep on Comin'*." Syracuse, N.Y.: Syracuse University Press, 1977. Pp. 169–276.

Betrock, Alan, comp. *Girl Groups: An Annotated Discography, 1960–65*. New York: A. Betrock, n.d.

Blair, John, comp. *The Illustrated Discography of Surf Music, 1959–1965*. Riverside, Calif.: J. Bee Productions, 1978.

Booth, Mark W. "Popular Music." In *Handbook of American Popular Culture – Vol. 1*. ed. M. Thomas Inge. Westport, Conn.: Greenwood Press, 1978. Pp. 171–93.

Brown, Len, and Gary Friedrich, comps. *Encyclopedia of Country and Western Music*. New York: Tower, 1971.

———. *Encyclopedia of Rock 'N' Roll*. New York: Tower, 1970.

Case, Brian, and Stan Britt, eds. *The Illustrated Encyclopedia of Jazz*. New York: Harmony Books, 1978.

Castleman, Harry, and Walter J. Podrazik, comps. *All Together Now: The First Complete Beatles Discography, 1961–1975*. New York: Ballantine, 1975.

———. *The Beatles Again?* Ann Arbor, Mich.: Pierian Press, 1977.

Clee, Ken, comp. *A Discography Collection of Artists and Labels*, 2d ed. Philadelphia: Stak-O-Wax Publications, 1979.

Cohen, Norm, with the assistance of Arnold Shaw and George Lewis. "Black Music Re-Issues: A Discography." *Billboard* (June 9, 1979):BM30, 36.

Cooper, B. Lee. "Popular Music Resources – Audio Collection Guidelines." *Library-College Experimenter* 4 (May 1978):11–22.

Csida, Joe, and June Bunny Csida. "Charting the Hit Songs, Artists, and Records: From Spotlighting Song Successes in 1903 to the Complex, Total Coverage Charts of 1976." *Billboard* (July 4, 1976):10ff.

Dachs, David. *Encyclopedia of Pop/Rock.* New York: Scholastic Services, 1972.

Dellar, Fred; Roy Thompson, and Douglas B. Green. comps. *The Illustrated Encyclopedia of Country Music.* New York: Harmony Books, 1977.

Denisoff, R. Serge, comp. *Songs of Protest, War, and Peace: A Bibliography and Discography,* Santa Barbara, Calif.: American Bibliographical Center—Clio Press, 1973.

_____. *Great Day Coming: Folk Music and the American Left.* Baltimore: Penguin, 1971. Pp. 190–92.

Dimmick, Mary LaVerne, comp. *The Rolling Stones: An Annotated Bibliography,* rev. ed. Pittsburgh: University of Pittsburgh Press, 1979.

Docks, L. R., comp. *The American Premium Record Guide, 1915–1965: Identification and Values of 78's, 45's, and LP's.* Florence, Ala.: Books Americana, 1980.

Edwards, Joe, comp. *Top 10's and Trivia of Rock and Roll and Rhythm and Blues, 1950–1973.* St. Louis: Blueberry Hill, 1974. (Supplements for 1974, 1975, etc. are also available.)

Escott, Colin, and Martin Hawkins, comps. *The Complete Sun Label Session Files,* rev. ed. Kent, Eng.: Martin Hawkins, n.d.

Ferlingere, Robert D., comp. *A Discography of Rhythm and Blues and Rock 'N' Roll Vocal Groups, 1945 to 1965.* Hayward, Calif.: California Trade School, 1976.

*The 45 RPM Handbook of Oldies: A Complete Guide to All the Available Hit Singles of the Past.* Los Angeles: Record Rack, 1976.

Gambaccini, Paul, comp. *Rock Critics' Choice: The top 200 Albums.* New York: Quick Fox, 1978.

Garland, Phyl. "Basic Library of Rhythm-And-Blues." *Stereo Review* 42 (May 1979):72–77.

_____. "Discography." In *The Sound of Soul: The Story of Black Music.* New York: Pocket Books, 1969. Pp. 199–202.

Gentry, Linnell, comp. *A History and Encyclopedia of Country, Western, and Gospel Music,* 2d ed. Nashville: Clairmont Corporation, 1969.

Gillett, Charlie. *The Sound of the City: The Rise of Rock and Roll.* New York: Outerbridge and Dienstfrey, 1970. Pp. 343–46.

Goldstein, Stewart, and Alan Jacobson, comps. *Oldies but Goodies: The Rock 'N' Roll Years.* New York: Mason/Charter, 1977.

John Goldrosen, with Bill Griggs. "Discography." In *The Buddy Holly Story,* rev. ed. New York: Quick Fox, 1979. Pp. 244–50.

Goldsworthy, Jay, ed. *Casey Kasem's American Top 40 Yearbook.* New York: Target Books, 1979.

Gonzalez, Fernando L., comp. *DISCO-FILE: The Discographical Catalog of American Rock and Roll and Rhythm and Blues Vocal Harmony Groups, 1902 to 1976*, 2d ed. Flushing, N.Y.: F. L. Gonzalez, 1977.

Green, Archie. "A Discography of American Labor Union Songs," *New York Folklore Quarterly* 1 (Autumn 1961):1–18.

Guralnick, Peter. "Selected Discography." In *Feel Like Going Home: Portraits in Blues and Rock 'N' Roll.* New York: Outerbridge and Dienstfrey, 1971. Pp. 212–17.

————. "Selected Discography." In *Lost Highway: Journeys and Arrivals of American Musicians.* Boston: Godine, 1979. Pp. 341–50.

Hardy, Phil, and Dave Laing, comps. *Encyclopedia of Rock, 1955–1975.* London: Aquarius, 1977.

Hill, Randal C., comp. *The Official Price Guide to Collectible Rock Records.* Orlando, Fla.: House of Collectibles, 1979.

Jahn, Mike. "A Selective Discography." In *Rock: From Elvis Presley to the Rolling Stones.* New York: Quadrangle, 1973. Pp. 295–302.

Jewell, Thomas N. "Rock: The Best Recordings of 1979." *Library Journal,* 107 (February 15, 1980):473–80.

Jorgensen, Ernst; Erik Rasmussen, and Johnny Mikkelson, comps. *Elvis – Recording Sessions.* Baneringen, Denmark: JEE Productions, 1975.

Keesing, Hugo A. "Annotated Bibliography of Pop/Rock Music." *Popular Culture Methods* 3 (Spring 1976):4–22.

Kirsch, Don R., comp. *Rock 'N' Roll Obscurities – Volume One.* Tacoma, Wash.: D. Kirsch, 1977.

Larkin, Rochelle. *Soul Music!* New York: Lancer, 1970. Pp. 181–89.

Leadbitter, Mike, and Neil Slaven, comps. *Blues Records, 1943–66*: A Discography. New York: Oak Publications, 1968.

Leibowitz, Alan "Bo," comp. *The Record Collector's Handbook.* New York: Everest House, 1979.

Lewis, George, Norm Cohen, Arnold Shaw et al. "Black Music Bibliography." *Billboard* (June 9, 1979): BM32, 40–41.

Lichter, Paul. "Discography and Films." In *The Boy Who Dared to Rock: The Definitive Elvis.* Garden City, N.Y.: Dolphin, 1978. Pp. 199–298.

Logan, Nick, and Bob Woffinden, comps. *The Illustrated Encyclopedia of Rock.* New York: Harmony Books, 1976.

————, eds. *The New Musical Express Book of Rock – No. 2.* London: Star Books (W. H. Allen and Company), 1973.

McGeary, Mitchell, comp. *The Beatles Discography*, rev. ed. Lacey, Wash.: Ticket To Ryde, 1976. Pp. 1–33.

Marchbank, Peace, and Barry Miles, comps. *The Illustrated Rock Almanac.* New York: Paddington Press, (Grosset and Dunlap), 1977.

Marcus, Greil. *Mystery Train: Images of America in Rock 'N' Roll Music,* New York: E. P. Dutton, 1975. Pp. 209–64.

Marion, Jean-Charles. "Essential Recordings: Part 1 – A Beginner's Basic Library." *Record Exchanger* 4 (1975):25,30.

————. Essential Recordings: Part 2 – A Collector's Basic Library," *Record Exchanger,* 4 (1976):13, 19.

Marsh, Dave, with John Swenson, eds. *The Rolling Stone Record Guide.* New York: Random House, 1979.

May, Christopher. "A Basic List of Rock Records." *BRIO* 13 (Autumn 1976):34–38.

Miles, Daniel J., Betty T. Miles, and Martin J. Miles, comps. *The Miles Chart Display – Volume I: 1955–1970.* Boulder, Colo.: Convex Industries, 1973.

————. *The Miles Chart Display of Popular Music – Volume II: 1971–1975.* New York: Arno Press, 1977.

Miron, Charles, comp. *Rock Gold: All the Hit Charts from 1955 to 1976.* New York: Drake, 1977.

"The Motown Era Discography." In *The Motown Era.* New York: Grosset and Dunlap, 1971. Pp. 5–16.

Murrells, Joseph, comp. *The Book of Golden Discs.* London: Barrie and Jenkins, 1978.

Naha, Ed, comp. *Lillian Roxon's Rock Encyclopedia,* rev. ed. New York: Grosset and Dunlap, 1978.

Nicholas, A. X. "Discography." In *The Poetry of Soul.* New York: Bantam, 1971. Pp. 93–98.

————. "Discography." In *Woke Up This Mornin': Poetry of the Blues.* New York: Bantam, 1973. Pp. 119–22.

Nite, Norm N., *Rock On: The Illustrated Encyclopedia of Rock 'N' Roll.* New York: Crowell, 1974.

————. *Rock On – Volume II: The Illustrated Encyclopedia of Rock N' Roll – The Modern Years, 1964 to the Present.* New York: Crowell, 1978.

Nugent, Stephen, and Charlie Gillett, comps. *Rock Almanac: Top Twenty American and British Singles and Albums of the '50's, '60's, and '70's.* Garden City, N.Y.: Anchor Press/Doubleday, 1976.

O'Connor, Jim. "A Rock and Roll Discography." *School Library Journal* 22 (September 1975):21–24.

Olds, Michael. "From Sargeant Pepper to Captain Fantastic: A Basic Rock Collection." *Hoosier School Libraries* 16 (December 1976):17–19.

Oliver, Paul. "Discography of Quoted Blues." In *The Meaning of the Blues.* New York: Collier, 1972. Pp. 339–69.

Osborne, Jerry, comp. *55 Years of Recorded Country/Western Music.* Phoenix: O'Sullivan, Woodside, 1976.

————. *Popular and Rock Records, 1948–1978,* 2d ed. Phoenix: O'Sullivan, Woodside, 1978.

————. *Record Albums, 1948–1978,* 2d ed. Phoenix: O'Sullivan, Woodside, 1978.

———— and Bruce Hamilton, comps. *A Guide to Record Collecting.* Phoenix: O'Sullivan, Woodside, 1979.

Palmer, Robert. "A Chronological Listing of Records Produced by Leiber and Stoller." In *Baby, That Was Rock 'N' Roll: The Legendary Leiber and Stoller.* New York: Harcourt Brace Jovanovich, 1978. Pp. 128–31.

————. "Recordings of Works by Leiber and Stoller." In *Baby, That Was Rock 'N' Roll: The Legendary Leiber and Stoller.* New York: Harcourt Brace Jovanovich, 1978. Pp. 120–27.

Pitts, Michael R. and Louis H. Harrison, comps. *Hollywood on Record: The Film Star's Discography.* Metuchen, N.J.: Scarecrow Press, 1978.

Price, Dan. "Bibliography of Bob Dylan: Articles and Books, By and About; Albums and Singles Published; and Unreleased Recordings." *Popular Music and Society* 3 (1974):227–41.

Propes, Steve. *Golden Goodies: A Guide to 50's and 60's Popular Rock & Roll Record Collecting.* Radnor, Pa.: Chilton, 1975.

————. *Golden Oldies: A Guide to 60's Record Collecting.* Radnor, Pa.: Chilton, 1974.

————. *Those Oldies but Goodies: A Guide to 50's Record Collecting.* New York: Collier, 1973.

Quirin, Jim, and Barry Cohen, comps. *Chartmasters' Rock 100: An Authoritative Ranking of the 100 Most Popular Songs for Each Year, 1956 through 1975,* 2d ed. Covington, La.: Chartmasters, 1976.

Raschke, Ulrich. "One Hundred Times Pop Music: Concrete Advice for the Construction of a Basic Collection." *Buch und Bibliographie* 27 (July-August 1975):661–82ff.

Robinson, Richard, et al. "Creem's List of Top Rock Albums, 1955–75." In *Rock Revolution.* New York: Popular Library, 1976. Pp. 209–14.

Rodnitzky, Jerome L. *Minstrels of the Dawn: The Folk-Protest Singer as a Culture Hero.* Chicago: Nelson-Hall, 1976. Pp. 181–84.

Rosenberg, Neil V. "Rock Books: An Incomplete Survey (Parts I and II.)" *JEMF Quarterly* 8 (Spring/Summer 1972):48–56 and 109–16.

*Lillian Roxon's Rock Encyclopedia*. New York: Grosset and Dunlap, 1969.

Sander, Ellen, and Tom Clark, comps. "A Rock Taxonomy." In *Trips: Rock Life in the Sixties*, by Ellen Sander. New York: Scribner's, 1973. Pp. 162–258.

Schurk, William L. "Recommended Popular Records for a Non-Classical Record Library." In *Selected Recordings and Publications in the Popular Music Field*, ed. William Ivey. Nashville: Country Foundation Press, 1975. Pp. 1–9.

Scott, Frank, et al. comps. *Vintage Rock and Roll Catalog – 1979*. El Cerrito, Calif.: Down Home Music, 1979.

Shapiro, Nat, ed. *Popular Music: An Annotated Index of American Popular Songs, Vol. 1: 1950–1959*. New York: Adrian Press, 1964.

_____. *Popular Music: An Annotated Index of American Popular Songs, Vol. III: 1960–1964*. New York: Adrian Press, 1967.

_____. *Popular Music: An Annotated Index of American Popular Songs, Vol. VI: 1965–1969*. New York: Adrian Press, 1973.

Shaw, Arnold. *Honkers and Shouters: The Golden Years of Rhythm and Blues*. New York: Collier, 1978. Pp. 529–41.

_____. *Rock Revolution*. New York: Crowell-Collier, 1969. Pp. 242–50.

_____. *The Rockin' '50's: The Decade That Transformed the Pop Music Scene*. New York: Hawthorne Books, 1974. Pp. 282–88.

_____. *The World of Soul*. New York: Paperback Library, 1971. Pp. 361–68.

Shestack, Melvin, comp. *Country Music Encyclopedia*. New York: Crowell 1974.

Smith, John L., comp. *Johnny Cash Discography and Recording History, 1955–1968*, JEMF Special Series, no. 2. Los Angeles: John Edwards Memorial Foundation, 1969.

Solomon, Clive, comp. *Record Hits: The British Top 50 Charts, 1954–1976*. London, Eng.: Omnibus Press, 1977.

Stambler, Irwin, comp. *Encyclopedia of Pop, Rock, and Soul*. New York: St. Martin's Press, 1974.

_____. *Encyclopedia of Popular Music*. New York: St. Martin's Press, 1965.

Stambler, Irwin, and Grelun Landon, comps. *Encyclopedia of Folk, Country, and Western Music*. New York: St. Martin's Press, 1969.

Summan, Friedrich, and Manfred Jagnow. "A Basic Collection of Rock 'N' Roll Records and Tape Cassettes." *Buch und Bibliographie* 27 (July-August 1975):682–84.

"Sun Record Company Discography." *Mean Mountain Music*, 4 (1979):15–21.

Tudor, Dean, and Nancy Tudor. *Black Music.* Littleton, Colo.: Libraries Unlimited, 1979. Pp. 31–188.

———. *Contemporary Popular Music.* Littleton, Colo.: Libraries Unlimited, 1979. Pp. 35–232.

Vassal, Jacques. *Electric Children: Roots and Branches of Modern Folkrock.* New York: Taplinger, 1976. Pp. 252–57.

Voigt, John. "Rock Music: The Sacred Squeal of Now." *Wilson Library Bulletin* 46 (October 1971):130–31.

Vulliamy, Graham, and Ed Lee. *Pop Music in School.* Cambridge: Cambridge University Press, 1976. Pp. 195–204.

Welding, Pete. "The Best of Blues and Roots: A Guide to Blues, Gospel, R&B, and Ragtime on Records." In *Downbeat Music '68.* Chicago: down beat magazine, 1968. Pp. 56–59, 86–93.

Whitburn, Joel, comp. *Pop Annual, 1955–1977.* Menomonee Falls, Wis.: Record Research, 1978.

———. *Top Country & Western Records, 1949–1971.* Menomonee Falls, Wis.: Record Research, 1972. (Supplements for 1972–73, 1974, etc., are also available.)

———. *Top Easy Listening Records, 1961–1974.* Menomonee Falls, Wis.: Record Research, 1975. (Supplements for 1975, 1976, etc., are also available.)

———. *Top LP Records, 1945–1972.* Menomonee Falls, Wis.: Record Research, 1973. (Supplements for 1973, 1974, etc., are also available.)

———. *Top Pop Artists and Singles, 1955–1978.* Menomonee Falls, Wis.: Record Research, 1979.

———. *Top Pop Records, 1940–1955.* Menomonee Falls, Wis.: Record Research, 1973.

———. *Top Pop Records, 1955–1972.* Menomonee Falls, Wis.: Record Research, 1973. (Supplements for 1973, 1974, etc., are also available.)

———. *Top Rhythm and Blues Records, 1949–1971.* Menomonee Falls, Wis.: Record Research, 1972. (Supplements for 1972–73, 1974, etc., are also available.)

## Unpublished Resources

Anderson, Bruce W. "Popular American Music: Changes in the Consumption of Sound Recordings, 1940–1955." Ph.D. dissertation, University of Pennsylvania, 1974.

Appleton, Clyde Robert. "The Comparative Preferential Response of Black and White Students to Black and White Folk and Popular Music Styles." Ph.D. dissertation, New York University, 1970.

Basirico, Lawrence A. "Stickin' Together: The Cohesiveness of Rock Groups." Master's thesis, State University of New York at Stony Brook, 1974.

Bennett, Hilton Stith. "Other People's Music." Ph.D. dissertation, Northwestern University, 1972.

Berger, David G. "The Unchanging Popular Tune Lyric, 1910–1955." Ph.D. dissertation, Columbia University, 1966.

Booker, George Arlen. "The Disc Jockey and His Impact on Teenage Musical Taste as Reflected through a Study in Three North Florida Cities." Ph.D. dissertation, Florida State University, 1968.

Bruno, James Byron. "Folk Music Materials for Use in the Elementary School." Ed.D. dissertation, New York University, 1960.

Bucci, Jerry Michael. "Love, Marriage, and Family Life Themes in the Popular Song: A Comparison of the Years 1940 and 1965." Ed.D. dissertation, Columbia University, 1968.

Carloni, Alice Stewart. "The Audience Turns On." Ph.D. dissertation, Brandeis University, 1970.

Charles, Norman. "Social Values in American Popular Songs, 1890–1950." Ph.D. dissertation, University of Pennsylvania, 1958.

Cooper, B. Lee. "The Objectives of Teaching Survey History Courses in American High Schools and Colleges: A Content Analysis of Articles from Selected Periodicals, 1939–1969." Ph.D. dissertation, Ohio State University, 1971.

Dees, David Regan. "On the Theory of Art: A Structuralist Analysis with Examples from Contemporary Popular Music." Ph.D. dissertation, Notre Dame University, 1972.

DeWitt, Howard A. "Using Popular History in the American Survey: Rock and Roll as an Expression of American Culture in the 1950's." Paper presented at the 7th National Conference of the Popular Culture Association, Baltimore, Md., April 28, 1977.

Etzkorn, Klaus Peter. "Musical and Social Patterns of Songwriters: An Exploratory Sociological Study." Ph.D. dissertation, Princeton University, 1959.

Ferris, William Reynolds, Jr. "Black Folklore from the Mississippi Delta." Ph.D. dissertation, University of Pennsylvania, 1969.

Flippo, Chester W. "Rock Journalism and *Rolling Stone*." Master's thesis, University of Texas, 1974.

Gillett, Charles. "The Evolution of Rock and Roll." Master's thesis, Teachers College of Columbia University, 1966.

Goodykoontz, William M. "Studies in Popular Culture: The Sociology of Rock." Paper presented at the 5th Annual Convention of the Popular Culture Association, St. Louis, Mo., March 20, 1975.

Griffin, Alan. "A Philosophical Approach to the Subject-Matter Preparation of Teachers of History." Ph.D. dissertation, Ohio State University, 1942.

Gritzner, Charles F. "Country Music: A Reflection of Popular Culture." Paper presented at the 6th Annual Convention of the Popular Culture Association, Chicago, April 23, 1976.

Harmon, James Elmer. "The New Music and the American Youth Subculture." Ph.D. dissertation, United States International University, 1971.

Hirsch, Paul M. "The Organization of Consumption." Ph.D. dissertation, University of Michigan, 1973.

Jewett, Robert E. "The Use of Historical Evidence in Grounding Civic Beliefs." Ph.D. dissertation, Ohio State University, 1947.

Johnson, Joseph Steve. "Radio Music – The Gatekeepers." Ph.D. dissertation, Michigan State University, 1970.

Jolly, Howard Delcour. "Popular Music: A Study in Collective Behavior." Ph.D. dissertation, Stanford University, 1967.

Kaye, Stephen Arnold. "The Rhetoric Song: Singing Persuasion in Social-Action Movements." Ph.D. dissertation, University of Oregon, 1966.

Keesing, Hugo. "Culture in the Grooves: American History at 78, 45, and 33⅓ r.p.m." Paper presented at the 8th Annual Convention of the Popular Culture Association, Cincinnati, Ohio, April 21, 1978.

_____. "Pop Goes to War: The Music of World War II and Vietnam." Paper presented at the 9th Annual Convention of the Popular Culture Association, Pittsburgh, Penn., April 27, 1979.

_____. "Youth in Transition: A Content Analysis of Two Decades of Popular Music." Ph.D. dissertation, Adelphi University, 1972.

King, Algin B. "The Marketing of Phonograph Records in the United States: An Industry Study." Ph.D. dissertation, Ohio State University, 1966.

McLaughlin, Mary. "The Social World of American Popular Songs." Master's thesis, Cornell University, 1968.

Malone, Bill C. "A History of Commercial Country Music in the United States, 1920–1964." Ph.D. dissertation, University of Texas, 1965.

Metcalf, Lawrence. "A Theory of Conceptual Learning and Its Implications for the Teaching of the Social Studies for the Purpose of Clarifying Social Attitudes." Ph.D. dissertation, Ohio State University, 1948.

Nanry, Charles. "The Occupational Subculture of the Jazz Musician: Myth and Reality." Ph.D. dissertation, Rutgers University, 1970.

Parker, John W. "American Popular Music: An Emerging Field of Academic Study." Ed.D. dissertation, University of Kentucky, 1962.

Pearson, Barry Lee. "The Duality of the Blues Tradition: Ethnic Art and Mass Culture Stereotypes." Paper presented at the Seventh Annual Convention of the Popular Culture Association, Baltimore, Md.: April 30, 1977.

Petterson, James. "Using Popular Music to Teach Topics in American History since 1950 for High School Students." Master's thesis, University of Southern California, 1977.

Reuss, Richard A. "American Folklore and Left-Wing Politics, 1927–1957." Ph.D. dissertation, Indiana University, 1971.

# Song Title Index

# Subject Index